7⁹⁵

# The
# Hiker's Guide
## to Montana

# The
# Hiker's Guide
## to Montana

*By Bill Schneider*
*Revised by Ed Madej*

*Falcon Press Publishing Co., Inc.*
*Billings and Helena, Montana*

## More Guides from Falcon Press

The Traveler's Guide to Montana
The Floater's Guide to Montana
The Floater's Guide to Colorado
The Nordic Skier's Guide to Montana
The Hiker's Guide to Idaho
The Angler's Guide to Montana
The Bicyclist's Guide to Montana
The Bicyclist's Guide to Glacier National Park
The Bicyclist's Guide to Yellowstone National Park

Order extra copies of this book and get information and prices for the above books by writing Falcon Press, P.O. Box 279, Billings, MT 59103. Also, ask for a copy of our current catalogue.

Please report any errors found in this book to Falcon Press.

Library of Congress Catalog Card Number 82-84323
ISBN 0-934318-08-5
Manufactured in the United States of America.
Falcon Press Publishing Co., Inc.
P.O. Box 731, Helena, MT 59624
Cover photo by Bill Schneider

# Acknowledgements

Editing any book runs into lots of work, but editing this book would have been impossible without the kind help of so many people. First and foremost, I must thank the contributors who provided most of the hikes. Without them, *The Hiker's Guide to Montana* would not be. Although their by-lines follow their contributions, I want to acknowledge their help again by listing them here: Wayne Avants, Don Berg, Bill Brown, Pat Caffrey, Bruce Chesler, Mike Comola, Frank Culver, Bill Cunningham, Art Foran, John Gatchall, Herb Gloege, Linda and Tom Hurlock, Jack Johns, Loren Kreck, Ed Madej, Joe Mussulman, Dave Orndoff, Bob Oset, Don Reed, Karen Renne, Mike Sample, Elaine and Art Sedlack, Elaine Snyder, Fred Swanson, Larry Thompson, Bob Wagenknecht, Rosemary Rowe, and John Westenberg. If you bump into any of these good folks on a mountaintop somewhere, please thank them for making *The Hiker's Guide* possible.

Perhaps as important as the text are the excellent maps. For these, thank Gary Wolf and Ed Madej. Larry Thompson provided the artwork for the title page.

Many of the photos are courtesy of the U.S. Forest Service. I especially thank the helpful public servants at the Regional Forester's Office of Information in Missoula. However, the Forest Service personnel from ranger districts throughout Montana helped in various capacities. Other photos in the book come from the cameras of Bruce Chesler, Art Foran, Joe Mussulman, Doug O'looney, Ed Madej, Tom Hurlock, Harry Engels, and Mike Sample.

T&R Engraving of Denver did an excellent in the difficult task of photographing topographic maps from the U.S. Geological Survey. And of course, the USGS itself deserves thanks for making the maps in the first place and allowing their reproduction.

As you can see, it takes much more than an editor to finally complete such a project.—*Bill Schneider*

# Contents

## Afterword

## Appendices

91

RIVER

39  86

RIVER

100

YELLOWSTONE

98
96 97 99

# Hikes Throughout Montana

Use this map to locate hikes in your general vicinity.
Then, use the detailed maps later in the book and
other maps to find trailheads.

# Foreword

## Hiking is for Everybody

Although we occasionally hear claims that only the young and rich elite use wilderness, quite the reverse is true. Families spend many pleasurable nights camping far from vehicles. And day hiking (or "walking for pleasure" as agencies sometimes call it) is undoubtedly one of the most popular forms of outdoor recreation.

The people who make such statements must do little, if any, hiking or they surely would see young, old, large, small, rich, and poor—all thoroughly enjoying the back country trails. Hiking and backpacking are available to all ages, sexes, and sizes. They only require a small amount of physical conditioning (which everybody should have anyway) and a minimal amount of equipment.

That's right—a *minimal* investment. Hiking and backpacking *can* be expensive—like any other sport—*if* one chooses to make them so. On the other hand, they can be among the most economical forms of outdoor recreation—especially day hiking which requires nothing except a pair of hiking shoes that are probably already in the closet.

For overnight trips, more expense is required. But even this can be a small investment. The cost of one two-week vacation, staying in motels and eating in restaurants, would be sufficient to outfit an entire family for backpacking. And this equipment can be used year after year. Once a small initial investment is made, hikers can see millions of acres of spectacular, roadless country without spending another penny on equipment. They only need a few dollars for food and for transportation to the trailhead. After the trailhead, it's free.

Not only is hiking free in the economic sense, but also free of the stress and regulation of modern America. Once on the trail, hikers can forget (albeit only temporarily) the tension of their work, the Internal Revenue Service, the unpaid bills, the noise and pollution—it's all behind them for a few hours or days. They can't even hear the bad news on the radio.

Hiking provides an escape—a chance to smell only natural odors; to hear the wind whistling through mature pines, a mountain stream whisper by, or the elk

1

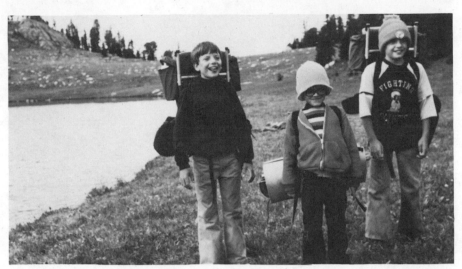

*Backpacking clowns. Bill Schneider photo.*

bugle; to hook a native trout instead of a hatchery-raised catchable; to see the sunset across a mountain lake or a mountain goat race across cliffs man would need climbing gear to negotiate; to drink from a gin-clear stream; and study vegetation that evolved without man's influence.

All this is here for the taking. Fortunately, Montana offers plenty of opportunity to do so.

Hikers can, of course, figure out their own trips by talking to local hikers or agency personnel and by searching through topographic maps. But to make it easier, we published this guide. It contains enough hikes for a lifetime of back country thrills.

We've included hikes from almost every roadless portion of Montana. Although we have trails from the more famous areas such as Glacier National Park and the Bob Marshall and Mission Mountains wilderness areas, we've been careful not to forget the many splendid areas that haven't gained a national reputation—yet.

We've also included hikes for all kinds of hikers—beginners, families, experienced backpackers. In fact, most of the hikes are short, day hikes—usually well-suited for families or inexperienced hikers. Since we've picked hikes from throughout Montana, one of the trailheads is most likely only a short drive.

Also, we feel the *way* this guide was written makes it particularly valuable. Instead of relying on the experience of one or a small group of hikers, we've listed the favorite hikes of veteran Montana hikers—people who wish to share their experience with others, hoping that new users will appreciate and fight to preserve these areas. The topographic maps included with most hikes add the final touch to the already detailed and accurate descriptions. With this guide, hikers shouldn't have any trouble discovering and enjoying wild Montana.

Happy hiking.—*Bill Schneider.*

# Introduction

In Montana, the potential for hiking seems almost endless. So any hiking guide can only include a small minority of the hundreds—perhaps thousands—of spectacular hikes. However, each of these hikes can be viewed as only an introduction to another hiking area; there are, of course, many more lakes, mountains, alpine basins and trails in the area to lure the hiker back the following summer.

The contributors to this guide have hiked these trails recently and recorded the directions in this book. But even more recent road or trail construction or natural phenomena could have changed something. This is why a source of updated information accompanies each hike.

The maps are good reproductions of sections of USGS Quadrangles and can provide many details to the course of the hike. In the book, the scale is always on the south side of the map—whether it lies horizontally or vertically on the page. Although you can probably get by without taking other maps in addition to those in the book, it would be better to do so. They will be especially helpful in identifying distant landmarks not included on the small maps in the book.

Unfortunately, there aren't topographic maps for every hike in the book, as some sections of Montana aren't covered by USGS Quads. In these cases, the Forest Service map was used. Likewise, FS maps were used when a hike transversed both 7.5 and 15 minute Quads.

## Touch the Land Lightly

Compare your favorite hiking area with your living room.

You don't mind visitors. Often, you invite them. But you want them to treat your home with respect.

If you have six obnoxious visitors who put their cigarettes out on the floor, spill drinks, and use foul language; your living room has, in your mind, exceeded its carrying capacity. And these visitors will leave lasting marks.

On the other hand, if you have a dozen quiet, polite, neat guests, the thought that your living room is being overused never enters your mind. And after they've gone home, there is no sign of their presence.

Using wilderness can follow the same theme. There is a large capacity as long as everybody behaves. But a few thoughtless or uninformed hikers can ruin it for others. An important addition to the checklist on page 245 would be *proper wilderness manners*. Don't leave home without them.

Most hikers treat wilderness gently, but some aren't aware that they have poor manners. Often, their actions are dictated by outdated remnants of a past generation of wilderness campers who cut green boughs for evening shelters and beds, set up camp close to alpine lakes, built fire rings, dug trenches around tents, etc. Twenty years ago, these "camping rules" may have been okay. Today, they leave unacceptable, long-lasting scars. Such behavior can no longer be tolerated.

The wilderness is shrinking, and the number of hikers is mushrooming. In fact, use has increased by more than 300% in some western wilderness areas in past years. In some national parks, it has increased even more. Without question, some camping areas show unsightly signs of this craze.

Thus, a new code of ethics is growing out of necessity to cope with unending waves of hikers—all wanting a perfect wilderness experience. Indeed, they should have it and probably can have it *if* all hikers educate themselves on proper and courteous use of fragile country.

As a general rule, touch the land as lightly as possible. Canoeists can look behind them and see no sign of their passing. The next canoe party has no idea another canoe is around the next bend. It should be the same with hiking and backpacking. Leave only memories and good times behind.

Nowadays, nobody dares litter—in or out of the wilderness. This means everything, including orange peels, flip tops, cigarette butts, and gum wrappers. Leave nothing, regardless of how small it is, along the trail or at the campsite.

Try to camp below timberline. Alpine areas are delicate and require special care. Often, it's only a short hike to a good campsite below timberline.

Also, keep your camp off the shoreline or streambank. Take alternate routes to water to avoid leaving a beaten path.

Hikers seek solitude and silence, so avoid making loud noises that may disturb others. This is only common courtesy.

Be very careful with food wastes to prevent unsightly messes and bad odors. If fires are allowed, burn food wastes. Throw cans and foil into the fire to burn off food scraps and odors. Then before breaking camp, dig them out of the ashes and pack them out.

Likewise, burn fish viscera if fires are allowed. If fires aren't allowed, wrap fish viscera and leftover food in plastic bags and carry it out or at least to the next fire area. Never throw fish viscera into mountain streams and lakes.

Waste water from boiling foods should be poured around the perimeter of the fire to keep it from spreading. This also protects natural vegetation. Wash dishes and clothing well away from streams and lakes and carefully discard dish water, such as in a small sump hole that can be covered with soil later. Never wash dishes in a mountain stream or lake: a glob of instant oatmeal is almost as ugly as an aluminum can on the bottom of a crystal-clear lake or stream. If you use soap, make sure it's biodegradable.

As with food wastes, be careful with human wastes. If toilet paper is used, burn it or carry it out. Thoroughly bury human wastes to avoid any chance of bad odor. This is an excellent reason to carry a lightweight trowel. Obviously, wastes must be kept away from lakes and streams.

Perhaps fires cause more damage than any part of back country camping. In many areas, avoid fires completely. (Sometimes regulations prohibit fires.) This goes double for alpine areas where wood is scarce and aesthetic and topsoil is sparse.

If a fire is allowed and appropriate for the campsite, dig out the native vegetation and topsoil and set it aside. Don't build a fire ring with rocks. When breaking camp, douse the fire thoroughly, scatter or bury the cold ashes, and replace the native soil and vegetation.

Another acceptable method is spreading several inches of mineral soil on a flat rock to avoid fire-scarring the rock. Later, scatter or bury the ashes and expose the rock—which should still look natural.

Build fires away from trees to prevent damage to root systems. Keep them small. And widely disperse any partly burned wood.

Don't make a mess tearing apart trees to get firewood. Don't use a saw or axe on a tree and leave a lasting scar. And never build a fire ring or light a fire near a reflector rock which will be permanently scarred.

Take a bath by jumping in water and then moving away from the water to lather yourself. Rinse off by pouring cans of water over your body. This allows soap to biodegrade quickly as it filters through the soil. Of course, use only biodegradable soap.

Avoid cutting switchbacks. And leave "souvenirs" for the next hiker to see; don't carry them out.

Finally and perhaps most importantly, strictly follow the pack in-pack out rule. If you carry it in, you must consume it, burn it, or carry it out.

## Make it a Safe Trip

Perhaps the best safety advice has guided scouts for many decades—be prepared. For starters, this means carrying survival and first aid equipment, compass, and topographic map—and knowing how to use them.

Perhaps the second best advice is to tell somebody where you're going and when you plan to return. Pilots must file flight plans before every trip, an excellent safety rule that can be used by hikers. File your plan with a friend or relative before taking off.

After those two points, safety advice can go on and on. There are probably other tips besides those listed here, but if hikers adhere to the following suggestions, they should have a safe trip.

• Watch the weather, being especially careful not to get caught on a ridge during a lightning storm or at high altitude by a snow storm.
• Be super careful with fires.
• Check the long-term forecast to avoid extended periods of cold, often snowy, weather.
• Don't hike at night.
• Never split up in the back country; always keep your party together.
• Avoid temptations to swim across cold, alpine lakes.

- Stay on the trail unless you are a very experienced hiker.
- Don't slide down snowbanks with cliffs or rocks at the bottom.
- Know the symptoms and treatment of hypothermia, the silent killer.
- Study basic survival and first aid before leaving home.
- Don't eat wild mushrooms or other plants in the back country unless you are positive of the identification.
- Find out as much as you can about the hike, especially any potential hazards, before you leave.
- Never hike alone.
- Don't wait until you're confused to open your topo map. Follow it as you go along, starting from the moment you start up the trail.
- Don't exhaust yourself or weaker members of your party by trying to travel too far, too fast.
- If you get lost, don't panic. Sit down and relax for a few minutes while you carefully check out the topo map and take readings with the compass. Confidently plan your next move. Thousands of hikers have spent unplanned nights in the woods and survived. A few—usually those who panicked and ran wildly around—didn't survive. If you've followed the rules and left your "flight plan" with somebody, they will be looking for you in the morning.
- If your hike calls for fording a large stream, take special precautions to cross safely. Remove your socks and put your boots back on. This makes for more secure footing on the slippery streambottom. Avoid the current's full force by keeping sideways to the flow. Slide—don't lift—your feet one at a time, making sure that one foot is securely anchored before seeking a new hold with the next one. Go slowly and deliberately. Some hikers use a walking stick or branch for additional support.
- In general, don't take any chances while in the back country such as climbing cliffs, jumping over objects, challenging shaky tree "bridges" over streams, etc.
- Last, but definitely not least, stay clear of all wild animals, and this goes tri-

## Survival kit

Compass, whistle, matches in waterproof container, candle, surgical tubing, emergency fishing gear, sixty feet of six-pound line, six hooks, six lead shot and six trout flies, safety pins, copper wire, signal mirror, fire starter, aluminum foil, water purification tablets, space blanket, and flare.

## First aid kit

Sewing needle, snake bite kit, 12 aspirin, antibacterial ointment, two antiseptic swabs, two butterfly bandages, adhesive tape, four adhesive strips, four gauze pads, two triangular bandages, 12 codeine tablets, two inflatable splints, moleskin, one roll of three-inch gauze, and lightweight first aid instructions.

# Hypothermia

Be aware of the danger of hypothermia—subnormal temperature of the body. Lowering of internal temperature leads to mental and physical collapse.

Hypothermia is caused by exposure to cold, and it is aggravated by wetness, wind, and exhaustion. It is the number one killer of outdoor recreationists.

The first step is exposure and exhaustion. The moment you begin to lose heat faster than your body produces it, you are undergoing exposure. Two things happen:

• You voluntarily exercise to stay warm, and your body makes involuntary adjustments to preserve normal temperature in the vital organs. Both responses drain your energy reserves. The only way to stop the drain is to reduce the degree of exposure.

• The second step is hypothermia. If exposure continues until your energy reserves are exhausted, cold reaches the brain, depriving you of judgment and reasoning power. You will not be aware that this is happening. You will lose control of your hands. This is hypothermia. Your internal temperature is sliding downward. Without treatment, this slide leads to stupor, collapse, and death.

To defend against hypothermia, stay dry. When clothes get wet, they lose about 90 percent of their insulating value. Wool loses less heat; cotton, down, and some synthetics lose more.

Choose rainclothes that cover the head, neck, body, and legs and provide good protection against wind-driven rain.

Understand cold. Most hypothermia cases develop in air temperatures between 30 and 50 degrees Fahrenheit.

If your party is exposed to wind, cold, and wet, think hypothermia. Watch yourself and others for these symptoms: Uncontrollable fits of shivering; vague, slow, slurred speech; memory lapses; incoherence; immobile, fumbling hands; frequent stumbling, lurching gait; drowsiness (to sleep is to die); apparent exhaustion; and inability to get up after a rest.

When a member of your party has hypothermia, he/she may deny any problem. Believe the symptoms, not the victim. Even mild symptoms demand treatment.

• Get the victim out of the wind and rain.
• Strip off all wet clothes.
• If the victim is only mildly impaired, give warm drinks. Get the person into warm clothes and a warm sleeping bag. Well-wrapped, warm (not hot) rocks or canteens will help.
• If victim is badly impaired, attempt to keep him/her awake. Put the victim in a sleeping bag with another person—both stripped. If you have a double bag, put the victim between two warm people.
• Build a fire to warm the camp.—*U.S. Forest Service*

*Fording streams such as the Middle Fork of the Flathead—one back country hazard that requires extreme caution, especially when children are along. Bill Schneider photo.*

ple for bears. In Montana, bears—particularly grizzly bears—present a hazard not faced by hikers in most other states. If hikers learn about bears and use proper back country etiquette, bear country can be very safe.

## Hiking Bear Country

The following chapter, compiled from interviews with authorities on bears and reviews of most of the literature on the subject, contains the basic information necessary to make hiking in bear country as safe as possible.

*General.* Be cautious and alert. Stay together. Never hike in bear country alone. Watch for bear sign and be extra careful when you find it. Leave your dog home. (Your pet may be "man's best friend" at home, but not in the wilderness where it could attract a grizzly.) Report all bear incidents to local authorities.[1]

*Hiking.* If you see a bear at a distance, make a wide detour on the upwind side so the bear can get your scent. If a detour isn't possible, slowly back down the trail until safely out-of-sight. Then, make lots of noise (the more, the better) and slowly and noisily make your way up the trail again. The bear should be gone when you get back to your earlier observation point. If the bear is still there and

---

[1]Keep in mind these are merely general rules. They're probably the best generalities anywhere, but, as always, it's dangerous to generalize. Certainly, there is no concrete formula for avoiding confrontations or for what to do when you are confronted. Dr. Charles Jonkel, upon reviewing these rules, suggested trying to evaluate each individual situation based on these general rules. And by all means, Jonkel emphasized, "try to avoid an encounter."

you can't safely get around him, abandon your trip.

Although it isn't a foolproof method, making noise while hiking helps avoid bears. Many hikers hang bells or a can of pebbles from their packs or belts. As a general rule, the noisier, the safer. Metallic noise seems more effective than human voices which can be muffled by natural conditions. Also, it's difficult to keep up steady conversation during long hikes.

*Camping.* Be careful and neat with food and garbage. Keep a clean camp. Don't camp in sites obviously frequented by bears. If you see a bear or fresh sign where you intend to camp, pick another campsite.

If possible, camp near tall trees that can be easily climbed. Sleep some distance from your campfire and cooking area. Keep food and garbage out-of-reach of bears at night (such as suspended between two trees) and away from your sleeping area. Keep food odors off clothes, tents, and sleeping bags. Avoid fresh, perishable, or "smelly' foods (i.e. bacon, lunch meat, sardines, etc.).

Burn combustible trash if regulations and natural conditions allow open fires. Burn cans and other incombustibles to remove odors. Then, dig them out of the ashes and pack them out. Never bury trash in the back country. If you can carry it in, you can carry it out.

Don't clean fish near camp. Burn fish entrails, if possible. Never leave them around camp. The smell of fish can attract bears. Camping at popular fishing sites requires extra caution.

*Special precautions for women.* Stay out of grizzly country during menstrual periods. Avoid using perfume, hair spray, deodorants, or other cosmetics. There is some evidence that bears are attracted and even infuriated by these scents.

*The confrontation.* Most important, try to remain calm. Never panic and run. You can't outrun a bear. And by rapid retreat, you may excite the bear into pursuit.

If the bear stands his ground and doesn't seem aggressive, stand still. If he continues the unaggressive behavior, back very slowly and quietly down the trail until out-of-sight.

If the bear looks aggressive, start looking for a tree to climb. If the bear moves toward you, get up it fast *if* you're sure you have enough time. Make sure it's tall enough to get you out-of-reach. Most such confrontations are with grizzly bears; only grizzly cubs can climb trees.

Before starting for the tree, drop something like a pack or a camera to distract the bear. Stay up the tree until you're positive the bear has left the area.

If you can't get up a tree, play dead. Curl up and clasp your hands over the back of your neck in the "cannonball" position. This takes courage, to say the least, but it's preferable to serious injury.

Physical resistance is, of course, useless.

## Giardia lamblia (Should I Drink the Water?)

There are few backpacking pleasures that can top a cool drink from a high country lake or stream. Whether on a day hike close to a large metropolitan area or miles into the back country, the refreshing sip along the trail is a tradition.

Unfortunately, that cool sip of water from a cold mountain stream may be hazardous to your health.

The most common problem is a waterborne parasite called *Giardia lamblia,* an invisible protozoan which, when ingested, can have results far from inconsequential. One hundred sixty-eight cases of *Giardia* were reported in Montana in 1981, and health authorities believe this may represent only 10% of actual cases.

The illness (called giardiasis, "Beaver fever," or "backpacker's diarrhea") is caused by ingestion of the dormant cyst form of the protozoan. These cysts can survive in cold (40°F) streams for up to three months and can be spread by the droppings of dogs, cats, horses, cattle, beavers, rabbits, marmots, ground squirrels, elk, and especially people.

The cysts are activated in the small intestine of the host, changing into the reproductive trophozoite stage, which attaches to the wall of the intestine. Symptoms may appear from within several days to three weeks after ingestion of the cysts and are characterized by severe diarrhea, weight loss, "rotten egg" belches, fatigue, and cramps. Apparently, some people are "carriers" of giardiasis and may have only very mild symptoms of the disease.

If you suspect you may have the disease, see your doctor immediately. Giardiasis must be treated by a doctor. Quinacrine and metronidazole (Flagyl) are most often used in treatment. Both have unpleasant side effects.

The only thing worse than coming down with giardiasis after a trip into the back country is coming down with it *during* a trip in the back country. There is little you can do, except try to get to a physician as best as you can. You probably won't feel like eating anything, but you should avoid foods such as dairy products (milk, cheese, etc.) which may only worsen your discomfort. It is important to drink plenty of fluids, in order to lessen the dehydrating effects of the illness. Also, stomach coating medicines, such as Peptobismol and milk of magnesia, may calm (but not cure) the intestinal cramps and allow you to hike out to civilization.

How can you prevent the spread of this nasty protozoan? By practicing good sanitary habits in the wilderness. Studies done in Colorado indicate that backpackers may be the most common cause of the spread of *Giardia,* because of improper human waste disposal. Bury feces at least 200 feet from any waterway, and cover them with six inches of organic soil to aid in decomposition. If you travel with dogs or horses, keep them out of streams and lakes as much as possible.

The *Giardia* cyst is a hardy little bugger, difficult to kill in the water. Halazone and chlorine don't work against it, and iodine (besides being dangerous in itself) will kill only 90-95% of all the cysts. Your best bet is to boil all water for at least one minute—and longer, especially above 6,000 feet, since water's boiling temperature decreases with altitude. This may prove impractical on longer trips, where you just can't carry enough fuel. Look for springs which can supply fresh, uncontaminated ground water in some areas.

The ultimate solution appears to be water purifying kits just coming onto the market. Designed for travelling in foreign countries where contaminated water is a problem, these water purifying kits weigh between four ounces and two pounds. *Giardia* cysts are removed by a resin column or a celluloid filter. The kits' major drawback appears to be the incredibly slow rate water passes through the filters, as slow as a quart every twelve minutes.

Improvements in these kits is sure to come as the seriousness of the *Giardia* problem becomes more widely known. Until some better solution is devised, boil your water, or take your chances, and remember to keep a clean camp.

# The Hikes

## 1  Northwest Peak

*General description:* An easy, scenic, uphill walk for almost anyone.
*General location:* Forty miles north of Libby in the northwest corner of the state, 3.5 miles from Idaho and 2.5 miles from Canada.
*Maps:* Northwest Peak USGS Quad and Kootenai National Forest, Yaak Ranger District.
*Special attractions:* An old lookout cabin on the peak, views of the Northwest Peak Scenic Area and, on a clear day, the Canadian Rockies.
*For more information:* Write the District Ranger, Yaak Ranger District, Kootenai National Forest, Route #1, Troy, MT 59935 or call (406) 295-4717.

Northwest Peak (elevation 7,705) is the central attraction of a high mountain ridge, the most striking portions of which are included in the Northwest Peak Scenic Area, an official designation of the Forest Service. Under this designation, the area's unique qualities are recognized and protected.

The area is seldom visited, simply because most people have never heard of it. Those that have hesitate to drive that far. But it's a great opportunity if you're in northwestern Montana with a half-day to kill.

The main access, Pete Creek Road #338, heads north off State Highway 508 two miles west of Yaak. After finding this paved road, drive thirteen miles north and then turn left (west) onto the West Fork Road. After two miles, turn right onto the Winkum Creek Road. Climb seven miles on this road. At 6,100 feet, you'll find the trailhead on the left (south) side of the road at the edge of a clearcut.

There are streams further up the road if you want fresh mountain water; there isn't any on the trail. This area usually has more than its share of snow, so wait until July to conquer Northwest Peak.

The trail follows a skid trail through the clearcut for about one-fourth mile before slipping into deep timber. The trail is marked with new signs, so it's easy to follow.

The trail climbs for two miles to the top of the peak, the last one-fourth mile consisting of open, talus rock. At the top is an old, unmanned lookout cabin,

*Northwest Peak*

complete with rusty pans and other nostalgic artifacts. The terrain drops down to alpine lakes on three sides of the peak.

The ridgetop to the south invites hikers, if you have time. The views are extensive, with the Cabinet Mountains to the south and the Canadian Rockies far to the north.

It's an easy place to pass the time without being in a hurry to do something or go elsewhere.—*Pat Caffrey*

## 2　*Hoskins Lake*

*General description:* An easy round trip to a mountain lake.
*General location:* Thirty-five miles north of Libby in the Purcell Mountains.
*Maps:* Bonnet Top USGS Quad (somewhat outdated) and Kootenai National

Forest, Yaak Ranger District.

*Special attractions:* A low-elevation, mountain lake with good fishing accessible by a short, well-maintained trail.

*For more information:* Write the District Ranger, Yaak Ranger District, Kootenai National Forest, Route #1, Troy, MT 59935 or call (406) 295-4717.

Take the Pipe Creek Road north of Libby for about thirty-three miles until the road forks right to Vinal Lake. Take Vinal Lake Road #746 (which isn't shown on Bonnet Top USGS Quad) for about nine miles or until you're about three miles past Vinal Creek. Here, you will find Forest Service Trail #162 to Hoskins Lake on the right side of the road.

Vigorous hikers will have a hard time calling this a "hike," as it's less than a half-mile to Hoskins Lake. However, for small children or less experienced hikers, it's perfect for an enjoyable day hike or "camp out." It takes only five minutes to reach the lake if you don't stop to smell the wildflowers.

The well-maintained trail has plenty of water along the way. There are no steep hills or hazards, and bear danger is almost nonexistent.

Mosquitoes can take the edge off this hike in the early summer, so it's best to wait until late summer or fall to see Hoskins Lake.

There are actually two lakes—a large lower lake with nice-sized cutthroat trout and a small, marshy, upper lake. Because of the good fishing, the lower lake is more heavily used, but not overused, mostly by local hikers. However, the upper lake offers an excellent opportunity to be alone with the wilderness.

A representative western larch forest, with some very large trees, surrounds the lakes. Deer and moose are frequently seen. Grouse are common, and a lucky hiker might spot an osprey or common loon near the lower lake. Some of the

*Hoskins Lake in the proposed Mount Henry Wilderness. Tom Hurlock, photo.*

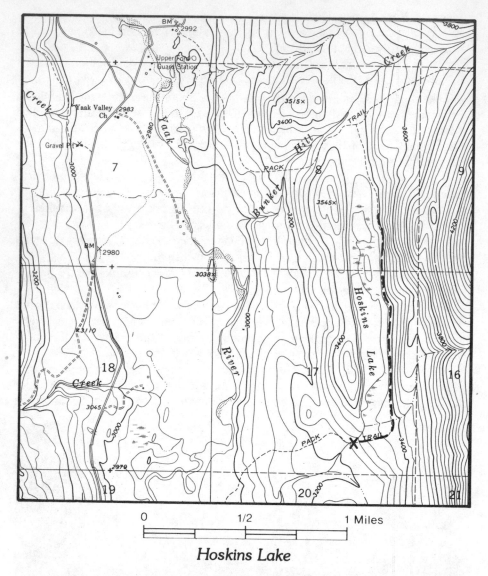

*Hoskins Lake*

more common wildflowers include wake robin, shooting star, wild rose, Pacific trillium, queencup beadlily and rock clematis.

A few hikers continue north past the lakes and go down Bunker Hill Creek. Simply follow this trail past the upper lake and stay with it for about one mile until it junctures with the trail up Bunker Hill Creek. Then, turn left, ignoring the un-maintained trail that goes to the right up Bunker Hill Creek. This makes a loop, since you come back to Vinal Lake Road about 1.5 miles north of the Hoskins Lake trailhead.

Although this is rarely an overnight hike, there are several good campsites. There is a developed Forest Service site at the lower end of Hoskins Lake. However, most backpackers prefer camping at the wooded FS campsite halfway up the lake where the fishing is better. You can also camp at the foot of Upper

Hoskins Lake about one hundred feet west of the trail. This spot gets little use, as it isn't a FS campsite.

Hoskins Lake is part of the Mount Henry Wilderness Study Area. Interim management for the area prevents roading and logging, until Congress says otherwise. However, in 1981, the Kootenai National Forest recommended against wilderness protection for Mount Henry, and has scheduled several timber sales for the area. Let your congressman know what you think is best for Mount Henry.—*Linda and Tom Hurlock*

## 3    Boulder Lakes

*General description:* A short, easy hike into two subalpine lakes.

*General location:* Thirty miles north of Libby or seven miles west of the bridge across Koocanusa Reservoir.

*Maps:* Boulder Lakes USGS Quad (outdated) and Kootenai National Forest, Rexford Ranger District.

*For more information:* Write the District Ranger, Rexford Ranger District, Kootenai National Forest, Box 666, Eureka, MT 59917 or call (406) 296-2536.

If you want to see a subalpine lake without vehicle access, this may be the easiest hike you could take. It's only about 1.5 miles to the Lower Boulder Lake along a slight incline—about 440 feet elevation gain.

To locate the trailhead, go west from Eureka for about fourteen miles on State Highway 37 over the Koocanusa Reservoir Bridge and then turn north at the end of the bridge. Continue north for about three miles until you turn left on the Boulder Creek Road #337. Stay on this logging road for about nine miles until you see the road to Red Mountain. Take the left fork here and go about two miles past this junction and turn right on the small road one-half mile past a sharp switchback. Follow this road for 1.5 miles until it ends and trail #91 takes off to the right. (If you find yourself driving on the level for miles, you've missed the last road junction, as the road levels off after the turn-off to Boulder Lakes).

The trail is well maintained and after one-fourth mile stays in the woods all the way. Just before the lake, this trail forks. Go left, as the right-hand trail continues to Purcell Marsh. (This last junction isn't shown on the Kootenai National Forest map.)

Bring drinking water; it can be very dry until you reach the lower lake.

The feeling of remoteness can be found on this hike, but not until after the first one-fourth mile which goes through a clearcut. Also, motorized vehicles are allowed on this trail throughout the year. The threat of bear trouble is slight, and mosquitoes aren't a significant problem. Midsummer is a good time for this hike.

For experienced hikers, there is an interesting side trip. From Lower Boulder Lake backtrack about one-fourth mile and take trail #91 west to the ridgetop at the head of Basin creek, which is about a 500-foot climb. Then, drop 900 feet to Purcell Marsh. Here, you will find few signs of man, and you have an excellent chance to see moose. It's an extra five-mile round trip to Purcell Marsh from Boulder Lakes.

Boulder Lakes country hosts the same diversity of wildlife found throughout northwestern Montana—deer, black bear, moose, elk, etc. Around the lakes,

*Boulder Lakes*

hikers will find beargrass, glacier lilies, and a variety of other wildflowers. On the Purcell Marsh side trip, you can find the uncommon alpine bog kalmia. Lower Boulder Lake has fair fishing for pan-sized cutthroat.

Although this is usually a day hike, there is an established Forest Service campsite at the lower lake. A few backpackers stay at Purcell Marsh, but this is a primitive campsite. Both sites have sufficient firewood and water.

Like Hoskins Lake, Boulder Lakes and Purcell Marsh are part of the Mount Henry Wilderness Study Area which may soon have roads throughout it—unless, of course, enough people object. —*Linda and Tom Hurlock*

# 4    West Branch of the South Fork of Big Creek

*General description:* An easy day hike perfectly suited for families because of the scant elevation gain.
*General location:* Fifteen miles north of Libby in the Purcell Mountains.
*Maps:* Banfield Mountain USGS Quad and Kootenai National Forest Map.
*Special attractions:* Easy hike that very few hikers use.
*For more information:* Write the District Ranger, Rexford Ranger Station, Kootenai National Forest, Box 666, Eureka, MT or call (406) 296-2536.

Most Montana hikes have at least one steep hill to climb, and the West Branch of Big Creek is no exception. The hill, however, is a short one, only half a block long and climbing only about seventy-five feet. Morever, it's at the very beginning while you're still fresh. After that, the trail winds along a slow-moving mountain stream which is frequently interrupted by beaver dams. Total elevation gain is only about 250 feet.

To find the trailhead, go about eight miles south of the bridge across Koocanusa Reservoir (near Rexford) and take the Big Creek Road from the west side of the reservoir. Follow this logging road west for about seven miles, swinging south along the South Fork of Big Creek for another eight miles to a three-way junction half-a-mile south of tiny Horse Lakes. Take the left-hand road past the marsh and continue for another four miles to the end of the road. (The last three miles are quite rough.) The trail takes off at the end of the road.

The trail can be reached more directly from Libby by following the Pipe Creek Road fifteen to twenty miles north from Libby to the junction a mile past the Pipe Creek campground. Take the right-hand fork up the East Branch of Pipe Creek for about six miles to a "T" junction. Turn right and go another mile and turn onto the South Fork Big Creek Road at the three-way junction by Horse Lakes. Continue to the right past the marsh and four miles to the end of the road where the trail begins.

After winding along the stream for about three miles, the trail is no longer maintained. By not going past the third trail junction (southeastern corner of section 28), you can avoid the unmaintained portion of this hike.

Late summer and fall are best for this hike. Earlier in the season, the trail can be quite wet and boggy. And mosquitoes can make the early summer hike unpleasant.

Since the hike is only six miles round trip, it's nicely suited for families. However, very few hikers use this trail. Even with frequent stops to watch the beavers, a slow hiker can make this trip in four hours.

*West Branch of the South Fork of Big Creek*

Motorized vehicles aren't allowed on this trail from April 1 through November 30. The area seems remote, with the signs of man disappearing once you're a hundred yards from the road. Fishing is fair for smaller cutthroat.

Few hikers make this an overnight backpack. But if you're so inclined, camp at the juncture of the East Branch and West Branch of Big Creek. It has lovely, grassy campsites and a few good fishing pools.

The hike traverses Big Creek/Gold Hill Roadless Area where two timber sales are proposed.—*Linda and Tom Hurlock*

## 5    East Branch of the South Fork of Big Creek

*General description:* A moderate, day hike into a seldom-used and ecologically unusual area.

The South Fork of Big Creek in the Kootenai National Forest. Tom Hurlock photo.

*General location:* Fifteen miles northeast of Libby in the Purcell Mountains.
*Maps:* Ural and Banfield Mountain USGS Quads and Kootenai National Forest, Rexford Ranger District.
*Special attractions:* A very moist site—unusual for Montana.
*For more information:* Write the District Ranger, Rexford Ranger Station, Kootenai National Forest, Box 666, Eureka, MT 59917 or call (406) 296-2536.

This hike is similar to the West Branch of Big Creek except for one addition common to most Montana hikers—a big hill. This hike is still easy, but it has one 700-foot ridge to climb.

Find the trailhead by driving east from Libby to Libby Dam, then north for about twelve miles along the west shore of Koocanusa Reservoir until you turn left (west) on the Bristow Creek Road. Follow the Bristow Creek Road for about two miles until you see Road #4874. Take this road north along the west side of Everett Creek. Go about six miles, crossing Ural Creek, to Trail #70 heading up Geibler Creek in the west side of section 23. The trail is marked with red "blazes."

The trail starts at about 4,900 feet and goes over a 5,600-foot ridge before dropping down to 5,300 where it starts leveling off and turns west to follow the north side of the East Branch. Big Meadow, perhaps the scenic highlight of this hike, lies at 5,000 feet, about two miles past the ridgetop. From here on, the trail crosses a number of small streams and meadows.

There is a clearcut about one-fourth mile from the trailhead. But you can see where the trail takes off from the right edge of the clearcut, about halfway up, by following the painted red arrows.

*East Branch of the South Fork of Big Creek*

From that point, the only sounds are nature's own. Like the West Branch of Big Creek, very few hikers use this trail—even though it's just right for families and beginners.

This is an eight-mile round trip that usually takes about five hours. Water is available along the trail, so there's no need to carry your own.

The trail is adequately maintained, but can be very boggy in the early summer—bad enough to make waterproof boots necessary. Mosquitoes are also abundant during early summer, so most hikers wait until late summer or fall for this hike. Motorized vehicles are banned from April 1 through November 30.

Although black bears are common in the area, bear/hiker conflicts are almost unknown. The area also has a large moose population as well as beaver, muskrat, barred owl, deer, mink, pine martin, spruce grouse, ruffed grouse, and many smaller birds. It's excellent for observing wet-site wild flowers like trillium and false hellebore. Also expect to see beargrass and Canada dogwood.

Most hikers take only one day to make this trip, but it can be an overnight backpack. The best campsite is in the northwestern corner of section 28 where an unmaintained trail crosses the East Branch trail. Firewood and water are plentiful, and the campsite is dry. However, fishing is marginal, as is the case throughout this hike.

An interesting side trip leaves the main trail at the junction on the ridgetop. Follow the side trail less than a mile to the northeast corner of section 27 and go through the openings shown on the Ural USGS Quad sheet to a 6,025-foot knob. From this high point, hikers get a scenic perspective of the entire area, including the Cabinet Mountains on the east horizon.

Perhaps the top attraction of this hike, however, is the gentle valley with meandering stream and wet meadows, the last such site remaining unroaded in the Kootenai area of northwestern Montana. On top of that, it's easily accessible to hikers.

The Forest Service has logging plans for the area around the trailhead, so check with the Rexford Ranger District for a status report before taking this hike.—*Linda and Tom Hurlock*

# 6    Fish Lakes Canyon

*General description:* One of the easiest and most scenic twelve-mile hikes in Montana.

*General location:* Thirty air miles north of Libby on the east side of the Yaak River.

*Maps:* Lost Horse Mountain, Mount Henry, and Yaak USGS Quads; and Kootenai National Forest, Yaak Ranger District.

*Special attractions:* A fifty-foot waterfall and a chain of five lakes in a rugged, low-elevation canyon.

*For more information:* Write the District Ranger, Yaak Ranger District, Kootenai National Forest, Route 1, Troy, MT 59935 or call (406) 295-4717.

To some, Fish Lakes is an overnight camp out. To others, it's a full day's hike. But to every hiker, it's one of the most scenic and diverse trips they've ever taken.

To find the trailhead, take the Pipe Creek Road north from Libby. Follow it for about thirty-one miles until you turn right on Vinal Lake Road #746. Vinal Creek trail #9 takes off to the east about six miles up this road. (This trail isn't shown on the Lost Horse Mountain USGS Quad.)

The trail is well-maintained, has plenty of drinking water, and gets rocky only along a few talus slopes. Elevation gain is a mere 600 feet to the northernmost lake.

It takes an average hiker twelve hours to make the complete round trip. However, if you only want to see South Fish Lake, the first in the series of five, the trip should take eight hours. This makes the Fish Lakes Canyon suitable for almost any hiker—families with children to veteran backpackers.

Forest Service regulations prohibit motorized vehicles from May 1 through October 31. The area is quite remote—except at the north end of the canyon where a few signs of man (i.e. clearcuts in the distance) are barely visible.

Wildlife and wildflowers abound and are characteristic of northwestern Montana—moose, deer, black bear, wakerobin, Canada dogwood, clematis—to name a few. Wild roses line Vinal Creek in great abundance.

Bear danger is low, but mosquitoes can be vicious in June and July. Take this hike anytime during the summer or fall.

For overnighters, there is an undeveloped campsite at Turner Falls, about 3.5 miles into the hike at the mouth of the canyon. It's so close to the falls that the roar of the crescendoing water dominates everything. It has firewood and dry spots to pitch tents.

There is a similar campsite at the foot of South Fish Lake, the second and largest of the chain. This has a great view and good fishing.

South Fish Lake perhaps has the best fishing in the canyon—with nice-sized cutthroat, rainbow, and eastern brook trout; Middle Fish Lake for pan-sized cut-

*The southernmost lake in a chain of lakes in the Fish Lakes Canyon, part of the proposed Mount Henry Wilderness. Tom Hurlock photo.*

*Fish Lakes Canyon*

throat; and North Fish Lake for smaller cutthroat.

Perhaps the most outstanding feature of the hike is Turner Falls. But even without the falls, this would be one of the most beautiful hikes in Montana. Here are five mountain lakes strung through a narrow, rugged canyon lined with a quiet forest of large cedar and larch trees.

Equally remarkable, however, is the fact that this area possibly won't be set aside from development even though it's part of the Mount Henry Wilderness Study Area. Like many other roadless areas in the Kootenai National Forest, timber cutters want to keep this forested valley "from going to waste." Perhaps a letter from hikers to their congressman explaining the value of such a place in its natural state might mean a better future for Fish Lakes Canyon and Mount Henry.—*Linda and Tom Hurlock*

# 7    Parsnip Creek

*General description:* A very short, easy hike.

*General location:* Twenty miles northeast of Libby in the Purcell Mountains.

*Maps:* Inch Mountain USGS Quad and Kootenai National Forest, Rexford Ranger District and Libby Ranger District.

*Special attractions:* Fine example of old-growth cedar woods just off the beaten path.

*For more information:* Write the District Ranger, Libby Ranger District, Kootenai National Forest, Route 2, Box 275, Libby, MT 59923 or call (406) 293-7741.

Parsnip Creek could be described as something besides a hike. Perhaps it would be more appropriately called a good place for a walk in the woods. Actually, it would be perfect for a weary traveler to take a short stroll to calm the nerves.

To find the trailhead, drive east from Libby on State Highway 37, and turn north and go about twenty miles up the west side of Koocanusa Reservoir. Watch carefully for a turn up Parsnip Creek. This road, which turns southwest, is shown on the 1978 Kootenai National Forest Map. It leaves the highway about one-fourth mile north of trail #70. Follow the Parsnip Creek Road until it ends. The trail takes off on the lower side of the road right where the road ends.

Although back from the stream slightly, the trail follows Parsnip Creek for about one-half mile, then it climbs steeply uphill. Hikers usually stroll up the trail to the point where it turns uphill enjoying wildlife and wildflowers, then return. Even with the slow pace, the round trip takes only an hour.

There is virtually no elevation gain. Bear trouble is slight. Mosquitoes aren't a problem. And water is available all along the trail.

Very few hikers camp out on this trail, but a few have stayed at a fair campsite at the end of the road.

Parsnip Creek is part of the Big Creek/Gold Hill Roadless Area which the Forest Service hopes to log in 1983.—*Linda and Tom Hurlock*

# 8    Roderick Mountain

*General description:* A strenuous day hike.

*General location:* Twenty miles north of Troy.

*Maps:* Sylvanite USGS Quad and Kootenai National Forest, Troy Ranger District.

*Special attractions:* Eye-opening scenery from the top of one of northwestern Montana's tallest peaks.

*For more information:* Write the District Ranger, Troy Ranger District, Kootenai National Forest, Box E, Troy, MT 59935 or call (406) 295-4693.

To find the trailhead, drive west of Troy on U.S. 2 for about twelve miles until you turn right on the paved Yaak River Road. After ten miles, watch for the Sylvanite Ranger Station in a clearing on your right. Go less than one mile past the ranger station and turn right on the Burnt Creek Road #472. The Roderick Mountain trailhead (trail #193) is on your right less than one-half mile up the Burnt Creek Road.

A word of caution: The Forest Service is rapidly developing the timber in this area, so new roads are continually under construction. If there is any confusion on the location of the trailhead caused by new road construction, drive back to the Sylvanite Ranger Station and ask for updated instructions.

*Parsnip Creek*

The trail is somewhat rocky and faint in spots, but still easy to follow. Although the trail cuts through deep timber most of the way, there are plenty of open parks with expansive vistas.

It's a gradual uphill pull all the way, going from 2,720 to 6,644 feet in seven miles. The first two miles are the toughest.

Although there are a few springs and intermittent streams, this is essentially a dry, fourteen-mile round trip. Bring plenty of drinking water.

Snow usually leaves the area by mid-July. So anytime in late summer or fall is right for climbing Roderick Mountain.

Actually, you climb three mountains on this hike. At about the four-mile mark, you traverse the western slope of 5,954-foot Skookum Mountain; and a mile later, the trail goes almost to the summit of 6,107-foot Pleasant View Mountain. Although impressive, these two peaks are belittled by Roderick Mountain.

Although few hikers make this an overnighter, you can camp at the base of Roderick Mountain. There are a few springs here, but you are still smart to bring your own water instead of depending on these springs.

From the top of Roderick, you can look east into the very remote country of Sheepherder, Flattail, and Papoose drainages which are trailless and support a struggling population of grizzlies. This takes the keen edge off a wonderful hike since much of this country has been allocated for timber development.—*Mike Comola*

*Black bear, common in most Montana mountain ranges. Harry Engels photo.*

*Roderick Mountain*

# 9   Ten Lakes

*General description:* A moderate two- or three-day backpack in a lake-filled alpine basin.

*General location:* Ten miles northeast of Eureka, on the Canadian border.

*Maps:* Ksanka Peak and Stahl Peak USGS Quads, and the Kootenia National Forest map (1978).

*Special attractions:* Lots of alpine scenery.

*For more information:* Write the District Ranger, Rexford Ranger District, Kootenai National Forest, Box 666, Eureka, MT 59917 or call (406) 296-2536.

The Ten Lakes area receives more than its fair share of snow in the winter, so don't attempt this hike before July 4. Also, Ten Lakes has a few resident grizzly you why Ten Lakes was chosen to be reviewed for wilderness protection under the Montana Wilderness Study Act.

To find the trailhead, turn off U.S. Highway 93 eight miles south of Eureka, onto Forest Service road #114. After thirteen miles, turn left onto FS road #319. Ten miles further, the Wolverine Flats road will take off over an old bridge on Wigwam Creek to the right. You'll want to park one car up Wolverine Creek, if the Wigwam Creek bridge is passable, and another vehicle at Big Therriault Lake, two miles further up road #319.

From Wolverine Creek, trail #89 will start from the end of an old logging road about one mile northeast of the creek road. The trail climbs steeply at first until it gains the ridge between the Ten Lakes Basin on the north, and the Wolverine Flats on the south. The views are expansive in all directions, with glimpses of ranges such as the ice-clad Bugaboos far into Canada.

Follow the ridge trail westward and then southward across the slopes of Poorman Mountain and Green Mountain into the Bluebird Lakes Basin.

The trail reaches Bluebird Lake some six miles from the trailhead, a good place to camp for the night and fish for dinner. Some of the lakes in this area receive heavy summer use, so try to leave your campsite cleaner than you found it.

Continuing to the southeast across the northern shoulder of St. Clair Peak trail #88 (which you've been following from just north of Poorman Mountain), will intersect with trail #339. Take #339 for three miles to Therriault Pass.

At the pass, it is worth your while to drop your packs and take an interesting side trip to the top of Stahl Peak, to visit the lookout and get a panoramic view of the southern portions of the Ten Lakes region. Keep your eyes open for bighorn sheep, which wander the crags during the summer months. The famous naturalist, Ernest Thompson Seton, wrote of the wild sheep in this area in several of his short stories published around the turn of the century. In fact, his namesake mountain, Mount Thompson Seton, lies some seven miles to the southeast of Stahl Peak.

Retracing your steps to Therriault Pass, pick up your packs and continue down the trail to the north, to Big Therriault Lake Campground and your waiting vehicle.

The Ten Lakes Area receives more than its fair share of snow in the winter, so don't attempt this hike before July 4th. Also, Ten Lakes has a few resident grizzly bears, so follow all the standard precautions for camping in bear country.

This spectacular scenery and the wild country of the Ten Lakes area should

*Ten Lakes*

prompt you into writing your congressman or senator in support of including the Ten Lakes Wilderness Study Area in the wilderness system.—*Bill Cunningham.*

# 10    *Pillick Ridge, Ross Creek*

*General description:* A day or overnight hike for experienced hikers, or if two cars are used, a rugged two or three-day, point-to-point hike.

*General location:* Thirty-five miles southwest of Libby in the West Cabinet Mountains (Scotchman Peaks).

*Maps:* Smeads Bench, Heron, and Sawtooth USGS Quads; and Kootenai National Forest, Cabinet Ranger District.

*For more information:* Write the Distict Ranger, Cabinet Ranger District, Kootenai National Forest, Route 2, Box 210, Trout Creek, MT 59874 or call (406) 847-2270.

Hikers who don't mind rugged, dry walking and appreciate wild scenery and solitude should like this trip. Pillick Ridge is the pristine, southeastern spur of the Scotchman Peaks and forms the scenic western backdrop to the Bull River Valley.

A Forest Service trail follows its crest for ten miles to a lookout on Squaw Peak. Views of the Cabinet Mountains, the Bull and Clark Fork Valleys, and Lake Pend O'reille in Idaho are superb.

The hiker stands a good chance of seeing deer, elk, bears, bighorn sheep, and mountain goats. In addition, the southern slopes of the ridge have an abundance of dry-site wildflowers.

To get to the Pillick Ridge trailhead, take State Highway 200 about forty miles west from Thompson Falls, through Trout Creek to the junction with Highway 56. Follow Highway 56 (marked Highway 202 on older maps) for nine miles to the signed trailhead on the west (left) side of the road.

The six-hour walk (twelve miles) to Squaw Peak gains 3,000 feet on trail #1036. Take plenty of water, especially if you're camping. There are sub-alpine basins below the northeast side of the ridge that have water and possible camp-sites. However, once off the ridge, the terrain becomes very steep and brushy, so don't expect easy going or an abundance of level camping spots.

You can return to your car from Squaw Point on the same route, or walk to a second car by way of the Napoleon (#1035) or Star Gulch (#1016) trails, both of which drop down into the Bull River Valley. Napoleon Creek trail takes off to the right two miles before Squaw Peak, as Star Creek does three-fourths of a mile before the mountain. The trailheads join up with Highway 56 thirteen and fourteen miles north of State Highway 200 respectively.

However, by far the best one-way trip entails leaving a second car at the Ross Creek Cedars Scenic Area, fifteen miles north on Highway 56 from the Pillick Ridge trailhead, and four miles west on the well-marked Forest Service Road.

Leaving a car at Ross Creek enables an experienced hiker to strike off north from Squaw Peak for six trailless, ridgetop miles to Sawtooth Mountain. Although the going is very rugged, the viewing is excellent and solitude assured. Be on the alert for elk and mountain goats or even one of the few grizzlies still in this area. Scramble up Sawtooth Mountain for a panorama of the heavily glaciated upper Ross Creek drainage.

Passing around Sawtooth Mountain from the right brings the hiker to the South Fork of Ross Creek. Another option is to wind around Sawtooth Peak and drop into the Middle Fork of Ross Creek. Follow either of these forks downstream for approximately six miles to the Ross Creek Cedars and your car. Only the last four miles will be on a trail; dropping down to the valley floor requires some difficult bushwhacking.

The very wild Ross Creek drainage contains some of the most beautiful forests in the state. However, this hike is strictly for woods-wise hikers with topo maps and compass.

*Bull elk still in velvet. Harry Engels photo.*

*Pillick Ridge, Ross Creek*

Miles

0 1 2 3 4 5

Although the Pillick Ridge and Lower Ross Creek area had broad support in the Forest Service's wilderness review process, the Forest Service has dropped most of those areas from the recommended 75,339-acre Scotchman Peaks Wilderness. Ross Creek and Pillick Ridge offer high quality wilderness recreation and are important to the integrity of the Scotchman Peaks area. Unfortunately, it is now possible that Pillick Ridge and Lower Ross Creek will be developed. The American Smelting and Refining Company (ASARCO), for example, has begun exploratory drilling at Ross Point in the South Fork of Ross Creek, an area that provides year-round mountain goat habitat.—*John Westenberg*

## 11    *Cedar Lakes Loop*

*General description:* A long day or overnight loop for experienced hikers.
*General location:* Ten miles southwest of Libby.
*Maps:* Scenery Mountain USGS Quad and the Cabinet Mountains Wilderness Map.
*Special attractions:* On clear days, spectacular views of the Cabinets, Glacier National Park, Canadian Rockies, Selkirk Mountains in Idaho, the Purcell Mountains, Scotchman Peaks, and Kootenai Falls 4,000 feet below.
*For more information:* Write the District Ranger, Libby Ranger District, Kootenai National Forest, Route 2, Box 275, Libby, MT 59923 or call (406) 293-7741.

For those interested in a fairly demanding hike that can provide many scenic rewards, this trip is ideal.

From Libby, take U.S. 2 west for four miles to the Cedar Creek Road. Turn left (south) onto this road and follow it about three miles until it ends at the trailhead.

The sixteen-mile hike requires a 4,300-foot gain in elevation and most of the walking is on waterless ridgetops. It begins with an easy one-mile walk up the Cedar Creek Trail (closed to motorcycles) to its junction with the Scenery Mountain Trail. Take this well-maintained trail north, then west for approximately five

*Cedar Lakes in the Kootenai National Forest. U.S. Forest Service photo.*

dry, uphill miles to Scenery Mountain. The views get more spectacular as you go, and an open forest of large ponderosa pine further improves the scenery. Most of the trail is on a ridgetop with cool breezes and few insect pests.

The view from Scenery Mountain is superb, particularly when looking down on the jade-colored Kootenai River. Kootenai Falls—the largest remaining falls in Montana—and the China Rapids Area upstream can be seen 4,000 feet below. Kootenai Falls is the site of a proposed hydro-electric facility which would divert most of the water from the falls through underground turbines and would back water three miles covering the China Rapids.

From Scenery Mountain continue west on an unmaintained trail that generally follows the ridgetop for three miles to Grambauer Mountain. Here, the view expands to include Lake Creek and Lower Kootenai Valleys and the Scotchman

0          1          2 Miles

*Cedar Lakes Loop*

Peaks. From Grambauer Peak, head south along the main Cabinet Divide. After a mile of ridge walking, veer slightly to the left, leaving the ridgetop. Bushwhack until intercepting either Lower Cedar Lake or the trail leading to it. Along the way, stop to fill up on some of Montana's largest huckleberry patches.

Both Cedar Lakes have campsites, but avoid those suffering from abuse and overuse—except perhaps to clean them up.

The loop is closed by following the Cedar Creek Trail through a beautiful forest back to the trailhead. Less experienced hikers can make this a twelve-mile round trip by retracing their steps back to the trailhead from Scenery Mountain.

Grizzlies are present in the Cabinets, but sighted less frequently at this northern end of the range. Black bears and many more wild animals are common, however.

Clear weather adds to the enjoyment of this hike. Late August through September is the best time. The bugs are mostly gone, and the shorter, often rainy, days of late fall haven't begun.

The entire trail to Scenery Mountain lies outside the Cabinet Mountains Wilderness, and the Forest Service has refused to study it as a possible addition to the wilderness.—*John Westenberg*

# 12    *Baree and Bear Lakes*

*General description:* A long day hike or leisurely, three-day backpack.
*General location:* Thirty miles south of Libby in the Cabinet Mountains.
*Maps:* Goat Peak and Silver Butte Pass USGS Quads; and the Kootenai National Forest's Cabinet Mountain Wilderness Map.
*For more information:* Write the District Ranger, Cabinet Ranger District, Kootenai National Forest, Route 2, Box 210, Trout Creek, MT 59874 or call (406) 847-2270.

Hikers who like to avoid retracing their steps, but dislike the difficult, two-car logistics that most one-way hikes involve, should like the Baree/Bear Lakes hike. The trailheads to the two lakes are less than a mile apart, and the lakes are connected by a trail along the top of the Cabinet Divide.

A quick study of the Cabinet Wilderness Map shows that there are a number of short hikes in the Cabinets. This hike has the advantage of being among the least traveled routes. Also, these trails are generally open a couple of weeks earlier (late June) than most of the Cabinets.

From Kalispell, take U.S. 2 west for sixty-five miles to the East Fisher River Road. Turn left (south) and proceed up the road for six miles until it forks. Take the right fork, the Silver Butte/Fisher River Road. The Baree Lake trailhead is approximately ten miles up the road.

Trail #489 to Baree Lake goes through a lush forest within earshot of Baree Creek most of the way. The three-mile hike to Baree gains 1,700 feet in elevation. Baree Lake has fair cutthroat fishing.

After Baree Lake, the trail makes an easy climb to the Cabinet Divide, then follows trail #560 along the divide to the north. The viewing from the ridge is excellent, particularly to the west and northwest into Swamp Creek, Wanless and Buck lakes, and the peaks surrounding them. Although grizzlies are uncommon along the Cabinet Divide, making noise along the trail provides extra security.

After a mile of ridgeline hiking, trail #63 to Bear Lakes splits to the right (east). This trail runs just below the top of a spur ridge off the Cabinet Divide. However, a five-minute detour to the top of the ridge affords a nice view of the upper Trail Creek Basin. Stay on the ridgetop until it intersects the trail a mile to the east where it crosses the ridge and drops down into the Bear Lakes.

Only one of the Bear Lakes (the largest and northernmost) has fish. It has one good campsite.

Trail #531 back to the Silver Butte Road cuts east across the outlet of the southernmost Bear Lake, then generally southeast through forested country. After reaching the powerline corridor than runs parallel to the Silver Butte Road, follow it southwest for three-fourths mile to the Baree Lake trailhead and your vehicle.

0          1          2          3  Miles

*Baree/Bear Lakes*

Most of the trail after Bear Lake, much of the Baree Lake trail, and two of the three Bear Lakes lie on Burlington Northern land. The Kootenai National Forest land use plan for the upper Fisher River Country recognized that this and other adjacent private land is important to the integrity of the Cabinet Mountains Wilderness and should be bought or traded for public land in other areas. So far, no steps towards acquisition have been made.

The Trail Creek and Iron Meadows areas to the north and east of Bear Lakes offer interesting variations on the Baree/Bear Lakes hike. This variation requires leaving a car at the Trail Creek trailhead, seven miles up the West Fisher River Road. Rather than returning to the Silver Butte Road from Bear Lake, take the Iron Meadow Trail. This takes the hiker through some of the Kootenai Forest's best elk country. From Iron Meadows, take the Trail Creek trail to the waiting car. Although small, Trail Creek is a productive cutthroat stream.

Like the Bear Lakes area, much of the Trail Creek area is owned by Burlington Northern. BN has announced plans to begin logging in this area in the near future, and the Kootenai National Forest plans to log parts of the Trail Creek drainage. Contact the Kootenai National Forest for an update on logging activities, and express your opinion on how they could affect back country recreation in the area.—*John Westenberg.*

# 13    Leigh Lakes

*General description:* A fairly rigorous, three-mile round trip for beginners.
*General location:* Twelve miles south of Libby
*Maps:* Snowshoe Peak USGS Quad and Kootenai National Forest's Cabinet Wilderness Map.
*For more information:* Write the District Ranger, Cabinet Ranger District, Kootenai National Forest, Route 2, Box 210, Trout Creek, MT 59874 or call (406) 847-2270.

The Cabinet Wilderness is small in size but large in diversity. It contains high peaks, glaciers, rain forests, and numerous lakes. Leigh Lake is the largest lake, nearly a mile across.

Take the Big Cherry Creek turnoff on U.S. 2 about seven miles south of Libby. After three miles, turn right and go seven miles on the Leigh Creek Road to the trailhead at the end of the road. Trail #132 climbs about 1,000 feet in 1.5 miles and ends at the 5,144-foot elevation lake.

At the west end of the lake is a massive, 3,000-foot wall, the high point being 8,712-foot Snowshoe Peak, the highest peak in the Cabinet Range and the highest peak between Glacier National Park and the Cascades.

Hikers can climb this peak from the lake, but it takes most of the day. From the outlet of the lake, head northwest straight up the face of a large east ridge. Once on the ridgetop, follow it southwest to the main ridge, being careful to notice Blackwell Glacier to your right and also being careful not to fall in that direction. After intersecting the main ridge, work your way up along the west side of this ridge until it levels out at the peak. Don't venture out on the snowfields on the east side of the main ridge unless you're properly trained and equipped for ice work.

Leigh Lake is good fishing. The trout (good-sized rainbows and brookies) are under ice most of the year and get particularly excited over fresh bait. If you're a hardy soul, you can pack a small rubber raft for use on the lake.

This area records phenomenal amounts of snow (20-30 feet). In July, the lake is still full of icebergs. The waves lap them into strange designs, and paddling around them, looking down and seeing the odd shapes down in the deep blue water gives one an eerie feeling. Some ice floes are quite large, and one can land

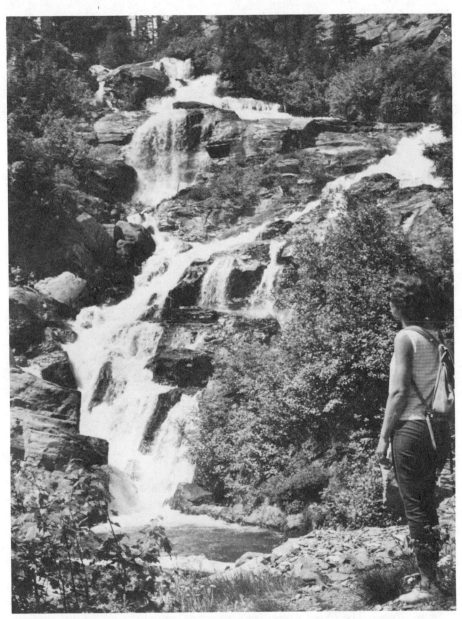

*Waterfall on the way to Leigh Lake in the Cabinet Mountains Wilderness. U.S. Forest Service photo.*

*Leigh Lake*

(wearing a life vest, of course) and fish from them.

The lake is well within the Cabinet Mountains Wilderness but easy to reach. This makes it popular locally, so hit this one on a weekday.—*Pat Caffrey*

## 14    *Three Lakes Peak*

*General description:* A fairly demanding one-day climb.

*General location:* Thirty-five miles northwest of Missoula on the Reservation Divide.

*Maps:* Perma and Tarkio USGS Quads and Lolo National Forest Recreation map. (Note: The Quad maps are somewhat outdated and do not show the road to the trailhead. Recent Lolo National Forest Travel Plan Maps show the trail clearly.)

41

*Special attractions:* Pleasant hike along a subalpine ridge, with great views of much of Western Montana.

*For more information:* Write the District Ranger, Nine-mile Ranger District, Lolo National Forest, Huson, MT 59846 or call (406) 626-5201.

Squaw Peak, the highest peak on Reservation Divide and a well-known landmark for Missoula residents, is easily and frequently climbed. Three Lakes Peak, a dozen miles northwest of Squaw, provides a slightly more demanding, but more interesting, hike.

To find the trailhead, take I-90 west from Missoula to the Nine-mile exit; follow the county road north to the Nine-mile Ranger Station. Turn left at the ranger station and follow the road that heads up the Nine-mile valley. Go thirteen miles before crossing a cattle guard and entering the Lolo National Forest. One mile

0          1          2 Miles

*Three Lakes Peak*

after entering the National Forest, the road forks. Take the right fork (north) toward the Reservation Divide. Follow this road for five miles to the trailhead.

The trailhead to Three Lakes Peak is marked as the Burnt Fork Pinnacle Trail #418. The trailhead is located at the west end of a clearcut on the north side of the road. The trail begins as a winding logging road skirting the edge of the clearcut. The logging road soon becomes a trail and climbs up to the Reservation Divide by way of the Burnt Fork Pinnacle, the former site of a lookout tower. Some stretches of trail between the trailhead and Burnt Fork Pinnacle show signs of erosion from trailbike abuse.

Soon after Burnt Fork Pinnacle, the trail intersects the Reservation Divide pack trail. Turn right (east) onto this trail. Here, the trail is usually above timberline and offers excellent views of the Nine-mile Valley, Nine-mile Divide, and the higher portion of the Great Burn recommended wilderness area on the Montana/Idaho border to the southwest.

Continue east for 2.5 miles until directly below the south summit of Three Lakes Peak. Scramble up the talus slope to the south summit, then on to the higher summit.

From the summit of Three Lakes Peak you can see the Cabinet Mountains to the northwest, the National Bison Range and Flathead Lake to the north, the Mission Mountains to the east, and the Bitterroots to the south. Below the summit to the east is a picturesque glacial cirque with, appropriately, three lakes. East along the Reservation Divide is conical-shaped Squaw Peak.

The ten-mile round trip to the peak and back takes a full day. And it's dry, so take plenty of water. Wait until late June for the snow to melt.

There are a number of enjoyable hikes along the Reservation Divide. The Three Lakes Peak hike is a good introduction to an area that is rarely used and quite wild.

Oddly, it wasn't wild enough to warrant serious wilderness study by the Forest Service. Thus, the future of this *de facto* wilderness is uncertain.—*John Westenberg*

# 15  *Hub Lake, Ward and Eagle Peaks*

*General description:* An excellent day or overnight family trip, with a number of short day trips from Hub Lake.

*General location:* Seventy miles northwest of Missoula in the Bitterroot Mountains.

*Maps:* Haugan SW and Haugan SE USGS Quads and Lolo National Forest Recreation Map.

*Special attractions:* Beautiful subalpine country on a scale small enough to be easily enjoyed by families with small children.

*For more information:* Write the District Ranger, Superior Ranger District, Lolo National Forest, Box 457, Superior, MT 59872 or call (406) 822-4233.

The Ward and Eagle Peak area is a "pocket wilderness" that, in spite of its small size, holds many scenic and recreational attractions.

It can be reached by taking I-90 west from Missoula for fifty-seven miles to St. Regis. About eight miles past St. Regis, turn south (left) onto the Ward Creek Road. Follow the Ward Creek Road for about eight miles, until it crosses Ward

*Hub Lake, Ward and Eagle Peak*

Creek. The trailhead is on the right side of the road just before it crosses the creek.

The three-mile trail (#262) to Hub Lake follows Ward Creek much of the way so don't worry about carrying drinking water. Soon after the trailhead, it enters a beautiful, fern-bottomed, cedar grove with some cedars over six feet across at the base. Soon after leaving the grove, the trail overlooks Dipper Falls, a pleasant spot for a break.

After turning right at the first intersection onto trail #280, the next mile of walking is steep, consuming most of the 1,500 feet of altitude gained in the hike to Hub Lake. Here, the main diversion is picking huckleberries. About 2.5 miles from the trailhead, the trail passes Hazel lake, which has pan-sized cutthroat, but its shore is too steep and brushy for camping.

Hub Lake is only a half-mile beyond Hazel Lake, not 1.5 miles as indicated on the Forest Service sign at the trailhead. Take this hike anytime after June.

There are two campsites at Hub Lake. The one near the outlet is brushy, but generally dry. The remains of an old prospector's cabin, now almost hidden in brush, lie between the trail and the campsite, and an abandoned mine overlooks the upper end of the lake. When dry, the meadows at the upper end of the lake offer good camping. Both campsites have plenty of firewood.

Although Hub Lake only offers fair fishing for cutthroat, it does lie in a picturesque subalpine setting. Hub Lake is also a good jumping-off spot for day hikes to Ward or Eagle peaks (both are within the capabilities of children) or fishing trips to Clear (rainbow), Gold (rainbow), Square (brook), and Hazel (cutthroat) Lakes. You won't catch anything large, but you will probably add fish to your camp fare. You'll want the Haugan SW USGS Quad for the cross country hiking needed to reach some of these lakes. Mary Lake, in the cirque below Warm Peak, has no fish, but is a pleasant stop enroute to Ward Peak.

Most of western Montana's big game species are found in this area, and the alert hiker has a chance of seeing them. Although grizzlies are gone from the Bitterroots, a good population of black bears remains.

The Lolo National Forest has not banned motorcycles from the trail to Hub Lake. However, there is little sign of cycle use, and, except for the clearcuts that can be seen from the peaks, there is no significant sign of man. The abandoned mining ruins gradually being reclaimed by nature contribute to the sense of being in the back country.

The Ward-Eagle Peak area offers small doses of the medicine that give Montana's mountains their healing power—beautiful forests, waterfalls, wildlife, berries, interesting history, and fishing. And they are accessible to all hikers.—*John Westenberg.*

# 16   Great Burn Loop

*General description:* A long, thirty-mile loop trip through the heart of the Great Burn proposed wilderness.

*General location:* Thirty miles west of Missoula.

*Maps:* Straight Peak USGS Quad and the Lolo National Forest Map (1975).

*Special attractions:* Beautiful subalpine country along the Bitterroot Divide.

*For more information:* Write the District Ranger, Superior Ranger District, Lolo

*Great Burn Loop*

National Forest, Superior, MT 59872 or call (406) 822-4233.

The Great Burn is a huge roadless area of almost 200,000 acres straddling the Idaho-Montana border, due west of Missoula. This superb loop hike will take you through long, timbered valleys and along open subalpine country on the Bitterroot Divide as well. Even this long, thirty mile hike will only touch a small portion of the back country hiking in the Great Burn.

Drive west from Missoula on Interstate 90, and turn south at the Fish Creek exit onto Forest Service road #343. After seven miles on #343 (which passes the largest ponderosa pine tree in the state), turn right on FS road #7750 and drive the remaining six miles to the trailhead at Clearwater Crossing.

The loop hike can be done in any direction, but this description goes counterclockwise up the North Fork of Fish Creek, along the Bitterroot Divide, returning to the trailhead via the West Fork of Fish Creek. The loop starts by heading north on trail #102 which eventually changes into trail #103.

The first ten miles of the hike follow the North Fork of Fish Creek as it curves north and then west up to the Bitterroot Divide. From the five to seven mile mark, the trail passes through private land next to the Greenwood Cabins. If you choose to camp before the trail reaches the divide, try to camp on Forest Service land after the trail leaves private cabins.

It's a steep, thousand-foot ascent out of the upper North Fork basin to a low pass on the state line, where the trail descends into Idaho to Goose Lake and several good campsites. Fill up with water here, since the trail stays high and dry for the next nine miles. If you choose to wet a hook in pursuit of some of Goose Lake's elusive trout, remember that you're in Idaho and need an Idaho license.

From the low point on the pass near Goose Lake (5,840 feet in elevation), the trail rolls up and down over the minor summits of the northern Bitterroot Range, eventually reaching a high point of 7,334 feet. The trail (#738 on the Lolo Forest map) crosses the broad meadows and knife-edged ridges as it follows the crest of the divide south to Fish Lake. Here, you are in the very center of the proposed Great Burn Wilderness, and views extend in every direction. On clear days, the tops of the Mission Mountains appear far to the east; the crumpled ranges of the huge Bighorn-Weitas roadless country stretch off to the west in Idaho. Wildflowers are spectacular early in the summer, and ghostly snags remind the hiker of the Great Burn which swept through this country during August of 1910.

The trail is dry all the way to Fish Lake, but it may be possible to bushwhack down to several of the subalpine lakes which hug both sides of the range and camp within reach of the divide trail.

The route turns northward down the West Fork of Fish Creek some nine miles after leaving Goose Lake. Hikers wishing to enjoy another day high on the divide can take a short detour southward to Fish Lake on the Idaho side of the range before continuing down the West Fork.

From the divide trail, it is about ten miles down to Clearwater Crossing and your vehicle. The central portion of this stretch is quite boggy and might slow your progress enough to encourage you to linger at one of the several campsites along the West Fork. The trail (#101) also passes through groves of old western red cedars, western larch, and big lodgepoles, which make this valley hiking much more pleasant than most valley trails.

Bear problems seem nonexistent along this hike, although there are reports of an occasional grizzly siting in the wild country of the Great Burn.

The Bitterroot Divide gets more snow than most parts of Montana, so don't attempt this loop before July 4. It might be worth your while to check about snow conditions with the Forest Service before you try an early July hike in a heavy snow year. Being wet country, bugs can be a problem, so bring something to keep them at bay.

Although recommended for wilderness protection by the Forest Service during RARE II, timber sales continue to nibble away at the edges of the Great Burn. Check with your local conservation organization for a progress report on the Great Burn wilderness proposal.—*Ed Madej*

# 17    Heart and Dalton Lakes

*General description:* A short day hike to a subalpine lake basin.
*General location:* Thirty miles west of Missoula.
*Maps:* Straight Peak USGS Quad and the Lolo National Forest Map (1975).
*Special attractions:* Cutthroat trout in the lakes and huckleberries in the bushes.
*For more information:* Write the District Ranger, Superior Ranger District, Lolo
   National Forest, Superior, MT 59872 or call (406) 822-4233.

The proposed Great Burn Wilderness sprawls for nearly forty miles along the Bitterroot Divide due west of Missoula. This short hike is sure to tantalize you with the hiking possibilities in this 200,000-acre area, which is one of the wilder roadless areas in Montana.

Drive west from Missoula on Interstate 90 and turn south on the Trout Creek Road (FS road #250) from the Superior exit. After about nineteen miles, the road makes a sharp switchback to the right. At this switchback, the trail to Heart Lake heads south from the road.

The trail climbs some 1,200 feet in two miles to the shore of Heart Lake, crossing the South Fork of Trout Creek several times. In late August and early September, ripe huckleberries line the trail and make this trek memorable for its incredible edibles.

Heart Lake has a good population of fishable cutthroat, and makes a good turnaround point for day hikers. Those wishing to explore a little further have three options.

An unmarked trail climbs higher up the lake basin, past Pearl Lake and over a low pass to Dalton Lake. Pearl appears to be too turbid for good fishing, but Dalton Lake has small trout and the advantage of being more remote (and less fished) than Heart Lake.

A steep trail leads westward to the Bitterroot Divide (see the Great Burn Loop hike description) and the Idaho border, providing astounding views of vast roadless country in the forested mountains of our neighboring state.

A third trail leads to the 7,440-foot summit of Lightning Peak, just east of Heart Lake, and eventually drops down into Cement Gulch and returns to the Trout Creek road. However, most hikers will want to return by way of Heart Lake to their vehicles and skip this eight mile long side trip.

Late summer is the best time to appreciate this hike, when the bugs are gone, the berries are ripe, and hunting season has not yet begun.—*Bill Cunningham*

Heart & Dalton Lakes

49

# 18 Stateline Trail South

*General description:* An easy day hike.

*General location:* Forty-five miles west of Missoula in the Bitterroot Mountains.

*Maps:* Illinois Peak NW, Illinois Peak SW, Illinois Peak SE, and Hoodoo USGS Quads; and Lolo National Forest Recreation Map.

*Special attraction:* A grassy mountaintop with an excellent view of the northern Bitterroot Mountains.

*For more information:* Write the District Ranger, Superior Ranger District, Lolo National Forest, Superior, MT 59872 or call (406) 822-4233.

Perhaps because the higher portions of the Bitterroot Mountains north of Lolo Pass aren't visible from a major highway, they remain relatively unknown. On a

Stateline Trail South

map they are easily overlooked and underrated; none of the peaks reach 8,000 feet.

Because they're among the westernmost of Montana's mountain ranges, they receive an abundance of rain and snow. The result is an abundance of alpine scenery at lower elevations than most mountain ranges. At 7,690 feet, Illinois Peak is one of the highest peaks in the northern Bitterroots. The walk to the top goes through pleasant subalpine country and offers lots of scenic views, as does the peak itself.

From Missoula, take I-90 west to Superior. After taking the Superior exit, turn left and go under the freeway, then turn left again onto the gravel road on the far side of the underpass. About 1.5 miles down the county road, the Cedar Creek Road takes off into the foothills to the right. Follow this winding road for twenty miles to the Bitterroot (or Stateline) Divide, which is clearly marked.

At the divide, take the Stateline Trail #738 on the left to the southeast. In 1981, this trail was designated as a national recreation trail, in recognition of its outstanding recreational qualities. The route along the divide has been used since aboriginal times, and the national recreation trail portion stretches twenty-eight miles from near Eagle Cliff on the north to Hoodoo Pass on the south. The trail and the pass are dry, so stock up on water at one of the creeks you'll cross while driving to the trailhead.

The trail is faint in places, but by sticking close to the divide you'll be sure to find it again. It's about five miles from the trailhead and Illinois Peak—making this a ten-mile round trip.

The Mission and southern Bitterroot Mountains and vast roadless areas in the Idaho Panhandle are frequently in view. Illinois Peak, 1,200 feet higher than the trailhead, offers a good view of much of the recommended Great Burn Wilderness to the southeast. Illinois Peak's grassy top is a good place to sit back and enjoy lunch.

On this hike, the wind keeps the hiker cool and the bugs down. This is a good hike from mid-July to mid-October.

The only fly-in-the-ointment is the motorcycle use of the trail. They have begun to tear up some of the subalpine vegetation along the trail. Contact the Lolo National Forest in Missoula, if you're interested in protecting this trail from noise and erosion.—*John Westenberg*

# 19   *Stateline Trail North*

*General description:* An easy, overnight or day round trip, or, if two vehicles are used, a mostly downhill point-to-point hike.
*General location:* Fifty miles west of Missoula in the Bitterroot Mountains.
*Maps:* Illinois Peak SE and Illinois Peak SW USGS Quads; and the Lolo National Forest Recreation Map.
*Special attractions:* An abundance of easily accessible subalpine country.
*For more information:* Write the District Ranger, Superior Ranger District, Lolo National Forest, Superior, MT 59872 or call (406) 822-4233.

Most Montanans think of the spectacular eastern front of the Selway-Bitterroot Wilderness when the Bitterroot Mountains are mentioned. However, from Lolo Pass north to Lookout Pass lies a section of the Bitterroots with a slightly dif-

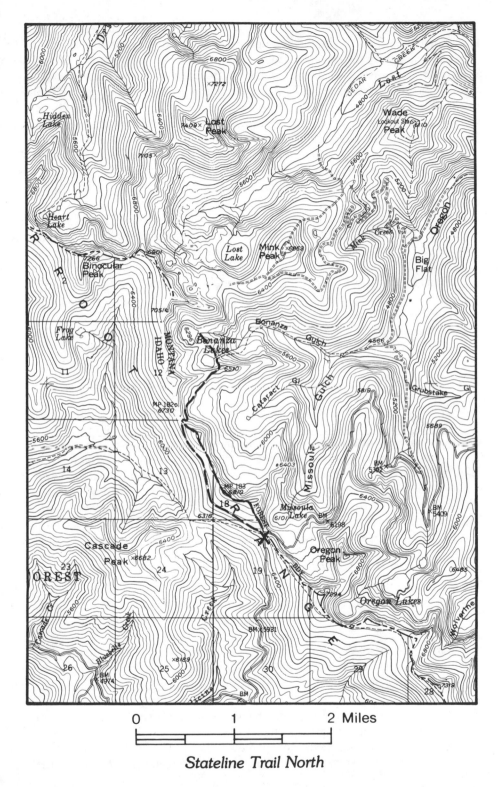

**Stateline Trail North**

ferent, but equally appealing, character. Although the northern Bitterroots are less craggy than their southern counterparts, they are heavily dotted with lakes. There are over forty fishable lakes on the Montana side of the Bitterroot Divide, most within an easy walk from a trailhead. Because of the fire which swept through much of the area in 1910, these mountains feature a more open, easily traversable terrain.

The Stateline Trail goes northwest from where Cedar Creek Road crosses the Bitterroot (or Stateline) Divide. To get there from Missoula, take I-90 west of Superior. Exit at Superior, and turn left to go under the freeway. Take another left just beyond the underpass onto the paved county road. After 1.5 miles, turn right onto the Cedar Creek Road. Follow it for twenty winding miles to the clearly marked divide and trailhead.

At the trailhead, you have two options. One is to take Stateline Trail #738 taking off just to the left (Idaho) side of the divide. It quickly splits with the left fork dropping down into Idaho. Take the right fork, which follows a contour along the Idaho side of the ridge.

The trail forks again 1.5 miles beyond the trailhead. Again, take the right fork back across the divide into Montana and through a grassy basin for about one mile to Bonanza Lakes.

The other option at the trailhead is to follow the jeep road that straddles the crest of the divide. The jeep trail soon disappears, and you follow the trailless but open ridge—with good views both ways—until you intersect the trail mentioned in the first option, 1.75 miles later. Follow it to the right down into the basin holding Bonanza Lakes.

Both routes are about two miles and have a small elevation loss from trailhead to lakes, so they are suited for hikers of all ages and abilities. Bring drinking water, as both routes are dry.

A pleasant, open campsite with plenty of firewood is located between the two lakes slightly closer to the larger, upper lake. Both lakes contain small brookies.

The Stateline Trail, which was designated a national recreational trail in 1981, goes beyond Bonanza Lake along the divide past Eagle Cliff to the northwest. This makes an excellent through hike if one leaves another car on the Dry Creek Road #342 where it crosses the Bitterroot Divide.—*John Westenberg*

## 20    Blodgett Canyon

*General description:* An easy day or overnight hike.

*General location:* Five miles northwest of Hamilton in the Bitterroot Mountains.

*Maps:* Printz Ridge USGS Quad and the Selway Bitterroot Wilderness Map (1980).

*For more information:* Write the District Ranger, Stevensville Ranger District, Bitterroot National Forest, Stevensville, MT 59870 or call (406) 777-5461.

There is a tendency to think of a hike as something that's done to get somewhere. In Blodgett Canyon, no object is necessary beyond the hike itself. Just a hundred yards from the car, the hiker is walking along a beautiful stream and looking up at spectacular canyon walls.

These basic scenic ingredients continue throughout the hike. Because there is no need to get to any particular point and there are ample campsites along the

*Scenic delights along Blodgett Creek in the Bitterroot Mountains. U.S. Forest Service photo.*

way, a hike up Blodgett Canyon is ideal for families and anyone who enjoys unhurried walking with lots of pleasant stops.

To get to Blodgett Canyon trailhead, take U.S. 93 south from Missoula up the Bitterroot Valley. Turn west (right) onto the county road two miles north of Hamilton just before U.S. 93 crosses the Bitterroot River. Follow this road west for one-half mile, south for 1.75 miles, then west again for the last two miles to

*Blodgett Canyon*

the trailhead.

Blodgett Canyon is the most spectacular of the many canyons penetrating the east front of the Selway-Bitterroot Wilderness. The vertical relief from canyon bottom to ridgetops is nearly 4,000 feet. Blodgett Creek itself, like all the streams in the Bitterroots, is clear and cold. It also has good fishing for pan-sized rainbows. The trail, which is never steep for extended periods, generally goes through pleasant forest environment, sometimes crosses talus slopes, and is always close to Blodgett Creek. (So don't worry about drinking water.) Sheer granite faces of 500-600 feet are common on the north side of the canyon, and there are several waterfalls between three and six miles into the hike.

Because it stays low, this trail is open earlier than many hikes. Chances of seeing wildlife increase further up the canyon. Moose, elk, and deer are found in Blodgett, and mountain goats range the ridgetops. Hikers willing to tackle the steep, 1,400-foot climb up to High Lake, on the south rim of the canyon, have a good chance of seeing mountain goats.

Although you can hike a full twenty miles up the canyon, most hikers take shorter day or overnight hikes into the area. Go until you feel like stopping and either pick a campsite (all with plenty of firewood) or turn back to the trailhead.

Though surrounded by the Selway-Bitterroot Wilderness, Blodgett Canyon is not part of it. When the Selway-Bitterroot Wilderness was set aside in 1939, Blodgett Canyon was excluded because it was considered a possible site for a dam and reservoir for Bitterroot Valley water users. Although the Forest Service has recommended Blodgett Canyon for wilderness, there has been some local

*Blodgett Canyon in the Bitterroot National Forest. U.S. Forest Service photo.*

opposition to the proposal. Contact the Bitterroot National Forest for an update on the issue.—*John Westenberg*

# 21    Canyon Falls

*General description:* A pleasant day hike in the Bitterroot Range.
*General location:* Seven miles west of Hamilton in the Selway Bitterroot Wilderness.
*Maps:* Printz Ridge and Ward Mountain USGS Quads and the Selway-Bitterroot Wilderness Map (1980).
*Special attractions:* The spectacular drops of Canyon Falls.
*For more information:* Write the District Ranger, Stevensville Ranger District, Bitterroot National Forest, Stevensville, MT 59870 or call (406) 777-5461.

Canyon Falls is one of the prettier, more accessible waterfalls in the Bitterroot Range. It's an easy day hike up from the Bitterroot Valley.

Turn west onto a county road from U.S. 93 just before it crosses the Bitterroot River, two miles north of Hamilton. Follow this road west for one-half mile, south for 1.75 miles, then west until it intersects FS road #735. Follow FS road #735 to the trailhead on Canyon Creek.

The trail stays to the northern side of the creek, avoiding stream crossings, and reaches Canyon Falls in about three miles. Canyon Falls is actually a series of cataracts along the stream, with the total drop approaching 200 feet. The views of the falls from the trail are spectacular, especially in May or June when the creek is swollen with snowmelt. Don't be tempted to clamber closer, though; the rotten rock and slippery footing virtually invite an accident.

If you're out for more than just a day hike, continue up past the falls for one-half mile to Canyon Lake, which has a few campsites along its northern shore. From a camp on Canyon Lake, it's an easy stroll further up the Canyon to Wyant Lake. Those inclined for a little mountaineering can go beyond Wyant Lake and ascend Canyon Peak (9,153 feet) via its rocky southern ridge.

Canyon Creek drains one of the smaller canyons penetrating the east side of the Bitterroots, but what it lacks in size it makes up for in scenic beauty; one of the smaller gems in the vast Selway-Bitterroot Wilderness.—*Don Reed*

# 22    Kerlee Lake

*General description:* A steep, overnight hike to a subalpine lake on the southern flanks of the Como Peaks.
*General location:* Seven miles west of Hamilton in the Selway-Bitterroot Wilderness.
*Maps:* Como Peaks and El Capitan USGS Quads and the Selway-Bitterroot Wilderness Map.
*Special attractions:* The high peaks of the southern Bitterroot Range.
*For more information:* Write the Distict Ranger, Darby Ranger District, Bitterroot National Forest, Darby, MT 59829 or call (406) 821-3913.

The jagged peaks of this portion of the Bitterroots are the highest mountains in the entire range, which stretches over 300 miles along Montana's western border. This hike will take you in to see some of the more interesting peaks of the

*Canyon Falls*

Selway-Bitterroot Wilderness, such as El Capitan, the Lonesome Bachelor, and the Como Peaks.

The trailhead starts from the end of FS Road #639, which leaves U.S. 93 just south and west of Darby. The Tin Cup Creek Trail (#96) starts up the canyon on the south side of the stream from the road just before it enters a parcel of private land within the forest.

The trail winds its way through dense timber in the lower reaches of the canyon, crossing Tin Cup Creek twice. These crossings can be tricky early in the summer, so it's best to wait and attempt this trek after July 4.

Some 5.5 miles from the trailhead, watch for a bridge crossing to the north side of the creek and the trail to Kerlee and Goat Lakes. It's a very steep 1,500-foot climb to tiny Goat Lake and the much larger Kerlee Lake. But the altitude gain has its rewards; although the main Tip Cup Creek Trail receives a moderate amount of use, few people bother to do the steep grunt up to these subalpine lakes.

Both lakes offer a choice of campsites, but Kerlee has the edge on scenery, with views of the high, rocky peaks to the north of the lake. Those exhausted by the climb to the lake basin can lounge around and fish, but the more ambitious hiker can attempt the scramble to the summit of massive El Capitan, two miles to the northwest. Climb the hillsides to the northwest of Kerlee Lake making sure to stay low enough to avoid the vertical rock walls on the southern slopes of the Lonesome Bachelor.

After reaching a low pass between the Bachelor and El Cap, cautiously follow the eastern ridge to the windswept summit, 9,983 feet high. Here are stupendous views of the Como Peaks, the Lonesome Bachelor, and the lakes in Little Rock Creek far below. To the west lie the forested ridges of the vast Selway-Bitterroot Wilderness and the canyons centered around the wild Selway River. To the south is a sawtoothed ridge with granite towers separating the valley of Tin Cup Creek from the North Fork of Trapper Creek. Few views of the Bitterroots are better than those from the summit of El Capitan.

Technical rock climbers will find the many faces of El Cap, the Bachelor, and Como Peaks to have challenging routes. Hikers should steer clear of the more difficult mountains thereabouts and limit themselves to the east edge of El Capitan.

In all, this trip makes a superb three-day or longer introduction to the high country of the Selway-Bitterroot.—*Don Reed*

# 23   Overwhich Falls

*General description:* A moderate, two-day backpack.

*General location:* Eight miles southwest of Sula or about eighty miles south of Missoula.

*Maps:* Medicine Hot Springs and Piquett Mountains USGS Quads; and Bitterroot National Forest, Sula Ranger District.

*For more information:* Write the District Ranger, Sula Ranger District, Bitterroot National Forest, Sula, MT 59871 or call (406) 821-3201.

Drive south of Missoula on U.S. 93 and keep going until you're thirteen miles past Sula at the Lost Trail Ski Area. From the ski area's parking lot, take the Saddle Mountain Road (signed) and follow it about four miles to where it ends and

*Kerlee Lake*

**Overwhich Falls**

the trail begins. The Saddle Mountain Road is rough and rocky, so expect a bumpy ride.

Leave a vehicle or have somebody pick you up at the Crazy Creek Campground, twenty-two miles north by road. To find this campground, drive 4.8 miles north of Sula on U.S. 93 to Warm Springs Road #370. Turn southwest at the Moosehead Museum and follow Road #370 for 4.5 miles to Crazy Creek Campground.

From the trailhead, take Trail #605 to the junction with trail #83 at Colter Creek. Take #83 to Overwhich Falls. Then, turn north on Trail #103 and stay on it all the way to Crazy Creek Campground. There are several trail junctions along the way, so keep your map handy. Most junctions are well marked.

All of these trails are well maintained except for a small relocation just before

Overwhich Falls on #605 and a few brushy spots on #103. Although not abundant, drinking water is usually available. Trail #605 has two good springs, and Trail #83 follows Shields Creek. Trail #103 follows streams most of the way, but since the lower portions are grazed by domestic cattle, you should treat water before drinking.

Since there isn't a steep climb—as is the case with most long hikes—the Overwhich Falls trip is suitable for all hikers. Most hikers are interested in a leisurely hike and take at least two days, but ambitious hikers could hike this in one day.

All three trails are open to motorcycle use, and cattle graze the Warm Springs area during summer months. With these exceptions, the signs of civilization are rare. Wait until July for snow to melt and make the Saddle Mountain Road passable.

The highlight of the trip is, of course, 200-foot Overwhich Falls, which can be viewed from the trail. For a closer look, drop your pack and bushwhack a short way to the creek below the falls.

Just past the falls, you can take a short side trip up Trail #400 to Pass and Capri lakes. Although both lakes have a few cutthroat, fishing is considered marginal, as it is in the streams along the way— with the possible exception of Warm Springs Creek, which can be good. The area is noted for its large, productive huckleberry patches, so consider substituting berry-picking for fishing.

The hike has several good campsites—Pass or Capri Lakes, or on the trail between them, or Three Forks and Sheepshead Flat. All have plenty of firewood. Overwhich Falls doesn't have readily available water, but the other sites do.—*Wayne Avants*

## 24 Blue Joint

*General description:* A four-day backpack.
*General location:* Thirty-five miles southwest of Hamilton on the Idaho/Montana border.
*Maps:* Painted Rocks Lake NW, Painted Rocks Lake SW, and Nezperce Peak USGS Quads; and the Bitterroot National Forest Map. Also useful is the Forest Service's River of No Return Wilderness Map.
*For more information:* Write the District Ranger, West Fork Ranger District, Bitterroot National Forest, Darby, MT 59829 or call (406) 821-3269.

Getting to the Blue Joint area involves a long drive for most hikers, but it's well worth it, especially if you like long backpacking trips into wild country seldom visited by hikers.

To find the trailhead, drive south from Darby on U.S. 93 for about five miles. Just before you cross the Bitterroot River, turn right up the West Fork of the Bitterroot. There is a sign for Trapper Creek Job Corps Center and West Fork Ranger Station at this junction, along with the Peaks & Pines trailer court.

Drive up this road for about thirteen miles until you see the Forest Service's West Fork Ranger Station. Go past the ranger station, and after only one-half mile, turn right on the Nezperce Road and drive about sixteen miles to Nezperce Pass. At the pass, turn left and park in a parking lot where the trail starts.

This is a twenty-nine-mile loop starting and ending at this trailhead. It can be taken in either direction, but it would be easier to take the stateline trail first and

Blue Joint

then come back to the trailhead by hiking down Blue Joint Creek.

The trail continues on a ridgetop hill all the way to Reynolds Lake—about thirteen miles. Be careful not to get on the Castle Rock trail which junctures with the stateline trail about one fourth mile from the trailhead. The trail down Jack the Ripper Creek takes off to the left about one mile from the trailhead. This is the trail that will bring you back to your vehicle, three days later.

With the exception of Two Buck Springs (about seven miles from the trailhead), there is no drinking water until you reach Reynolds Lake. So leave the vehicle with full water bottles and fill them again at Two Buck Springs which, incidentally, is a good place to spend the first night.

All along this trail, including from Two Buck Springs, the view of the Selway River country in Idaho is spectacular. This is subalpine country, featuring whitebark pine and lots of standing snags. Although firewood is available, it's often scarce and aesthetic. Be sure to bring your backpack stove.

The second day's hike is more ridgetop hiking with scenic vistas on each side. It's about six miles to Reynolds Lake, a good second campsite. Don't miss the trail junction just before Reynolds Lake. It occurs in a small, grassy valley with water. Take the lefthand trail to the lake. Reynolds Lake has fishing for cutthroat to add to the evening's entertainment.

About two miles after leaving Reynolds Lake, you reach the Blue Joint Creek trail junction. There is a primitive road leading to this trail junction, and it's possible to have a vehicle left here to make this a point-to-point hike. However, it would be your big loss to miss the Blue Joint Creek. The trail down this drainage is twelve miles long and well maintained with plenty of drinking water. It winds through a wide valley with grassy meadows and a meandering Blue Joint Creek. The stream has good fishing for small cutthroat.

Blue Joint Meadows (six miles from Reynolds Lake) is especially beautiful and a wise choice for your third campsite. This leaves eight miles for the last day.

The trail up Jack the Ripper Creek takes off about five miles from Blue Joint Meadows. Watch carefully for this junction. It juts off to the left just after a creek crossing. It's easy to see, but there is no sign.

The trail gradually climbs up Jack the Ripper for about three miles along a small, troutless stream and through small but gorgeous meadows. The last half-mile is fairly steep as you approach the ridgeline.

Then, retrace your footsteps from three days hence for about one mile to the trailhead and your waiting vehicle, leaving some of Montana's most spectacular, yet gentle, back country behind you.

Although you won't see grizzly bears along this hike, black bears are fairly common, so be careful with your food and keep a clean camp. The area also has adequate supplies of most other wildlife associated with western Montana, including mountain lions, mountain goats, elk, deer, and moose. Mosquitoes usually aren't a big problem after June. You'll want to wait until at least July anyway to let the snows free the area.

The 61,400-acre Blue Joint Wilderness Study Area is actually a portion of the immense River of No Return Wilderness country which extends across the Idaho border into Montana. The 2.2 million-acre River of No Return is the largest designated wilderness in the lower 48 states, and Blue Joint would make a fine addition to this spectacular area.

On the way home, your enthusiasm for the grandeur of this area might be dampened by the fact that it might not be the same for the next generation. Although the area is undergoing a congressionally mandated wilderness study, there is intense pressure to develop the minimal timber resource in the Blue Joint Wilderness Study Area instead of setting it aside. Check with the Bitterroot National Forest for a progress report on this controversy.—*Bob Oset*

# 25   *Stoney Lake, Dome Shaped Mountain*

*General description:* An overnighter for families with the option—for hikers in good condition—of climbing Dome Shaped Mountain.

*General location:* Twenty-five miles northeast of Hamilton in the Sapphire Mountains.

*Maps:* Mount Emerine, Burnt Fork Lakes, Skalkaho Pass, and Stoney Creek USGS Quads; and Deerlodge National Forest Map.

*For more information:* Write the District Ranger, Philipsburg Ranger District, Deerlodge National Forest, Philipsburg, MT 59858 or call (406) 859-3211

Part of the enjoyment of hiking in the Sapphires is the feeling that you've discovered an area that most hikers would ordinarily drive past without a second glance. The Sapphires (once they've got your attention) prove that there is more to the "wilderness experience" than craggy peaks and snowfields.

Stoney Lake is one place where this point is well made. To find it, take U.S. 93 south from Missoula to its junction with the Skalkaho Road #38, three miles south of Hamilton. Turn east (left) on this winding mountain road going past Skalkaho Falls and over Skalkaho Pass. About two miles over the pass is Crystal Creek Campground, a good place to park.

The trail goes steadily but gradually uphill, much of the time through meadows. Upon reaching the divide, the trail heads north for a little over a mile Crystal Creek on the right and a clearcut on the left. The road changes into a hiking trail (#10) after a few hundred yards, but continues to follow Crystal Creek for three miles to its beginning at the Sapphire Divide—also called the Bitterroot Divide or Rock Creek Divide on some Forest Service signs.

The trail goes steadily, but gradually, uphill, much of the time through meadows. Upon reaching the divide, the trail heads north for a little over a mile before the trail down to Stoney Lake splits off to the right.

Stoney Lake offers average fishing for cutthroat, a good campsite with firewood near its outlet, and a chance of seeing mountain goats on the cliffs across the lake from camp.

If you have an extra day or you are a strong hiker, it's possible to return to the divide trail (#313) and follow it north to Dome Shaped Mountain. Dome Shaped Mountain has a broad grassy summit, criss-crossed with snowdrifts which may linger well into July. Also of interest are the thickets of whitebark pine on the summit ridge.

With the Burnt Fork Game Preserve on your left (west), you stand a good chance of seeing deer and elk. Although they don't appear to be what is generally considered mountain goat country, the Sapphires are home for a surprisingly large population, particularly around Dome Shaped Mountain. The occasional

*Stoney Lake, Dome Shaped Mountain*

open spots along the divide provide views of the Pintlers (southeast), the Flint Creek Range (northeast), the Bitterroots (west), and to the south across the Skalkaho Pass, the higher peaks of the Sapphire Wilderness Study Area.—*John Westenberg*

## 26    *Legend and Spud Lakes*

*General description:* A three-day trip for ambitious hikers who want to explore the Sapphire Mountains.

*General location:* Thirty miles southeast of Hamilton.

*Maps:* Gibbons Pass, Whetstone Ridge, Kent Peak, and Jennings Creek Camp USGS Quads; and Bitterroot National Forest Map.

*Special attractions:* Solitude, wildlife, and an introduction to a little-known mountain range.

*For more information:* Write the District Ranger, Sula Ranger District Bitterroot National Forest, Sula, MT 59871 or call (406) 821-3201.

Facing the rugged Bitterroot Mountains across the Bitterroot Valley, the Sap-

*Legend/Spud Lakes*

phire Mountains seem like low, rolling hills. However, they offer first-rate wilderness recreation. This hike takes the hiker into the center of the Sapphire's largest remaining roadless area.

To reach the trailhead from Missoula, take U.S. 93 south eighty-two miles to Sula. Then take the road up the East Fork of the Bitterroot for about twenty miles to its junction with the Moose Creek Road just beyond the East Fork Ranger Station. Take the Moose Creek Road north until it ends five miles later at the trailhead.

For the first three miles, the trail (#168) borders Moose Creek, going up its narrow, talus-filled canyon. The trail then turns east and climbs up the ridge between Moose Creek and Cuba Creek. This one-mile climb marks the beginning of a dry section, so stock up with water before climbing out of Moose Creek.

The trail then heads north along the ridge for 3.5 miles until intersecting with an abandoned jeep road. Although not as pleasant as a trail, the road is gradually going to seed, with little sign of vehicle use. Turn west (left) and follow the abandoned road for approximately three miles, passing Shadow Lake (no fish) and several meadows on the right.

After entering a particularly beautiful meadow, you come upon a second fork in the trail. The right fork takes you into country you'll probably want to investigate tomorrow. However, by this time you'll probably be more interested in the left fork, leading to Legend and Spud lakes (only one mile further) and your campsite along trail #39. A final fork in the trail comes just beyond this point, with the right fork climbing the ridge above the lakes and the easily-missed left fork leading directly to the lakes. Missing this fork and finding yourself on top of the ridge is no cause for regret. You can explore the ridge, looking down on the lakes, south and east to the Pintlers and west to the Bitterroots. In the foreground to the west are the scars of the huge Sleeping Child fire of 1953. The easiest place to scramble back down to the trail leading to the lakes is at the north end of the ridge.

After passing fishless Snow Lake, you come to Legend and Spud lakes. Although both are small lakes, they contain pan-sized cutthroat trout. They're also good vantage points for seeing mountain goats. This is heavily timbered country, so there's no shortage of firewood.

If you have a second night at the lakes, you can spend the next day exploring the country to the north. Climb 9,000-foot Kent Peak, exploring the meadows and watching for deer, elk, and goats enroute; or drop down into the upper Rock Creek drainage to Lake Abundance, a rarely visited lake with good cutthroat fishing.

There are two possible variations for the return trip. If you're taking two cars, leave one at the trailhead at the end of the forest road that runs north through the Martin Creek Recreation Area. To find this trailhead, take the road that leaves the Moose Creek Road about one-third mile past the junction of the East Fork and Moose Creek Roads. This makes it possible for the backpacker to return to the ridge above the lake, and follow the trail seven miles along the ridge and down to the waiting car.

Hikers with one car can return by dropping directly down to Moose Creek from the lakes. This means cross-country hiking and carefully descending some steep slopes while clinging to underbrush—definitely not for novice hikers or families. Once down in the Moose Creek bottom, follow the game trails parallelling Moose Creek for approximately three miles until you intercept the trail you came in on as it crosses Moose Creek. This option gives the hiker an excellent chance of seeing elk or moose and also takes the hiker through beautiful groves of huge Engelmann spruce.

The third return trip option is, of course, retracing your steps back to your vehicle.

The Forest Service has plans to log and build roads into Moose Creek. For the time being, however, Moose Creek is safe within the boundary of the 90,000-acre Sapphire Mountains Wilderness Study Area, one of nine such areas contained in the late Senator Metcalf's Montana Wilderness Study Act. Watch for developments on Forest Service plans for the Sapphires.—*John Westenberg.*

## 27    Welcome Creek

*General description:* A moderate round trip suitable for a day hike or overnighter.

*Welcome Creek*

*General location:* Twenty-five miles east of Missoula in the Sapphire Mountains.

*Maps:* Cleveland Mountain and Ravenna USGS Quads and the Lolo National Forest map.

*Special attractions:* A very accessible, pleasant hike in one of Montana's smallest wilderness areas, the Welcome Creek Wilderness.

*For more information:* Write the District Ranger, Missoula Ranger District, Lolo National Forest, 2801 Russell, Missoula, MT 59801 or call (406) 329-3111.

Besides offering scenic, timbered hiking trails, the Welcome Creek Wilderness

*The flush of a blue grouse can rudely jolt hikers from their daydreams. Harry Engels photo.*

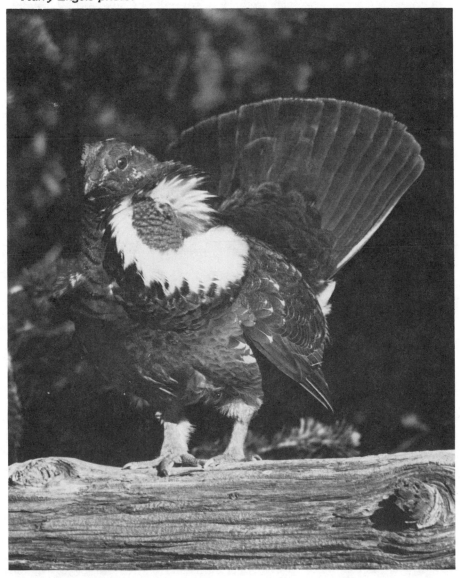

has a rich history. Mined extensively around the turn of the century, the area has many haunting reminders, now abandoned and decaying into the landscape, to greet Welcome Creek travelers.

The trail starts thirteen miles up well-known Rock Creek east of Missoula. Drive east from Missoula for twenty-five miles on I-90 and turn right (south) at the Rock Creek exit. Go up the gravel Rock Creek Road for thirteen miles and watch for a sign on your right (west) marking the Welcome Creek trailhead.

After leaving your car, you cross over Rock Creek on a large pack bridge. Then veer right, following the creek downstream for one-half mile before turning west up Welcome Creek. From there, you gradually climb, following Welcome Creek, until you feel like camping or turning around and returning to your vehicle. The trail continues some five miles to the low summit of Cleveland Mountain.

It isn't really a canyon, but the valley is steep and narrow. It has a mystery and loneliness of its own, as you walk by old mining sites and see how the forest is gradually reclaiming them.

This is a wet area, so wait until July for hiking. If you go earlier, expect a boggy trail and mosquitoes out in force. However, drinking water poses no problem, as clear, clean water is everywhere. Although Welcome Creek has small brookies, the fishing there takes a back seat to famous Rock Creek running past the trailhead.

If you're camping, you have a wide selection of sites. Perhaps the best are where Cinnabar and Spartan creeks join Welcome Creek. Both sites have old mining ruins to explore after supper.

Although some protesters of wilderness classification claimed that Welcome Creek has too many signs of civilization to qualify for wilderness, the reverse is true. Man's hold on the area has long faded into history. Now, the ghosts of old timers (such as outlaw Frank Brady who was shot in 1904 in Welcome Creek) only enrich the wilderness experience. It also shows how fast nature heals the wounds of past carelessness.—*Don Berg*

## 28    Stuart Peak, Twin Lakes

*General description:* A two or three-day backpack for hardy hikers.

*General location:* In the Rattlesnake Wilderness, Missoula's municipal watershed, just north of Missoula.

*Maps:* Northeast Missoula and Stuart Peak USGS Quads, and the Lolo National Forest Map (western half).

*Special attraction:* Vistas of at least four major mountain ranges from the summit of Stuart Peak.

*For more information:* Write the District Ranger, Missoula Ranger District, Lolo National Forest, 2801 Russell, Missoula, MT 59801 or call (406) 329-3111.

Probably no other town has such a spectacular, yet accessible, wild area virtually within the city limits, as does Missoula with its Rattlesnake Wilderness. This hike will take you into some of the alpine lake country around Stuart Peak.

Drive north on Van Buren Street from the Van Buren I-90 interchange, bearing to the right until you find yourself on Rattlesnake Drive. Turn left onto the unmarked road just beyond Wildcat Road, four miles from the interchange. The parking area and entrance to the Upper Rattlesnake Area are located at the

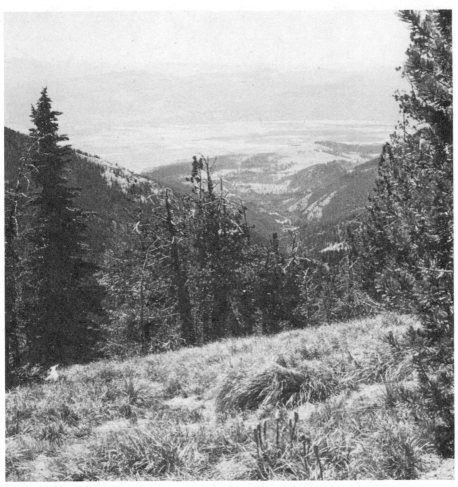

*The Missoula Valley from Stuart Peak, deep in the Rattlesnake Wilderness. Joseph A. Musselman photo.*

mouth of Sawmill Gulch, just a few yards beyond the bridge. A large wooden map at the gate provides an overview of the entire drainage.

The hike along trail #517 is a popular trip with beginning backpackers, possibly because it appears from the wooden map that Stuart Peak and the enticing lakes to the north are but a short distance from the gate. Also, it would seem that one would be comfortably close to civilization throughout the trip. (Indeed, from time to time en route, one is within sight—and sometimes even sound—of Missoula.) However, the sign at the entrance to Spring Gulch, less than a half-mile north of the gate, reads "Stuart Peak, 9.5 mi.; 7 hrs.," a tip-off that the hike actually is somewhat challenging. And a quality of wildness pervades the atmosphere.

The first three miles up the bottom of Spring Gulch are quite easy regardless of whether you follow the old cow paths to the west of the creek or the farm lane to the east. Both routes lead past the sites of homesteads established a century or more ago, though all that remain are traces of foundations and hearths, a few

*Stuart Peak, Twin Lakes*

persistent lilac bushes and apple trees, and two alien Lombardy poplars.

From the head of Spring Gulch, trail #517 begins winding relentlessly upward, 6.5 miles to Stuart Peak. There is usually water at the 5,800-foot level, but no more until you reach Twin Lakes, which lie in the cirque just north of 7,960-foot Stuart Peak.

The Twin Lakes are barren, but Cliff and Peterson lakes, accessible by poor trails to the southeast, contain fish.

Given the time and energy, one might prefer to proceed northward along the ridge to the Lake Creek drainage, whose principle lakes (McKinley, Worden, Carter, Big, and Sheridan) also provide some fishing.

If you're primarily out for exercise and scenery (or for huckleberries, in season) you might wish to pitch camp one evening at the upper end of Spring Gulch, spend the following day walking to Stuart Peak and back, and pack out on the morning of the third day. There are half a dozen pleasant campsites along the creek on the fringes of Kench Meadow.

Much of the Rattlesnake high country remains untrailed or served by only the faintest tracks. Despite the Rattlesnake's popularity, secluded, almost un-discovered basins and lakes dot the far reaches of this high country. There are those who make a habit of exploring these untrailed areas, and they report that they frequently travel several days without encountering other hikers.

Proximity to Missoula results in high use over much of the area. This—plus the fragile nature of the high country itself and the area's status as Missoula's municipal watershed—demand that the hiker take every precaution to leave no trace of his visit. Evidence of high country campsites is proliferating. Make every effort to go light on this fragile terrain. Camp well back from the lakes, and don't add to the blight of fire rings.

Spectacular scenery and access from a large metropolitan area make the Rat-tlesnake a unique area. In 1980, after a long public debate, the Rattlesnake became Montana's newest wilderness area. Hopefully, wilderness designation will protect this area for years to come.—*Joseph A. Mussulman and Bill Brown.*

# 29   Rainbow Lake

*General description:* An ideal hike for campers willing to work hard for a round trip to a high lake in the heart of the Anaconda-Pintlar Wilderness.

*General location:* Thirty miles southwest of Anaconda.

*Maps:* Warren Peak USGS Quad and the Deerlodge National Forest Map.

*Special attractions:* A secluded wilderness lake ringed with spectacular scenery.

*For more information:* Write the District Ranger, Philipsburg Ranger Station Deerlodge National Forest, Philipsburg, MT 59858 or call (406) 859-3211.

Ever want to set up camp in a secluded alpine clearing away from the mainstream of wilderness traffic, where a diversity of peaks surround a small, deep lake loaded with trout? There are many of these secret spots in Montana, but those who find them usually keep them secret, which is a selfish way to han-dle any blessing. Rainbow Lake is one of these blessings. Promise not to tell?

To find the trailhead, take State Highway 38 south from Philipsburg, and

*Rainbow Lake*

eleven miles past the Georgetown-Anaconda turnoff, turn south onto the Moose Lake Road. Follow this road for twelve miles until you reach Copper Creek Campground. Then, take the Middle Fork Rock Creek Road and follow it until it dead ends five miles later. Here, take Falls Fork Trail #29.

It's a 4.5 mile uphill grind to Johnson Lake (elevation 7,720). Hike along the west shore of this lake to a trail junction at the south end, and take the left-hand fork to the east (Trail #9). Then, climb a 2.5-mile stretch with moderate switchbacks to 9,040-foot Rainbow Pass.

The snow usually clings to this high land until at least late June, so mid-July or later is best for this hike. There is plenty of water along the trail except for the stretch between Johnson and Rainbow lakes.

This pass is a great place to relax and enjoy the surroundings. To the east is the ominous, broad pyramid of 10,793-foot West Goat Peak, highest in the Pintlar Range. To the south are slopes covered with rare alpine larch. And right below you is your destination—Rainbow Lake. You can see the trail switchbacking down to the 8,215-foot lake.

The outlet is the best spot to camp. The rainbow trout are especially active in the morning and evening. Dead trees provide plentiful firewood. Trails-to-explore and peaks-to-climb are in all directions.

The geology is rather striking. The range is mainly the more typical Montana sedimentary rock, but with granitic intrusions, which accounts for all the odd-looking granite boulders strewn about in unexpected places. This phenomenon is especially evident on the trail to Warren Lake. —*Pat Caffrey*

## 30   *Pioneer and High-Up Lakes*

*General description:* a fairly strenuous overnight round trip (well-suited for a three-day trip) to a small lake just below the Montana/Idaho border.

*General location:* On the east slope of the Continental Divide in the Beaverhead National Forest, fifteen miles southwest of Jackson, sixty-five miles west of Dillon.

*Maps:* Goldstone Mountain USGS Quad and Beaverhead National Forest Tavel Plan.

*Special attractions:* A remote high mountain lake way off the beaten path.

*For more information:* Write the District Ranger, Wisdom Ranger District,

*Johnson Lake in the Anaconda-Pintlar Wilderness. U.S. Forest Service photo.*

Beaverhead National Forest, Box 236, Wisdom, MT 59761 or call (406) 689-2431.

To get to the trailhead, drive one mile south of Jackson on State Highway 278 and turn right on a gravel road near the top of a hill. Follow this road south and west to Van Houten Lake Campground, crossing many of the upper tributaries of the Big Hole River on narrow bridges. Continue straight ahead at the South Van Houten Campground for approximately one-half mile along the newly constructed Bloody Dick reroute to the junction with the Berry Creek Road. Turn left at this junction, immediately crossing Pioneer Creek, and proceed driving on the Bloody Dick Road for two miles to the Jahnke Creek trailhead. Two-wheel drive vehicles with adequate clearance can go up the Jahnke Creek Trail for about half a mile, to the intersection of the Overland Trail #36. At this point, you should park your vehicle and continue on foot. The Overland Trail goes downslope and joins the Pioneer Creek Trail just before the creek crossing.

The track crosses Pioneer Creek on the remains of a primitive bridge, which some four-wheelers have avoided, resulting in deep ruts along the soft streambanks.

Shortly after this crossing is the junction with trail #442, which continues along the south side of Pioneer Creek as a primitive vehicle track. It's more pleasant to walk along this track as it winds among parks and groves. Watch for moose in the willow bottoms by the creek.

The trail climbs slowly and crosses the creek again about six miles from Van Houten Lake. Just past this crossing, the trail branches; the shortest route con-

*High-up Lake in the West Big Hole proposed wilderness. Fred Swanson photo.*

*Pioneer & High-Up Lakes*

tinues along the creek, while the right-hand trail climbs the hill to an old miner's cabin and eventually rejoins the main trail. The trail starts to climb more steeply as you approach the high peaks along the Continental Divide. Even at this high elevation (7,000 to 8,000 feet), there are large spruce and fir growing close to Pioneer Creek.

The route for the last few miles is a regular hiking trail. It crosses the north branch of Pioneer Creek and cuts across a slope to the south branch of the creek. Soon, it comes to a jumble of trees from a recent snow avalanche that started on the steep slopes to the south. This section of the trail away from the stream can be confusing, so consult your map and watch for faint blazes.

Pioneer Lake lies about one mile past the avalanche (about ten miles from Van Houten Campground). It offers some good camping spots and a close-up look at the Continental Divide.

Enterprising hikers may want to try a short climb up the hill west of Pioneer Lake on faint animal paths to High-Up Lake, actually a pair of alpine jewels just below the divide. There is a good campsite on the east end of the lake with a fine view back down the valley you've just labored up. A third lake, Skytop, lies over the next ridge, but its shores are rockier.

Try to catch the sunrise above the Big Hole Valley over the high peaks of the East Pioneer Mountains. A moonrise is also worth staying up for—ghostly light silhouetting the limbs of dead whitebark pine surrounding the lake. Pine beetles killed these trees decades ago, but this treeline forest is renewing itself.

Enjoy a small fire from deadfall at one of the fire rings in place at the lake. Chances are you will be the only people at this remote spot; try to leave the lakeshore as undisturbed as it was when you came.

High-Up Lake is a great place to spend an extra day exploring. The Continental Divide is a short climb on steep talus above the south end of the lake. On top of the Divide it's fairly common to see mountain goats among the crags. The west slope of the Divide is more gentle than the steep glacier-carved east wall, and it's possible to walk north and south along the crest amid wild scenery. Center Mountain rises three miles north along the ridge and is a moderate, nontechnical climb, but use caution among its loose sliderock. To the west are the rugged Big Horn Crags in the great wild area of central Idaho, the River of No Return Wilderness.

Both Pioneer and High-Up lakes have small cutthroat, but neither are noted for fishing.

Trail hints: The Big Hole and its surrounding mountains are notorious for their mosquitoes. Plan a late summer hike or bring plenty of repellent. The trail along Pioneer Creek stays close to water most of the distance. Fishermen and less ambitious hikers will enjoy ambling along the willow-bordered stream on the lower portion of the trail.

High-Up Lake and most of the Pioneer Creek valley are within a wilderness area proposed by local sportsmen's groups. The Forest Service has also proposed a smaller wilderness area, but they have plans to cut timber and build roads in the lower slopes of this range. As roads increase along the fringes of the Big Hole, some of the remoteness that makes it special will be lost. —*Fred Swanson.*

# 31  Bobcat Lakes

*General description:* A moderate, eight-mile day hike or overnight trip in the West Pioneer Mountains.

*General location:* In an eastern drainage of the West Pioneer Mountains, twenty miles south of Wise River and sixty miles southwest of Butte in the Beaverhead National Forest.

*Maps:* Odell Lake and Shaw Mountain USGS Quads and the Beaverhead National Forest Travel Plan.

*Special attractions:* Lower Bobcat Lake is one of several lakes in the West Pioneers that support the rare southern grayling.

*For more information:* Write the District Ranger, Wise River Ranger District, Beaverhead National Forest, Box 86, Wise River, MT 59762 or call (406) 839-2201.

Bobcat Lakes lie in small glacial cirques in the middle of the gentle West Pioneer Mountains. There are two good trails to the lakes, and it is possible to make this a loop trip. Both trails begin from Forest Service Road #90 which follows Lacy Creek, a tributary of Wise River.

To get there, drive south from the town of Wise River on the Wise River Road about fifteen miles. A mile or so after the Wise River Road leaves the river canyon and enters a broad meadow, turn right on Road #90 (Lacy Creek Road) and go west. About two miles up Lacy Creek Road a narrow, not-too-obvious, old wagon road angles steeply uphill to the right, climbs out of Lacy Creek valley, and meets trail #26 in about a mile. There is a gate where the old wagon road leaves Lacy Creek, so you must park and walk up the road.

Trail #26 heads west along a small stream through thick stands of lodgepole, spruce, and fir. After a little over two miles, you come to a pretty meadow near the junction of the trail to the Bobcat Lakes. Turn southwest on this trail and hike for about two more miles to the lakes. The total distance from Lacy Creek Road is about six miles.

A more direct route to the Bobcat Lakes begins just past the end of road #90, about four miles from the Wise River Road. Park at the primitive campground, cross Lacy Creek and take trail #50 up the Bobcat Creek canyon about four miles to the lakes. This trail passes through attractive stands of lodgepole pine and fir, with occasional vistas across the broad slopes of the West Pioneers.

Lower and Upper Bobcat Lakes lie just below Bobcat Peak. At 9,241 feet, it is one of the higher points in the range. From the upper lake, a steep trail leads west to the ridge separating the Bobcat Creek and Pattengail Creek drainages, the latter dissecting the heart of the West Pioneers. Elk often frequent the small meadows that dot this high area. Further west is a long ridge topped by Odell Peak. Several cirque lakes lie at the base of this ridge.

An interesting feature of Lower Bobcat Lake is its grayling population. These native fish are now mostly restricted to the Big Hole River drainage. The grayling have specialized habitat requirements which make it hard for them to compete with other sport fish in lower elevation waters. The remoteness of the Bobcat Lakes helps them survive. Please take care to avoid disturbing the small stream that drains Lower Bobcat Lake—the grayling depend on the fine gravels in the

*Bobcat Lakes*

streambed for spawning.

As with any back country lake, it's best to avoid camping on the lakeshore. There are, however, several suitable campsites along the margin of the woods surrounding Bobcat Lakes. If you're diligent, you can find enough deadfall for a good fire.

For an enjoyable loop trip, leave your car at the end of road #90, take trail #50 to the lakes, and return via trail #26. Where you rejoin the Lacy Creek Road, stow your pack and walk a mile or so up the road to retrieve your car. There is drinking water near both trailheads, but fill your canteens here, as the rest of the hike may be dry.

In 1981, the Forest Service recommended against wilderness protection for the West Pioneers wilderness study area, and instead proposed increased logging for these remote mountains. Conservation groups are attempting to acheive special wildlife management status for the West Pioneers, but will not succeed without your help and the help of your congressman.—*Fred Swanson*

## 32    Torrey Lake

*General description:* A seventeen-mile round trip for hikers, backpackers, fishermen, and climbers.

*General location:* Twenty-five miles northwest of Dillon, in the East Pioneers.

*Maps:* Torrey Mountain, Maurice Mountain, and Vipond USGS Quads; and Beaverhead National Forest Map.

*Special attractions:* The lake itself, nearly 9,000 feet in elevation, one-half mile long by one-quarter mile wide, with good fishing. Torrey Mountain and Tweedy Mountain are available for mountaineers, and many granite features are available for technical climbers.

*For more information:* Write District Ranger, Wise River Ranger District, Box 86, Wise River, MT 59762.

The eastern portion of the Pioneer Range is such a confusing jumble of formations that geologists have yet to come up with a complete explanation for what happened here. Torrey Lake is in the middle of an area where molten rock intruded into the older formations from below and cooled there. After time and erosion removed the overburden of older rock, the granite backbone of this range was exposed.

The trail to Torrey Lake starts from the Mono Creek Campground. You can drive there from the north or south. The northern approach involves leaving State Highway 43 at Wise River and heading up the Wise River Road for about twenty-two miles. The southern approach leaves State Highway 278 and takes you past Polaris and the Maverick Mountain Ski Area. It's about twenty-two miles from the highway this way, also.

The first 2.5 miles of the trail wander through some open timber, and then the trail skirts Jacobson Meadows. Then you'll go back into the timber and, just above Jacobson Creek, you'll hit a trail junction. Take the right fork, which immediately drops down to cross Jacobson Creek and then heads up David Creek. You'll now have four miles of gently climbing trail through lodgepole stands, intermittent meadows, and spruce bottoms. The last two miles ascend 1,000 feet as the trail winds its way up through granite boulders to the lake.

Torrey Lake

The lakeshore is fragile, and you should camp back from it a bit in the whitebark pine forest. Looking south across the lake one sees the ragged igneous hump of Torrey Mountain, 11,147 feet high. Behind to the northeast are the shredded granite cliffs and buttresses of Tweedy Mountain, 11,154 feet high. Granite towers stand on the divide between Tweedy and Torrey, west of Torrey. If you decide to climb around on the large rockslide between Torrey Peak and the lake, note that this slide shifted dramatically in 1981 and is still very unstable. Avoid the steep pitches of rubble, which *will* start to slide under your weight.—*Pat Caffrey*

## 33  Hollowtop Lake

*General description:* A moderate twelve-mile, overnight round trip to an attractive lake in a high mountain basin.

*General location:* On the east side of the Tobacco Root Mountains in the Beaverhead National Forest, fifty-five miles west of Bozeman or ninety miles south of Helena.

*Maps:* Harrison USGS Quad and the Beaverhead National Forest Travel Plan.

*Special attractions:* Hollowtop Lake is bordered on three sides by the high peaks of the Tobacco Root Mountains.

*For more information:* Write the District Ranger, Madison Ranger District, Beaverhead National Forest, Box 366, Ennis, MT 59729 or call (406) 628-4253.

The trailhead is 2.5 miles southwest of Pony, an interesting old mining town in the foothills of the Tobacco Roots, six miles southwest of Harrison. Drive west through Pony and proceed up a narrow dirt road 1.5 miles to the fork. Take the lower, left-hand road downhill to the North Fork of Willow Creek. There is a good place to park at a bridge over the creek about two miles from Pony. Beyond the bridge a rocky jeep trail follows the creek, becoming a foot trail after about five miles.

Starting from the parking area at the bridge, walk up a moderate grade one-half mile along the south side of the creek to a primitive bridge. In the spring, watch for fuzzy blue pasqueflowers in the grassy meadows.

Above the primitive bridge, the trail climbs steadily along the north side of the creek, passing a good camping spot. Three miles from the trailhead, the jeep trail forks. The south fork (trail #333) heads over the ridge to Albro Lake; the other fork (trail #301 to Hollowtop Lake) continues along the north side of the creek through groves of spruce and fir and back into open meadows. Above this fork, the trail is closed to vehicles over forty inches wide.

About 3.5 miles from the trailhead, the trail again crosses the creek. Pause here to fill canteens, as the trail heads away from the main creek at this point. This stream crossing can be tricky during early summer runoff, and a stout staff selected from among the deadfall will help. Later into the summer, you can more easily cross the stream on jammed logs.

Above the crossing, the trail climbs more steeply to the 8,550-foot lake. You will pass some beautiful, sloping meadows with great views east into the Bozeman valley and the Spanish Peaks. Hollowtop Lake (which has pan-sized rainbows) is about six miles from the trailhead and is the source of the stream

*Hollowtop Lake*

you have been following.

This hike is within the boundaries of the Tobacco Root Further Planning Area, an area the Forest Service is studying for possible wilderness designation.

There is a good campsite near the outlet. Northwest of the lake is Mount Jefferson, at 10,600 feet the highest point in the Tobacco Roots. Hollowtop Mountain (10,513 feet) lies west of the lake, and to the south is Potosi Peak, named by miners after a fabulous mine in the Andes. All three mountains are technically easy scrambles, but be prepared for rough weather on the windswept alpine slopes.—*Fred Swanson*

# 34    *Lake Louise*

*General description:* A short, but steep, overnighter.
*General location:* Forty miles southeast of Butte in the Tobacco Root Mountains.
*Maps:* Waterloo USGS Quad and the Deerlodge National Forest Map.
*For more information:* Write the District Ranger, Jefferson Ranger District, 405
    E. Legion, Whitehall, MT 59759 or call (406) 2878-3223.

The Tobacco Roots aren't well known as a hiking area, but the range has much to offer—particularly short hikes suitable for families, such as Lake Louise.

To find the trailhead, take the turn south off I-90 at the Cardwell exit 31 miles east of Butte. Instead of taking U.S. 10 along the Jefferson River, veer south on State Highway 359. After about four miles turn right (southwest) on the South Boulder Road. Stay on this road for about twenty miles, past a small town named Mammoth, to the trailhead. The road gets steadily worse as you proceed, but in dry weather late in the summer, a two-wheel drive vehicle can make it. The trail leaves the South Boulder Road to the left about five miles past Mammoth and just before the Bismark Reservoir.

*Lake Louise*

Four-wheelers sometimes travel the first half-mile or so of this trail, but they can't make it to the lake. Motorcycles frequently use the trail, however.

You cross the South Boulder immediately after hoisting your packs on. It's a safe crossing, but there isn't a bridge, so you'll get your feet wet.

After this, the trail (which isn't shown on the topo map) climbs for three long

*Lake Louise in the Tobacco Root Mountains. Bill Schneider photo.*

miles to the lake. The elevation gain—2,800 feet—makes it seem longer. Carry your drinking water, as there are only a few water holes along the way.

The lake sits in a bowl-shaped cirque with massive, 10,353-foot Middle Mountain to the south. The best campsite is to your left when you hit the lake. Although firewood isn't readily available, there's enough for a healthy fire.

The lake has a small population of large cutthroat trout that can be very fussy about which fly they take. If you find the fly that works, only catch enough for supper, returning the rest for the next angler.

Although the trail is steep, the hike is popular with families. With children, plan on at least four hours to reach the lake—and probably more.

This fine hike has been recognized by the Forest Service as a national recreation trail, for its outstanding scenery and exceptional recreational oportunities. The trail also passes through the Tobacco Root Further Planning Area, an area being studied for possible wilderness designation.

Climbers in your party will be tempted to scramble up Middle Mountain, a nontechnical climb.—*Bill Schneider*

## 35    Trask Lakes

*General description:* A moderate overnighter.
*General location:* About twelve miles west of Deer Lodge in the Flint Creek Range.
*Maps:* Rock Creek Lake, Pike's Peak, and Pozega Lakes USGS Quads; and the Deerlodge National Forest Map.
*For more information:* Write the District Ranger, Deer Lodge Ranger District, Deer Lodge National Forest, 91 N. Frontage Road, Deer Lodge, MT 59722 or call (406) 846-1770

Although this area lies close to Butte, Deer Lodge, and Helena, it remains relatively unknown.

Without doubt, the Flint Creek Range is among the most scenic in the state. Unfortunately, much of this beautiful range has been roaded. The parts that haven't are included in the 52,340-acre Flint Creek Range Further Planning Area, which is being studied for possible wilderness designation by the Forest Service.

To find the trailhead, go down the main street of Deer Lodge and turn west at the corner with the bank. Follow this road for two miles until it splits. The left-hand fork goes to the prison farm. Take the right fork (actually straight ahead) and follow it ten more miles to Rock Creek Lake. Park at the upper end of the lake, where the good road turns into a rugged jeep road. (It may be too rugged even for jeeps.) The parking area is private land with limited space for vehicles.

The first three miles of the trip to Trask Lakes are on an old jeep road (road #168.2), which is not officially closed to motorized vehicle travel. This is an old county road which the Forest Service is wisely trying to close, since it is almost completely impassable except to four-wheel drive vehicles.

At the three-mile mark, watch for a trail junction. The road continues on, but you must turn left, crossing Rock Creek and then following the South Fork of Rock Creek to the lakes. Forest Service Trail #63 continues climbing gradually for four miles to Lower Trask Lake, one of four lakes (plus several potholes) in this small but gorgeous cirque. Once you're off the jeep road, the signs of civiliza-

0                   1               2 Miles

## Trask Lakes

tion fall behind and the hike becomes more of a quality back country experience.

The 7,800-foot Trask Lakes offer excellent fishing for small brookies. In fact, fish are so abundant and hungry that even the youngest angler can expect a good catch. (The fishing is also good in the main Rock Creek along the jeep road in the first three miles of the hike.)

The good fishing and moderate, fourteen-mile round trip (1,900-foot elevation gain) make Trask Lakes perfect for family backpacking. But don't forget the insect repellent or your kids won't want to leave the tent. Drinking water is available all along the trail.

The basin has many suitable campsites. However, firewood is scarce, so use your stove and avoid fires. Also, take a few minutes and carry out garbage left by thoughtless visitors.

After you're bored with hauling in fish, you might try an interesting side trip to Racetrack Peak. Stay on the trail for three miles past the lakes until it climbs to the top of 8,507-foot Racetrack Pass. Then, turn right (west) and make a one-mile scramble to the summit of 9,524-foot Racetrack Peak for an outstanding view of the entire area.

The low point of the Trask Lakes trip is the knowledge that without increased support for preserving this area, it will probably be developed like the rest of this mountain range.—*Frank Culver*

## 36   *Humbug Spires*

*General description:* An easy day hike or overnighter into a unique primitive area.

*General location:* Twenty-six miles south of Butte in the Humbug Spires Recommended Wilderness.

*Maps:* Butte South USGS Quad and the Bureau of Land Management's Public Lands in Montana-Dillon Map, #32.

*Humbug Spires*

*For more information:* Write District Manager, Bureau of Land Management, Butte District, P.O. Box 3388, 106 N. Parkmont, Butte, MT 59702 or call (406) 494-5059.

Of all the roadless country in Montana, the 11,174-acre Humbug Spires area must rank among the most intriguing. Besides the granite protrusions, for which it is named, the area has a lovely, trout-laden stream (small cutthroat) and a forest of primeval Douglas fir, somehow overlooked by early timber cutters.

After driving south of Butte for twenty-six miles, turn left (east) at the Moose Creek Interchange. Drive for three miles up the Moose Creek Road to the BLM parking lot where the trail begins.

Upon leaving the parking area, you cross a culvert to the west side of Moose Creek where there is a BLM sign announcing the primitive area and notifying recreationists that motorized vehicles aren't allowed. In the first 1.3 miles, you pass by numerous ancient trees, possibly 200 years or older, truly noble reminders of what it was like when the pioneers arrived.

At the 1.3 mile mark, the trail forks. Take the left fork and continue up the east side of the stream. Stay on this trail for about two miles until you reach the only private inholding in this tract of public domain. Make sure to respect private property rights here, since access is granted by the good will of the owners. At this point, take a right turn up a small gulch which has a small stream.

This turns into a deep gulch, steep in a few places and containing the beginnings of the spires. About a mile up this steep gulch, you leave the small stream, climbing off to the left over a short pitch to the ridge where the incredible Humbug Spires unfold before you in all their majesty.

It's four miles to this point, making this an eight-mile round trip. The trail has only a few steep, but short, upgrades. In places, the trail becomes indistinct, but careful scrutiny will reveal its presence.

Although this is usually a day hike, you can camp along the stream just before you climb out of the gulch. You could also camp on the ridge—if you feel the scenery pays for the extra work of hauling water up from the stream.

If you camp, plan on spending the first half of your second day wandering around, possibly awe-struck, among the spires. You'll come home exclaiming about the beauty and uniqueness of the Humbug Spires.—*Herb B. Gloege*

# 37   Snowcrest Trail

*General description:* A twenty-mile loop hike along the top of the Snowcrest Range.

*General location:* Forty miles southeast of Dillon.

*Maps:* Antone Peak and Stonehouse Mountain USGS Quads, and the Beaverhead National Forest Travel Plan Map.

*Special attractions:* High alpine scenery on the crest of the Snowcrests.

*For more information:* Write the District Ranger, Sheridan Ranger District, Beaverhead National Forest. P.O. Box 428, Sheridan, MT 59749 or call (406) 683-2337.

The Snowcrest Range stretches for twenty miles north to south right next to the Gravellys in the far southwestern corner of Montana. This hike will take you along eight miles of the southern portion of the crest of the range, mostly at eleva-

**0        2        4 Miles**

*Snowcrest Trail*

tions greater than 9,500 feet. Make sure to check in with the Forest Service about snow conditions if you are attempting the hike before mid-July.

After leaving I-15 at Dillon, look for the Blacktail Deer Road which heads eastward just south of Western Montana State College. Nine miles east of Dillon, the pavement ends, but continue on the gravel road for another eighteen miles. At this point, turn left at the sign indicating the road to the East Fork of Blacktail Creek and the Department of Fish, Wildlife and Parks Winter Game Range. It is ten miles more down this road to the trailhead.

From the trailhead, you'll want to follow the East Fork of Blacktail Deer Creek Trail (#69) to Honeymoon Park on the Snowcrest Divide. Here at another trail intersection, take the right fork (trail #4), which leads to Honeymoon Park.

The next eight miles of hiking are all along the Snowcrest Divide, on the Snowcrest Trail. Stonehouse Mountain is the highest elevation near the trail at 10,075 feet. Look for the small stone hut built by shepherds.

The views in all directions are impressive, but this stretch has a major problem: lack of water. This is especially problematic later in the season. If you go earlier in July, snowbanks may linger and can be used for water sources. Otherwise, you can drop down off the crest into the heads of drainages to find water or settle for a dry camp.

Large cirque basins hug the eastern side of the crest, as the trail skirts several minor summits along the divide, always remaining above 9,500 feet. At the fifth trail intersection since leaving Honeymoon Park, some 5.5 miles ago, the main Snowcrest Trail continues southward and drops down into Peterson Basin. Take the right fork to the west toward Antone Peak. This portion of trail is not marked on Forest Service Maps, but is present on the USGS topo.

About a mile before reaching Antone Peak, the trail splits again. Follow the northern trail down Lawrence Creek, which leads to the main East Fork Blacktail Creek Trail that you started on.

Although few other hikers use this country, there is extensive cattle use in some areas, and you may run into a sheepherder or two. This means that you should take special care to treat your water supplies, unless snowfields are available.

Elk, deer, and mountain goats are all inhabitants of the Snowcrest Country, but the fishing is poor except for the main East Fork of Blacktail Deer Creek. With grazing in the area, don't expect any trouble from the few black bears which call the Snowcrests their home.

This trip might impress you with enough hiking possibilities in the Snowcests to interest you in other hikes thoughout this small but interesting mountain range.—*Bob Wagenknecht and Ed Madej*

## 38   *Deadman Creek Nicholia Creek*

*General description:* A three or four-day hike for experienced hikers in the little-visited Italian Peaks proposed wilderness.

*General location:* Twenty miles southwest of Lima, Montana.

*Maps:* Scott Peak USGS Quad and the Beaverhead National Forest Travel Plan Map.

*Deadman Creek Nicholia Creek*

*Special attractions:* The huge glacial cirque of Italian Peak, high on the Continental Divide.

*For more information:* Write the District Ranger, Dillon Ranger District, Beaverhead National Forest, Box 1258, Dillon, MT 59725 or call (406) 683-2312.

Few hikers visit this remote, isolated mountain range in the far southwestern corner of the state, but its spectacular alpine scenery is sure to make it more popular in the years to come.

The trailhead is rather remote, but easy to find, using the Beaverhead National Forest Travel Plan map. Turn off I-15 at the Dell exit, forty-five miles south of Dillon. Follow the gravel road which parallels the interstate's western side for 1.5 miles south, where a road turns westward up Big Sheep Canyon. After eighteen miles the road branches; take the left branch toward Nicholia-Deadman. In two and a quarter miles the road branches again. Continue left up the broad valley of Nicholia Creek.

Another 4.5 miles will bring you to a creek crossing, half a mile inside the National Forest boundary, and a good place to start the hike. If you have two vehicles, take one with high clearance over the road to Deadman Lake toward the southeast; if not, start walking the three miles to Deadman Lake.

Deadman Lake is a small pond lying in a steep, V-shaped valley, which offers some cutthroat fishing. Once it heads south up the right side of the lake, the trail (such as it is) enters the proposed wilderness boundary and leaves the rough jeep track behind.

The trails in this region receive little use and have a tendency to fade away in the many grassy meadows along the track. A few tips are in order: Don't trust the trail as shown on the Scott Peak USGS Quad. It is very old, and inaccurate to boot. Do trust the blazes on the trees, which look like upsidedown exclamation points. You will always find the trail if you stay in the valley bottoms near the stream and don't wander up the steep side slopes for any great distance.

For four miles the trail follows Deadman Creek, frequently fording the small stream to avoid the little lakes formed by avalanches and mudslides coming off the high, nameless ridge to the west. Even in late July, snow may remain at the base of these avalanche chutes, which can easily be avoided by remaining on the eastern side of the stream.

The valley at this point begins to take on a more alpine character, showing signs of the glaciers which once carved the U-shaped upper canyon. The pretty meadows here are a good place for the first night's camp, or, if you have the energy, you can hike up to Divide Lake. Divide Lake lies in a rocky depression just a few yards on the Idaho side of the Continental Divide. It is also perfectly invisible from the Deadman Creek side. The old trail used to climb the grassy slope up to a broad saddle on the divide to the lake, but is now grown over. Use your topo map and you shouldn't have any problem.

The advantage of camping at Divide Lake is that you may catch a few cutthroat for dinner (Idaho fishing license required). The disadvantage is having to climb the four hundred feet up to the lake and back down again to continue the hike.

The trail climbs gradually through the alpine meadows of the upper Deadman drainage, with the steep rocky ridge of the Continental Divide looming overhead to the left. At one point, a huge geological formation, called a *breach anticline,* forms a cliff along the divide, resembling a meteor impact crater. About four miles from the Divide Lake turnoff, the trail reaches the pass between Deadman and Nicholia Creek drainages. Here at 9,400 feet, the alpine scenery is spectacular, with the knife edged ridge of the divide rising up to the 10,998-foot summit of Italian Peak. Keep your eyes peeled for bighorn sheep and goats up on the high slopes.

The trail switchbacks down a steep talus slope into the rolling alpine meadows at the base of the north wall of Italian Peak. A snowfield lingers year round on Italian Peak's north wall, perhaps aspiring to become a glacier. This alpine basin makes a perfect second night's campsite and may convince you to spend an extra day exploring the meadows and talus slopes of this huge cirque. This is the southernmost point in Montana, and surely one of the prettiest.

Going northward, the trail descends the broad, green valley of Nicholia Creek, staying on the western side of the stream just above the bogs in the creek bottom. Once again, the trail tends to disappear in some of the meadows, but is blazed through the forested parts. At one large meadow, about three miles from the cirque basin, the route is marked by a series of five-foot-high posts. Past this meadow, the trail enters the lower reaches of Nicholia Creek and becomes very well defined, especially after it crosses to the eastern bank of the stream.

For six miles, the route follows an old, grass-grown jeep track through the sagebrush flats. Be sure to turn around frequently to see the changing views of Italian Peak and Scott Peak over in Idaho. Some 8.5 miles after leaving the cirque

*Panoramic views from the Continental Divide in the Italian Peaks. Rosemary Rowe photo.*

at the base of Italian Peak, you reach your waiting car.

Although there are several fresh springs in both the Deadman and Nicholia Valleys, hikers should be prepared to treat their water, since cows graze the meadows along nearly the entire route. The bugs can be bad as well, so bring lots of insect repellent.

The high pass between Nicholia and Deadman Creeks is usually clear of snow by the Fourth of July, but check local conditions with the Forest Service before you start. You might also want to check with the Forest Service on the status of the Italian Peaks, which is a further planning area, endorsed for wilderness designation by conservation groups.—*Ed Madej and Rosemary Rowe.*

## 39    *Sawtooth Mountain Antone Pass*

*General description:* A twelve-mile overnight loop hike through some little-known country.

*General location:* Forty miles southeast of Dillon.

*Maps:* Antone Peak USGS Quad and the Beaverhead National Forest Travel Plan Map.

*Special attractions:* Interesting alpine country among the 10,000-foot peaks of the Snowcrest Range.

*For more information:* Write the District Ranger, Sheridan Ranger District, Beaverhead National Forest, P.O. Box 428, Sheridan, MT 59749 or call (406) 842-5432. Also, you can contact the Resource Area Manager, Bureau of Land Management. P.O. Box 1048, Dillon MT 59724 or call (406) 683-2337.

Few people have ever heard of the Snowcrest Range. That's all the more reason to try one of the hikes in this little-visited but scenic area.

Turn off I-15 at the Dillon interchange (to be completed in 1984) and drive into town. Just south of Western Montana State College, look for the Blacktail Road, which takes off to the east. The pavement ends nine miles east of Dillon. Continue along the gravel road for another eighteen miles, while keeping an eye open for signs pointing to the East Fork of Blacktail Deer Creek and the Montana Fish, Wildlife and Parks Winter Game Range. Turn left up the East Fork and drive ten miles more to the trailhead.

The Sawtooth Trail leads up Indian Creek to the southwest of the trailhead (trail #68). Climbing steeply out of the creek bottom, the trail gains a shoulder at 9,300 feet on the north slope of Sawtooth Mountain, offering good views of Sawtooth's jagged north face.

The trail continues for about a mile on the high northern slope of Sawtooth before dropping down to a trail intersection and a series of springs. If cattle have not yet been here, the springs may be the best water source along this entire twelve-mile loop, as well as a good camping spot.

From the springs, the trail is now called the Cornell Trail and leads to Cornell Camp, a grazing headquarters on the South Fork of the West Fork of Blacktail Deer Creek. Here you'll have to walk eastward up a gravel road for one mile to the Antone Guard Station and the trail to Antone Pass.

Leaving the guard station, trail #670 leads to 8,600-foot Antone Pass and a pretty place to camp, if you can find water. A steep but worthwhile side trip from the pass follows a trail toward the southeast. This trail eventually bends away

97

*Sawtooth Mountain Antone Pass*

from the 10,247-foot summit of Antone Peak, but a short bit of scrambling will bring you to the top. The view here includes the rest of the Snowcrest Range stretching off to the north, the expanse of the Red Rock Valley, and the Centennial Mountains on the southern horizon.

Dropping down from Antone Pass, it is 2.5 miles along Rough Creek until the trail intersects with the main East Fork of Blacktail Deer Creek Trail. Turn left on this route and hike the mile-and-a-half back to your car.

Wildlife may be plentiful along this hike, especially if there aren't too many cattle around. Blacktail Creek is home to a large elk herd, and mountain goats are found on many of the high peaks. With cattle in the area, make sure to treat your water, unless you travel early enough in the season (early July) to make use of snowfields.

There is some fishing for cutthroat and brown trout in the East Fork, but the rest of the streams along the way are too small to support much of a fishery.

The lower reaches of the East Fork of Blacktail Creek were studied by the Bureau of Land Management in their wilderness study process, and, in general, the area had a high wilderness rating.—*Bob Wagenknecht and Ed Madej*

## 40 Murr Canyon

*General description:* A moderate day trip.
*General location:* Forty-five miles southwest of Kalispell.
*Maps:* Shroder Creek USGS Quad and the Lolo National Forest Map (Idaho and Montana).
*For more information:* Write the District Ranger, Plains Ranger District, Lolo National Forest, Plains, Mt 59859 or call (406) 826-3821.

Murr Canyon is part of a roadless management area, established by the Lolo Forest, and is managed for its dispersed recreation values. The canyon isn't well known by hikers, although it has many scenic attractions.

To find the trailhead, drive west from Kalispell on U.S. 2 for forty miles to the Thompson River Road. Turn left (south) here and go slightly over six miles until you see a trail sign on your left (east) for Murr Creek Trail #145.

The trail gradually climbs through deeply forested country along Murr Creek for about four miles to a junction with trail #118, which juts off to the northeast to Pinehill. About a half-mile past this junction, a short spur trail takes off to the right just after crossing a creek in a deep gully. This spur trail, which goes about a half-mile to a good viewpoint over Murr Canyon, is marked but hasn't been maintained for several years. It's possible to climb down into Murr Canyon, but this requires rugged, cross-country hiking—for the very experienced only.

Murr Canyon is a lovely, steep-walled gorge with a waterfall at the east end where Murr creek once again becomes a normal stream. On the way up, you can leave the trail and hike along the creek for about a mile to see this waterfall. To see the waterfall, however, you must fight through heavy brush. It's best to try this in the spring.

The well-maintained trail gains only about 300 feet in elevation on the way to this hidden gorge. Although the trail has several places to get water, it also has some dry sections. The nine-mile round trip is easy enough for any hiker.

Motorized vehicles are allowed, but they aren't commonly seen in the area. Ex-

Murr Canyon

4 Miles

cept for a clearcut at the beginning of the hike, the signs of civilization are few.—*Elaine Snyder*

## 41    St. Mary's Peaks

*General description:* A demanding, cross country hike for experienced hikers.
*General location:* Thirty miles north of Missoula in the Mission Mountains.
*Maps:* St. Mary's Lake USGS Quad.
*Special attractions:* A spectacular view of the rugged southern Mission Mountains and much of northwestern Montana.

*For more information:* Contact the Wilderness Manager, Confederated Salish and Kootenai Tribes, Ronan, MT 59864

The hike to the top of St. Mary's peaks is physically demanding, but requires no special climbing skills. Along the way expect a view of some of the most spectacular mountain terrain in western Montana.

It's only a short drive from Missoula. Take U.S. 93 north, past Ravalli, to the blacktop road that takes off to the east (right) from U.S. 93 one mile south of St. Ignatius. After one mile turn right onto the road that skirts the south of St. Ignatius and follow it for about twelve miles as it heads southeast to St. Mary's Reservoir.

Since you are on the Flathead Indian reservation, be sure to get a tribal recreation permit. They are available at many sporting goods stores on or near the reservation.

Park at the northwest end of the reservoir, and strike out cross country north-by-northeast up the mountain.

Your compass and topographic map will help you find and follow the ridge that eventually becomes the east shoulder of the peaks. It's a steep, dry walk, not an idllyic stroll through the woods. Although the 9,400-foot peaks are only four horizontal miles (eight miles round trip) from the trailhead, they're a vertical mile higher.

The alpine area to the northeast of the peaks is very enticing. If you have the time or have taken overnight gear, it is well worth investigating. Although this area does not have the highest concentration of grizzlies in the Missions, it supports a few big bruins, so exercise standard precautions.

The view of the other Mission Mountain peaks from St. Mary's peaks is outstanding. Although anyone seeing the Missions from the Flathead Valley floor can recognize the Missions as rugged, the view from St. Mary's peaks gives their rugged character a new dimension. Also, on clear days the more distant viewing is incredible, particularly in late fall when the larch begin to color in the Rattlesnake Mountains, which lie just across the Jocko Valley from St. Mary's peaks. Fall often means hazy days, due to slash burning that takes place across western Montana, so try to hike close on the heels of an air-scouring front.

The Flathead Tribe, in 1979, designated the west slope of the Mission Range as a tribal wilderness, a fitting tribute to these magnificent mountains.—*John Westenberg*

## 42    Morrell Falls

*General description:* A fairly easy, five-mile round trip for any hiker.

## St. Mary's Peaks

*Morrell Falls*

*General location:* Ten miles north of Seeley Lake.

*Maps:* Morrell Lake USGS Quad and the Lolo National Forest Map for the eastern half of the forest.

*Special attractions:* Large waterfalls, small lakes.

*For more information:* Write District Ranger, Seeley Lake Ranger District, Drawer G, Seeley Lake, MT 59868 or call (406) 677-2233.

The Morrell Falls is a series of large cascades which drop about one hundred feet. In winter, it qualifies as one of Montana's larger icicles. The Forest Service has designated the route as a national recreation trail.

To find the trailhead, turn east onto the Morrell Creek Road one-fourth mile north of the Seeley Lake Post Office. Go for slightly more than a mile and take a left on the Morrell-Clearwater Road and drive seven miles. Then, hang a right, cross the bridge over Morrell Creek and take a left at the next junction. From here, it's one mile to the trailhead.

The trail is mostly flat and wanders 2.5 miles through open, lodgepole stands. There's only one short steep stretch and a few streams to cross (most of which are bridged). About one-fourth mile from the falls, you'll pass Morrell Lake, a handy place to swim, but the Forest Service discourages camping here, due to overuse of the one small site.

The main trail goes to the lower falls. But there's a steep subsidiary trail (which leaves the main trail just before it reaches the falls) that offers more viewpoints of the falls. After climbing to the upper falls, this subsidiary trail leads back into Grizzly Basin, a portion of the Swan Range recommended by the Forest Service as an addition to the Bob Marshall Wilderness.

The trail is generally free of snow mid-May through October, and there's enough drinking water. June is the best time to feed the mosquitoes, or you can shoot them for sport. They are as overwhelming as the volume of water coming over the falls, so don't forget your repellent.—*Pat Caffrey*

# 43  Sapphire Lake

*General description:* A short, steep hike to a high alpine lake in the wild Swan Range.

*General location:* Twenty miles north of Seeley Lake.

*Maps:* Holland Lake USGS Quad and the Flathead National Forest Map, south half (1975).

*Special attractions:* Spectacular views of the Swan Range and the Mission Mountains.

*For more information:* Write the District Ranger, Swan Lake Ranger District, Flathead National Forest, Bigfork, MT 59911 or call (406) 837-5081.

Although hordes of people use the main trail up Holland Creek as a major access route into the Bob Marshall Wilderness, far fewer hikers bother to climb past Sapphire Lake and take the old trail which used to serve the old Holland fire lookout. Possibly, the four thousand foot elevation gain in eight miles discourages people, but the scenery is definitely worth it.

Drive north from Seeley Lake for about twenty miles on Montana Highway 209 and turn east on the Holland Lake Road, which leads eventually to the trailhead.

The hike can be done as a twelve-mile loop day hike, or hikers can camp overnight at Sapphire Lake. If you want to avoid the traffic on the main Holland Trail, and enjoy climbing steep switchbacks, the trip can be done as an up and back, while remaining just on trail #42. This description will focus on the loop hike done in a counter-clockwise direction.

Start up the main Holland Trail (#35 on the Forest Service maps), which leads through dense forest for a mile and begins to climb the grade into the Swan Range. In a mile, a trail sign will indicate the steep Holland lookout trail leading to the Necklace Lakes and Sapphire Lake, taking off uphill to the left. You'll descend this path on the way back to lower Holland Lake.

Continuing along the main trail, the route cuts across steep sidehills, which offer beautiful views of lower Holland Lake, the Swan Valley, and the Mission Mountains. You might recognize this view as the Garry Wunderwald photo which has been appearing on the Montana Vacation and Information Guide, the state's

*The hoary marmot, not as common as its cousin, the yellow-bellied marmot, but still commonly seen in certain high country hiking areas. Harry Engels photo.*

*Sapphire Lake*

The roar of waterfalls becomes overwhelming as the path passes above Holland Falls. Another separate trail leads to the base of the falls and takes off from the main trail back near the trailhead. As the trail climbs parallel to Holland Creek, several other falls and cascades appear, as the stream rushes down the abrupt western slope of the Swan Range. Early in the summer season, in late June, the thunder of the stream will be almost deafening, and almost drown out the buzzing of early season mosquitoes. Take care in crossing the narrow footlogs over Holland Creek during high water.

Six miles from the trailhead, the trail reaches Upper Holland Lake, situated in a gorgeous subalpine basin beneath the crest of the Swan Range. The trail to Sapphire Lake leads upward from the north shore of the lake, passing through sparse stands of spruce and fir and meadows filled with glacier lilies. For the next three miles, the trail is a hiker's delight, with views opening up to the south along the Swan Range and distant vistas of huge mountains appearing to the east, deep within the Bob Marshall Wilderness.

A mile from Upper Holland Lake, the trail reaches the rumpled plateau on which several ponds, including Sapphire Lake, are located. If you plan to camp here, you may end up pitching a tent on a snowfield, if you attempt the hike before July 4.

After leaving the upper basin above Sapphire Lake, the trail ascends a steep slope to a notch in a high ridge. Once through the notch, the trail continues along a south-facing slope, with the great pyramid of Carmine Peak rising over the deep canyon of Holland Creek below you. This spectacular skywalk through the alpine meadows on the western slope of the Swan Range brings you almost to eyeball level with the Mission Mountains peaks across the valley.

A sign indicates the old Holland Lookout trail climbing the ridge to the north. If you have time and energy, this is a very worthwhile side trip. But if you're satisfied with the views you've already gotten, continue down the endless switchbacks toward lower Holland Lake. Three miles on the trail from Sapphire Lake and another mile on the main trail will bring you back to the trailhead and the completion of the loop.

The Holland Trail is the second busiest access route into the Bob Marshall Wilderness (Benchmark on the Rocky Mountain Front is the busiest), so the main trail can get crowded at times. To avoid the hordes, try the loop as early in the season as snow conditions will allow. Once off the main drag and onto the Sapphire Trail, the crowds drop off dramatically.

The mosquitoes in the Swan are well known for their voraciousness. Bring lots of bug dope or a small handgun to keep them under control.

All of this hike is outside the western boundary of the Bob Marshall Wilderness. Hopefully, the Flathead National Forest will protect this spectacular portion of the Swan Range for roadless recreation under their new forest plan.—*Ed Madej and Rosemary Rowe*

# 44   Lion Creek

*General description:* A variety of back country hiking possibilities up Lion Creek Canyon in the wild Swan Range.

*Lion Creek*

*General location:* Forty miles southeast of Kalispell, just northeast of Condon.

*Maps:* Swan Peak and Sunburst Lake USGS Quads, and the Flathead National Forest Map, South Half (1980).

*Special attractions:* A grove of old growth western red cedars.

*For more information:* Write the District Ranger, Swan Lake Ranger District, Flathead National Forest, Bigfork, MT 59911 or call (406) 837-5081.

In contrast with most hiking in the rugged Swan Front, the trail up Lion Creek climbs gradually up from the Swan Valley to the large basin beneath the Swan Divide. As a result, Lion Ceek offers fine day hiking opportunities for families or more extensive two- or three-day trips for the more adventuresome hiker.

Turn east off of the Swan Highway (Montana 83) onto the Van Lake Road, about fifteen miles south of the town of Swan Lake. Follow the Van Lake Road for five miles to the trailhead for Lion Creek (trail #25).

The trail leaves the main Swan Valley, climbing rocky benches sprinkled with a few old ponderosa pines, as it enters the narrow canyon of Lion Creek. A few miles of trail take you to the first of the several waterfalls on Lion Creek, as it cascades down from the glaciers and snowfields of Swan and Union peaks.

Continuing on, the trail passes through a majestic grove of old western red cedars, which are becoming rare in Montana as loggers cut the remaining unprotected old growth timber. After the grove, another series of falls appears on the creek just after the South Fork of Lion Creek joins the main stream.

There is a good camp spot about eight miles from the trailhead, as you enter the grand basin which wraps around the southeast flank of Swan Peak. This campsite can be used as a basecamp to climb the southern ridge of Swan Peak, or hikers can continue up and over Lion Creek Pass into the Palisade drainage in the Bob Marshall Wilderness. In all, it is 7.5 miles from your car at the trailhead to Lion Creek Pass and the Bob Marshall boundary.

When you enter Lion Creek Canyon, you enter the grizzly's domain. Please respect the great bear, and take the standard precautions to keep a clean camp.

The Swan Ranger District is considering an extensive timber sale throughout the wild Lion Creek Canyon. However, residents of the Swan Valley have urged the Forest Service to allocate Lion Creek and the surrounding unprotected wildlands of the Swan Front for back country management, providing clean water, primitive recreation, wildlife habitat, and wildness for future generations to enjoy. The steep terrain, narrow canyons, and fragile subalpine basins make commodity production difficult and expensive at best.

You might want to take the time to express your views on the management of the wild Swan Front to the Swan District Ranger in Bigfork.—*John Gatchall*

# 45    Crater Lake

*General description:* An overnight hike through subalpine terrain to a good fishing lake.

*General location:* Twenty miles north of Swan Lake in Swan Range.

*Maps:* Jewel Basin and Crater Lake USGS Quads and Flathead Forest, Swan Ranger District.

*Special attractions:* An interesting hike through western forestland similar to Glacier National Park.

0         1         2         3      4 Miles

## Crater Lake

*For more information;* Write the District Ranger, Swan Ranger Station, Flathead National Forest, Bigfork, MT 59911 or call (406) 837-5081.

To reach high elevation lakes, hikers usually expect a healthy climb. Crater Lake is the exception. The trail starts high, so it's five easy miles to this scenic fishing lake, a ten-mile round trip. This is commonly known as Alpine Trail #7.

To reach this trailhead, go north on Highway 83 from Swan Lake. After thirteen miles, 209 turns left, but keep going straight (north) on Highway 83. After about three miles, turn right at Echo Lake Store on the Foothills Road. Follow this road with the help of the signs for about seven miles to a parking lot. Beyond this lot, the road is not maintained for public use; but can be driven to a smaller parking lot at a microwave station on the Mount Aeneas Ridge.

From the smaller parking lot, the trail heads southeast along the south face of

Mount Aeneas. A quarter-mile later, it splits. Take the trail to Birch Lake. Then, it cuts though a lush forest sprinkled with wet meadows for six miles before making a slight drop into Crater Lake. There are several trail junctions along the way, but they're unusually well-marked, so simply follow the signs to Crater Lake.

At two miles, you reach Birch Lake, and at three miles Squaw Lake can be seen a few hundred yards east of the trail.

The Forest Service adequately maintains this trail all summer. The area is remote, and motorized vehicles are banned. The trail is very popular, so expect to see other hikers.

Sharp-eyed hikers often spot a mountain goat on the crags above the trail or a deer or elk in one of the many open parks. Wildflowers abound, especially at the beginning of the hike along the face of Mount Aeneas.

An occasional grizzly is reported in this area, and black bears are fairly common. However, reports of bear trouble are almost nonexistent.

Crater Lake can be nearly perfect for a family overnighter. The hike is easy, about the right distance, cool, and can be taken anytime from July through October. Be sure to bring mosquito repellent, however, as Crater Lake also seems to have its share of these pesky insects.

Most campers stay at Crater Lake where the fishing for brook trout is excellent. However, a few stay at Squaw or Birch Lakes which are along the trail to Crater Lake. All three lakes have several Forest Service campsites. At Crater Lake, firewood is scarce, but it's everywhere at the other lakes.

Perhaps the highlight of this trip is the rocky, glacier-scoured basin around Crater lake. There seems to be more rock than vegetation in this basin. Except for the Crater Lake basin, the entire trail goes through a series of moist mountain glades similar to those of Glacier Park.

The Crater Lake hike has a wide selection of possible side trips. Perhaps the most popular is to continue south on the same trail for two more miles to Big Hawk Lake which is slightly larger than Crater Lake, but not quite as scenic.—*Larry Thompson*

# 46   *Jewel Basin*

*General description:* A collection of easy-to-moderate hikes.

*General location:* Ten miles northeast of Bigfork, on the northern tip of the Swan Range.

*Maps:* Jewel Basin, Crater Lake, and Big Hawk Mountain USGS Quads; and a special Forest Service handout and map on the Jewel Basin Hiking Area.

*Special attractions:* A beautiful chunk of back country set aside for hikers only.

*For more information:* Write District Ranger, Swan Ranger District, Bigfork, MT 59911 or call (406) 837-5081.

The Forest Service has designated Jewel Basin, with its twenty-eight lakes and thirty-five miles of trail, as a special hiking area, prohibiting pack stock and motorized vehicles. The 15,349-acre area is aptly named.

To find it, drive two miles north of Bigfork and turn east off State Highway 35 onto State Highway 83. Drive about 2.7 miles and turn north on Echo Lake Road. After 2.5 miles, take the Noisy Creek Road to the east and follow it until it ends at a parking area where several trails into Jewel Basin begin. A pick-up or similar vehicle with high clearance is a necessity for the last few miles of the Noisy Creek Road.

Instead of detailing a single hike, choose from the wide selection of scenic trips leaving from this trailhead. Five trails leave from the end of Noisy Creek Road, all of which will get you into Jewel Basin in two miles or less. Get a map and plan a trip that suits you.

Jewel Basin is perfect for beginning hikers wanting to see what backpacking is all about—or for families ready to introduce their children to the back country without working too hard the first time. The area is also just right for a leisurely day hike—perhaps with a brief sampling of the area's good fishing.

You can take a short hop into tranquil Picnic Lakes, or a longer hike covering most of the basin, stopping to fish and camp at several lakes. Almost all lakes have suitable campsites, but plan on using your backpack stove to keep the sites from showing the wear-and-tear of heavy use.

The Jewel Basin even has something for those who have irresistible urges to climb to the top of something. From the end of Noisy Creek Road, they can take a short hike on a trail along Aeneas Ridge to the top of 7,530-foot Mount Aeneas, which offers super views of Flathead Lake and the southern portion of Glacier National Park.—*Pat Caffrey and Loren Kreck*

*Because the above describes a general area instead of a specific hike, there is no map.—Editor*

# 47   Alpine Trail Columbia Mountain

*General description:* A long, three-day hike for experienced hikers.
*General location:* Just southeast of Columbia Falls.
*Maps:* Doris Mountain, Jewel Basin, and Hash Mountain USGS Quads; Forest Service's Jewel Basin Hiking Area map; and Flathead National Forest Swan Lake Ranger District.
*Special attractions:* Outstanding panoramic views of northwestern Montana and Flathead Lake from a delightful ridgeline trail.
*For more information:* Write District Ranger, Hungry Horse Ranger District, Hungry Horse, MT 59919 or call (406) 387-5243.

This twenty-seven-mile hike isn't for beginners or small children. It usually requires three days with a full pack and involves a 3,500-foot elevation gain.

To reach the trailhead, turn south off U.S. 2 about 1.3 miles east of the U.S. 2/State Highway 40 junction. This turn is marked with a "Columbia Mountain Trail" sign. Follow this road .8 mile to the trail marked "Columbia Mountain Trail #51."

Trail #51 climbs steadily up the slopes of Columbia Mountain where it intersects with Trail #7. Take #7 all the way to Strawberry Lake and then turn west on Trail #5 for a short drop down to Krause Road and the end of your three-day excursion.

This is a point-to-point hike, so it's best to leave a vehicle at the end of the hike (Strawberry Lake trailhead) or have somebody pick you up there. To find the Strawberry Lake trailhead, turn east from U.S. 2 (four miles north of Creston) on the Lake Blaine Road. Just after passing Lake Blaine, turn south on the Foothills

*Alpine Trail Columbia Mountain*

Road and go about eight miles. Then, turn left (east) up the Krause Creek Road to Strawberry Lake Trailhead.

Although there is water at many places along the trail, there are some stretches in the northern half of this hike where hikers must carry it. Mosquitoes can be a problem early in the season, but they seem less severe than many areas. Shelter from wind and drinking water can often be found by dropping over the ridge to the east into the high meadows.

Black bears and grizzlies inhabit this area, so there is a chance of a bear/man confrontation. The likelihood of such an encounter might be higher here than on many trails in Montana's national forests, but the probability of bear trouble is still much lower than in nearby Glacier National Park. Proper bear country manners will further lower the probability of bear trouble.

Except for the trail below Strawberry Lake, few motorized vehicles are encountered on this trail because of its remoteness. The signs of civilization—clearcuts, cities, etc.—can be seen in the distance, but the terrain is relatively untouched along the trail.

The twenty-seven miles can be made in two days, but to really enjoy the scenery on this high-altitude hike, allow three days. Although the trail is remote and primitive, it's still well-maintained—good enough to follow easily. There is a fair chance of spotting elk or deer, and a great variety of wildflowers greet summer hikers, particularly in mid-July. Snow may block this trail until early July.

The best campsites are Lamoose and Strawberry lakes, but there is a good selection from which to choose. Both of these lakes have fish and easily available water, but firewood is scarce, so bring your backpack stove.

Although there is some fishing in Strawberry and Lamoose lakes, this hike isn't known for its fishing. The main attraction is vistas inherent to crest trails.

There are many variations of this hike because of the extensive trail system in the area. For instance, hikers could easily be lured into extending into nearby Jewel Basin.—*Loren Kreck*

# 48    Logan Creek

*General description:* A steep day hike for experienced hikers.

*General location:* Just east of Hungry Horse Reservoir.

*Maps:* Felix Peak and Nimrod USGS Quads, the Great Bear Wilderness Map, and the Flathead National Forest Map (north half).

*Special attractions:* Scenery—especially rock cliffs and one very high waterfall.

*For more information:* Write the District Ranger, Hungry Horse Ranger Station, Flathead National Forest, Hungry Horse, MT 59919 or call (406) 387-5243.

Although the trip up and back Logan Creek usually makes a nice day hike for good hikers, a few decide to spend the night near where the trail ends—on the divide between the South Fork and Middle Fork of the Flathead River.

To find the trailhead turn south off U.S. 2 at Martin City and go along the east shore of Hungry Horse Reservoir for thirty-five miles until you reach Logan Creek. There should be a sign marking the turn off onto a smaller dirt road up Logan Creek. For the first two miles, the trail follows Logan Creek through deep spruce forests. After leaving the creek on the trail, look for the sheer cliffs to your

*Logan Creek*

left and a cascading waterfall on your right. Soon you'll break out into a luscious subalpine meadow.

Through the meadows flows a babbling brook lined with buttercups and other wildflowers. It also has a small pond, elk wallow, and a crescendoing waterfall. The last mile of the hike gradually climbs through subalpine meadows and large spruces and larch snags to the divide where you get an unsurpassed view into Dirtyface Creek and the Middle Fork of the Flathead River.

It's six miles from trailhead to divide with an elevation gain of 2,300 feet, which will take at least six hours for the round trip. Water is available all along the trail. The only possible hazards are two crossings of Logan Creek, which could be tricky at high water. Mosquitoes exist in tolerable densities, especially in July, August, and September, which is the best time for this hike.

If you prefer to make this an overnighter, the best campsite is in the meadow just as you break out of the brush and just below the divide. It has a delicious stream and carpets of wildflowers. Bring your backpacker stove, however, as firewood is scarce, unless you want to carry it from the edge of the meadow.

This trail continues down Dirtyface Creek through old clearcuts and hits U.S. 2 3.5 miles west of Essex. However, most hikers prefer to make it an out-and-back hike.

Apparently, part of this area was left out of the Great Bear Wilderness because of numerous mining claims. But it can still remain in its present roadless condition if enough people voice support for wilderness management.—*Elaine and Art Sedlack*

## 49   Ousel Peak

*General description:* A long day hike for experienced hikers.
*General location:* Just southwest of West Glacier in the Great Bear Wilderness.
*Maps:* West Glacier and Nyack USGS Quads, the Great Bear Wilderness Map, and the Flathead National Forest Map (north half).
*For more information:* Write the District Ranger, Hungry Horse Ranger Station, Flathead National Forest, Hungry Horse, MT 59919 or call (406) 387-5243.

Although the trailhead may be difficult to locate, the Ousel Peak hike warrants the extra time. To make sure you don't have trouble finding the trailhead, however, check with Hungry Horse Ranger Station on U.S. 2 in Hungry Horse.

Take U.S. 2 and turn south at Martin City on the Forest Service road along the east shore of Hungry Horse Reservoir. Go seven miles and turn east on the Emery Creek Road. Follow this road up onto the Highline Loop Road. The trail begins about 7.5 miles from the reservoir road or 2.5 miles from the only bend (180 degrees) in the road. The first 200 yards of the trail were eliminated by a clearcut in 1978, but the new trailhead, which is marked by a small sign, can be found twenty feet up a skid road in the cut.

This is a rugged, twelve-mile point-to-point hike that goes from Hungry Horse Reservoir on the South Fork of the Flathead River over the Flathead Range and through the Great Bear Wilderness down to U.S. 2 on the Middle Fork of the Flathead. After finding the trail, you move through an open forest of large tamaracks. Then, the trail enters a rocky drainage before breaking out on open,

*Ousel Peak*

rocky ridges with views of Deerlick Creek, Nyack Creek, the Middle Fork of the Flathead, Harrison Lake in Glacier National Park, and many of the highest peaks in the park. The trail follows the rocky ridges for about three miles before ducking around the back of Ousel Peak. Then, it drops abruptly down to U.S. 2, five miles east of West Glacier.

This point-to-point hike is actually two trails—trail #388 up from Hungry Horse Reservoir and trail #331 down to U.S. 2. The two trails both go to the vicinity of Ousel Peak, but do not actually connect. Plan on spending some extra time looking for the other trail, and referring to your topo map.

The trail is sometimes hard to find as it comes off Ousel Peak, so watch your topo map closely. the last three-mile drop to the highway cuts through alder thickets that can be bothersome.

This isn't a trip for beginners. It rises 2,700 feet (4,400 to 7,100), and the trail can be hard to follow on the rocky ridges. In addition, you have to bring drinking water for the entire trip, as the trail is quite dry. There are also a few blowdowns on the South Fork side to slow progess. On the plus side, mosquitoes are rarely a problem.

It takes a good hiker eight hours to make this hike. Unless you want to hike through snow, wait until mid-July to try it.

Most hikers leave a vehicle where the trail meets U.S. 2 or have somebody pick them up. Hitchhiking back to the trailhead would be most difficult.

Wild animals—elk, deer, black bears, and others—are fairly common. Even an occasional grizzly bear is spotted. And watch for glacier lilies, lupine, and other wildflowers. Later in the year, expect to find some excellent huckleberry patches.

Few—if any—hikers make this an overnighter. And there aren't any good campsites.—*Elaine and Art Sedlack*

## 50   Great Northern

*General description:* A mountain ascent through timbered undergrowth and up scree slopes for scramblers with good stamina.
*General location:* Thirty miles east of Kalispell, in the Great Bear Wilderness.
*Maps:* Mount Grant USGS Quad, the Great Bear Wilderness Map, and "Climbing Great Northern," a Forest Service handout.
*Special attractions:* Goat trails, fine scenery, Stanton Glacier, and spectacular views of seldom-seen southern Glacier National Park.
*For more information:* Write the District Ranger, Hungry Horse Ranger Station Flathead National Forest, Hungry Horse, MT 59919 or call (406) 387-5243.

Although named for a former railroad, the mountain's name suggests exactly what it is. Its graceful curves and broad faces are irresistible to the individual who has acquired a taste for the high places. With the incomparable peaks of Glacier Park close at hand, this mountain attracts many individuals solely on the merits of its own beauty.

Two popular routes are described on a Forest Service flyer available at the Hungry Horse Ranger Station. The following is a shorter variation of the western approach described in the flyer.

Take the East Side Road of Hungry Horse Reservoir, which leaves U.S. 2 as the main street of Martin City. About 8.5 miles past the Emery Creek boat land-

Great Northern

ing area, hang a left (uphill) and go one-half mile to the Highline Loop Road junction, where you will find a small bridge. Park at this bridge (elevation 4,249 feet), fill your canteen, and start climbing.

Look south of the bridge and notice the impenetrable thickets of brush and small trees. After briefly considering whether the whole idea is worthwhile, charge into these thickets. They don't last long and are the hardest part of the climb. Find a game trail to help escape this jungle.

Climb the ascending ridge on the south side of Hungry Horse Creek, where you just filled your canteen. Initially, work to the south, climbing and contouring to get out of the brush and windfalls on the north side of the ridge. In early August, be careful not to delay too long in these massive huckleberry patches.

Within one-half mile, a definite ridgetop, complete with definite trail, develops. Follow this ridge for one mile to where it peaks out at timberline. Ahead of you is a small timbered saddle, on the other side of which is the Great Northern.

From here, you have a choice of two routes. Note the rocky, open spur ascending directly to the peak. Save this route for the descent. It's loose scree, and with great care and concentration, you can run down its slopes in ten minutes.

Now, note another ascending spur to the left (north) of the main peak, with clumps of gnarled trees reaching almost to the summit ridge. Try climbing this way; the rock is firmer. Once on the summit ridge, after a few gasps at the scenery, follow intriguing little goat trails along ledges and around rock knobs to the 8,720-foot summit.

By now, you've noticed 120-acre Stanton Glacier which reaches all the way to the summit ridge on the east side. This is a "real" glacier of hard, slippery ice and deep crevasses, so stay off it unless you're properly equipped.

To the east is the Middle Fork of the Flathead River and across it the usually unseen array of peaks of southern Glacier Park. One unusually monstrous-looking peak sticks up above the others. The south portion of this peak is pyramid-shaped, with a chopped-off ridge to the north. This is Mount Stimson, at 10,142 feet the second highest peak and the most exhausting climb in the park. North of it is 10,052-foot Mount Jackson, with huge Harrison Glacier flung across the entire south face. A few miles to the south of Mount Stimson, you can pick out 9,376-foot St. Nicholas, the most difficult technical climb in the park. It's just north of Church Butte, a flat-topped rectangle. St. Nicholas is easy to spot because, quite literally, it sticks out like a sore thumb. And it appears impossible to climb.

With all these impressive peaks, Great Northern maintains its own magic lure. It's a true mountain, and is never mistaken for anything less.—*Pat Caffrey*

## 51    *Stanton Lake*

*General description:* A short hike suitable for any hiker.

*General location:* Thirteen miles southeast of West Glacier in the Great Bear Wilderness.

*Maps:* Mount Grant, Pinnacle and Stanton Lake USGS Quads, the Great Bear Wilderness Map; and the Flathead National Forest Map (north half).

*Special attractions:* An easy way to get a choice view of the mountains of Glacier Park and of Great Northern Mountain in the Great Bear Wilderness.

*Stanton Lake*

*For more information:* Write the District Ranger, Hungry Horse Ranger Station, Flathead National Forest, Hungry Horse, MT 59919 or call (406) 387-5243.

The Stanton Lake trail begins right on U.S. 2 just east of Stanton Lake Lodge about thirteen miles east of West Glacier. So, for once, the trailhead is easy to find.

Except for some motorcycle traffic on the first part of the trail, this hike is remote. The trail is well-maintained with a gradual incline, rising 500 feet in two miles. There isn't any drinking water until you reach the lake.

This trail receives fairly heavy use, and it's easy to see why. It's an easy hike, open from June through October. (Bring your insect repellent in June and July.) The fishing is good, and the likelihood of bear trouble is minimal.

Hikers often get a glimpse of a moose at the head of the lake or a beaver in the beaver ponds as the stream leaves the lake. Wildflowers are fairly common—beargrass, wild hollyhocks, cow parsnip, and others.

Some hikers carry in small rubber rafts for float fishing. Usually, this is worth the effort, as it increases the size of the catch of the lake's supply of rainbow and cutthroat trout. However, anglers can usually catch at least some smaller cutthroat from shore.

Although it's only two miles into the lake, the lake still receives substantial overnight use. Most backpackers use the campsite at the head of the lake where water and firewood are easy to find.

Perhaps the highlight of this hike is the vista of the mountains of Glacier National Park to the north and the massive Great Northern Mountain to the south.

Since this popular lake has an above average number of visitors, be extra careful not to leave signs of your passing. And do whatever you can to pick up or cover up the signs of others who weren't so careful—*Elaine and Art Sedlack.*

## 52   *Marion Lake*

*General description:* A leisurely day hike or overnighter into one of the many high altitude lakes in the Great Bear Wilderness.

*General location:* Just south of Glacier National Park.

*Maps:* Pinnacle USGS Quad, the Great Bear Wilderness Map, and the Flathead National Forest Map (north half).

*Special attractions:* An easily accessible wilderness lake.

*For more information:* Write the District Ranger, Hungry Horse Ranger Station, Flathead National Forest, Hungry Horse, MT 59919 or call (406) 387-5243.

Marion Lake is easily accessible and has good fishing. Thus, it probably receives above average use compared with other mountain lakes in designated wilderness areas.

The trailhead is also easy to find. Turn west on the Essex Creek Road which turns off from U.S. 2 one mile north of Essex or twenty-four miles south of West Glacier. Watch for a sign marking the trailhead about 1.5 miles from the highway.

The way to Marion Lake is a steady, uphill pull. The trail gains about 2,000 feet in three miles. This should take a family less than three hours into the lake and two hours or less out.

*Marion Lake*

The hike has a well-maintained trail, plenty of drinking water, and a tolerable number of mosquitoes—except some years in June and July. Since this lake lies within the Great Bear Wilderness, the hike has a remote feeling, and of course, motorized vehicles are banned.

Bear problems are minimal even though black bears are numerous and an occasional grizzly frequents this area. Skip this hike in June unless you want to risk hiking through snowbanks.

At the head of the lake lies a gorgeous, grassy swale blanketed with wildflowers—beargrass, fireweed, wild hollyhocks, dogwood, bunchberry, and others.

The trail comes to the foot of the lake. But there is a faint trail around to the head of the lake—about one-half mile.

For an excellent side trip, work your way through the swale to the pass on the horizon. It's only about one-half mile from where the trail hits the lake. At the top of the swale, you can look down over 1,000-foot cliffs into the headwaters of Essex Creek.

Backpackers almost always camp at the head of the lake where scenery is abundant and firewood scarce.

The lake has good fishing, particularly in June when the ice breaks up. Each winter, a few avid anglers ski or snowshoe in for ice fishing, and they usually have good success from the lake's healthy population of cutthroat and rainbow trout.

Fortunately, Montana has such choice spots within reach of everybody. Unfortunately, Marion Lake shows a little wear-and-tear as the result of this accessibility and popularity. Take a bag along and carry out any garbage a thoughtless hiker might have left behind.—*Elaine and Art Sedlack*

## 53    Nyack Loop

*General description:* A long backpacking expedition for experienced hikers.

*General location:* Fifteen miles southeast of West Glacier in the Middle Fork region of Glacier National Park.

*Maps:* Nyack, Mount Jackson, Mount Stimson, and Mount Saint Nicholas USGS Quads; and the large USGS topo map of the entire park.

*Special attractions:* A rare opportunity to get intimately close to the wilderness and totally away from everything else.

*For more information:* Write Superintendent, Glacier National Park, West Glacier, MT 59936 or call (406) 888-5441.

Many trails in Glacier Park are heavily used. But others receive surprisingly little use—even though they host as many back country rewards. The Nyack Loop is an excellent case-in-point.

It follows Nyack Creek as it flows over a gorgeous falls and colorful bedrock. Mount Stimson, an incredible hulk of a mountain, dominates the landscape for much of the hike. And wildlife—including the grizzly—is as abundant as any section of the park.

So what keeps the trail from heavy use or overuse? It's a long hike, thirty-five miles or more depending on how many side trips you take. There is no fishing. And it starts and ends by fording the Middle Fork of the Flathead River.

But if you aren't a fanatic angler, can tolerate getting your feet wet, and don't

### Nyack Loop

mind long walks, this could turn out to be the backpacking vacation of your life. Plan on at least three days, but you can easily spend a week without regretting it.

Another limiting factor for the Nyack Loop route is the difficulty in finding the trailheads and fords over the Middle Fork. The easiest way to avoid confusion is to stop at or call the Walton Ranger Station for detailed and updated directions and a special hand-drawn map to both the Nyack Creek and Coal Creek trailheads.

To start this hike, drive west from Walton Ranger Station until you cross the railroad tracks. After this crossing, take the first gravel road to your right. Follow it for a short distance and turn right where it dead ends just before the tracks. Drive about another one-fourth mile and park. Walk down the road a hundred yards or so, cross the tracks, follow a trail through a cottonwood stand, and then wade the river, keeping your eyes peeled for trail markers on trees on the opposite riverbank.

Leave a vehicle or have somebody pick you up at the Coal Creek trailhead which is about five miles southeast of Nyack on U.S. 2. Drive from Walton to a small parking area which is a short drive up a gravel road to your left. The trail takes off from the highway and crosses the tracks before merging into an old logging road. Ford the Middle Fork about seventy-five yards south of where the old logging road hits the river.

The trail starts at the abandoned Nyack Ranger Station and crosses Nyack Creek about one mile from the river. This is a large stream, and the bridge has been washed out; so be prepared for wet feet again. No, this isn't the last time; there are other streams to cross in the next few days.

The trail gradually climbs along Nyack Creek all the way to Surprise Pass. The

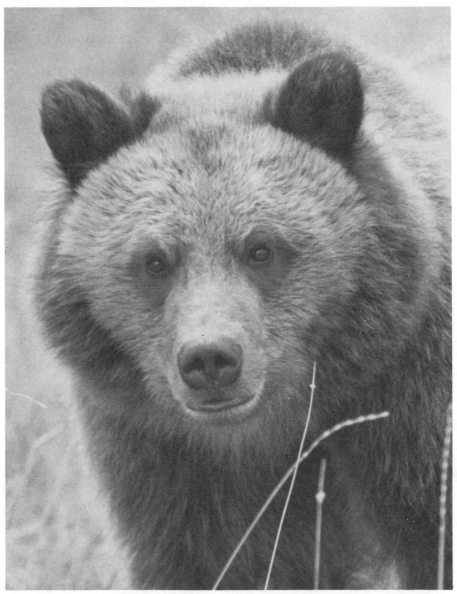

*The mighty grizzly, king of the wilderness. Doug O'looney photo.*

trail dips down to the stream occasionally, but stays high much of the way. Although there are a few dry stretches, you can usually find enough drinking water. Although the scenery leaves little to be desired all the way, the scenic highlight may be Nyack Falls with massive Mount Stimson forming the backdrop. On the way up Surprise Pass, spend a few hours gorging yourself on huckleberries. Keep very close watch for grizzlies, however, as this entire hike traverses some of the best grizzly habitat left in Montana.

Soon after dropping over Surprise Pass into Coal Creek, a trail to Buffalo Woman and Beaver Woman lakes juts off to the right. Even if you don't camp here, don't miss these "beautiful women." After the lakes, it's a long, scenic haul down Coal Creek to the Middle Fork.

On such a long hike, you have several side trip possibilities. You can take the Dawson Pass or Pitamakan Pass trails for good views of much of southern Glacier Park. Perhaps the most popular side trip is a climb up Mount Stimson. Plan to take a full day from timberline to the summit of Mt. Stimson, and back down again. Although one of the most—if not the most—rigorous climbs in the park, it's still nontechnical and within reach of most well-conditioned, experienced hikers.

Leave your fishing pole at home, as Nyack Creek, Coal Creek, Buffalo Woman Lake, and Beaver Woman Lake are all closed to fishing by the National Park Service. You'll need the extra room in your pack for food, anyway.

Before taking the hike, be sure to obtain a back country camping permit from any park ranger station. You can camp anywhere, and there are numerous excellent campsites. The NPS discourages camping at the patrol cabins along this hike. Also before leaving, check the current park regulations on campfires, as they are often prohibited during dry weather.

As to special precaution, carefully read the section on "Hiking Bear Country" in this book to reduce to almost nothing your chance of encountering a grizzly on unpleasant terms. Remember, this is the big bear's home, and you are the visitor, so behave accordingly.—*Bill Schneider*

# 54   *Akokala Lake*

*General description:* A moderate day hike or easy overnighter.

*General location:* Thirty-five miles north of West Glacier in the North Fork region of Glacier National Park.

*Maps:* Quartz Ridge and Kintla Peak USGS Quads, the large topographic map of Glacier Park available at retail stores in the area, and the National Park Service brochure/map given to every park visitor.

*For more information:* Write Superintenent, Glacier National Park, West Glacier, MT 59936 or call (406) 888-5441.

The North Fork of the Flathead River forms the west boundary of Glacier National Park. Inside the park, there are several lakes that drain into the river, with Akokala being one of the smallest. This hike extends through fairly typical North Fork country with lodgepole forests and rolling ridges, without the snow-capped crags found elsewhere in the park.

The trail leaves from the Bowman Lake Campground which can be found by driving into the park from West Glacier. Shortly after entering the park, turn

*Akokala Lake*

north on the Camas Creek Road and stay on this paved highway until it crosses the North Fork of the Flathead and leaves the park.

Immediately after crossing the river, the Camas Creek Road dead-ends with the North Fork Road, a partly paved Forest Service road going all the way to the Canadian border. Turn north on the North Fork Road and stay on it for about twenty-five miles until you reach Polebridge, which is little more than a General Store, the Northern Lights Saloon, and a few cabins.

Go through Polebridge and across the river into the park again at the Polebridge Ranger Station. Also drive through the ranger station and go about a quarter-mile north until you see a right-hand turn to Bowman Lake. It's six more miles up this gravel road to Bowman Lake Campground.

(There is also a road following the North Fork within the park. However, this is longer, slower, and dustier.)

From the campground, it's about 5.6 miles to Akokala Lake on an easy-to-follow trail. You have one big hill near the beginning of the hike and a few more small climbs later on, but it's generally easy all the way, only gaining about 600 feet in elevation. When you reach Akokala Creek, you might see a trail junction with a trail following the creek. You turn right and follow Akokala Creek upstream to the lake. The left-hand fork has more-or-less been abandoned by the park and doesn't appear on current hiking maps.

The first half of the hike can be dry in late summer or early fall, but the last half has plenty of drinking water. Be sure to bring your insect repellent—especially in June—as Bowman Lake is almost infamous for its fierce mosquitoes.

Akokala Lake has a good population of cutthroat and Dolly Varden trout. The fishing is best halfway around the left-hand (west) side where the water deepens close to shore.

The only campground is near the outlet where the trail hits the lake. However, be sure to check with the rangers at Polebridge or Bowman Lake for a back country camping permit and updated regulations before leaving on the hike. Fires are often prohibited in this area.

Don't forget you're in Glacier Park grizzly country. So be religious about every possible bear country precaution and sanitary rule.—*Bill Schneider*

## 55   *Mt. Thoma*

*General description:* A ten-mile round trip climb in the North Fork Flathead wildlands.

*General location:* Forty miles north of Columbia Falls near the British Columbia border.

*Maps:* Mount Hefty USGS Quad and the Flathead National Forest Map, North Half, 1980.

*Special attractions:* Some spectacular views of Glacier National Park from a little known area.

*For more information:* Write the District Ranger, Hungry Horse Ranger District, Flathead National Forest, Hungry Horse, MT 59919 or call (406) 387-5243.

The Mount Thoma trail lies in an area between Trail Creek Road and the Canadian border west of the North Fork Flathead road and east of the Whitefish Range.

*Mount Thoma*

To get to the trailhead, go north on the North Fork Flathead road for about forty miles from Hungry Horse to where a prominent sign marks the Trail Creek road and indicates that the Canadian border is six miles farther. Drive three miles up the Trail Creek road to where a Forest Service sign marks the Mount Thoma-Mount Hefty trailhead. Turn right and drive in about a hundred yards to where you can park your car, shielded from the main road.

The trail is quite clear with little brush. Except for a few short marshy places, the footing is good, although rather steep in spots for the entire distance to Mount Thoma. There are no streams to cross, which demands that one carry enough water for the entire hike.

The period of time the trail is passable is determined by the amount of last winter's snowfall. Expert skiers and persistent snowshoers can climb the trail nearly all year, but the casual hiker should wait at least until July. The trail is not heavily used at any time, although hunters use it to some extent in the fall.

Grizzly bears frequent the area, but have not been a problem to day hikers. This part of the North Fork of the Flathead is reported to have one of the densest grizzly concentrations in the state, so it is wise to keep alert along the trail. Deer and elk are also present, but probably not as conspicuous as the wilderness traveler would like.

The trail starts out in low key with a moderate climb up through lodgepole pine mixed with larch, spruce, and fir. Soon enough the trail becomes steeper, until it comes out on the open side of a ridge. With a little extra effort, the hiker can leave the trail and climb the bare ridge to get a view looking east over the Ketchikan drainage and over some low hills into Glacier National Park.

When the trail begins the final ascent to the summit, the climb is much steeper with no switchbacks to relieve the tedium. Once on top, however, the sweep and magnitude of the view are magnificent. East are the Rockies of Glacier Park, west is the Whitefish Range, north the view is blocked by the bulk of Mount Hefty, and to the northeast one can ponder over the pockmarked landscape of clearcuts adjacent to Waterton National Park. The view is both grandly aesthetic and morbidly educational.

If you have time and strength remaining, you can follow the trail north for another two and a half miles to the top of Mount Hefty, almost on the Canadian border.

There are no developed campsites near or on the trail, but there are many places to camp if you bring your own water.—*Jack Johns*

## 56    Pitamakan and Dawson Passes

*General description:* A two or three-day hike to two mountain lakes and over two spectacular mountain passes.

*General location:* On the east side of Glacier National Park about twelve miles northwest of East Glacier.

*Maps:* Cut Bank Pass and Mount Rockwell USGS Quads (Kiowa and Squaw Mountain cover the first two miles). The USGS also publishes a large contour map of the entire Glacier Park. Of additional help is the Backcountry Map and Trail Guide available at no charge from the National Park Service at all ranger stations.

*Special attractions:* Crossing the Continental Divide twice, this trail offers at least five separate panoramic views.

*For more information:* Write Superintendent, Glacier National Park, West Glacier, MT 59936 or call (406) 888-5441.

The trailhead is at the outlet of Two Medicine Lake. From the town of East Glacier, drive north on Highway 49 about four miles to a well-marked turnoff on the Two Medicine Road. Drive to the end of the Two Medicine Road and park in the lot near the ranger station.

Note these two points: 1) In order to camp at Oldman and/or No Name Lakes, you must have a back country camping permit, which can be secured the day before or the day of your hike at any park ranger station. 2) This is a loop trail and can be taken in the reverse direction from the way it is described below.

From the parking lot, cross the bridge below Pray Lake and turn right at the marked trail junction. The first segment of the trail stretches a little less than six miles to Oldman Lake. In the first two miles, the hiker moves around the base of towering Rising Wolf Mountain and across Dry Creek (which is knee-deep in springtime) to a marked trail junction where you turn left (west). From here, you face a steady climb up an open valley. Very wet Dry Creek cascades the length of the valley, while several smaller streams drop out of hidden cirques to add to the volume. Paintbrush and lupine add splashes of color to the scene.

At the head of the valley, you enter a thick forest which is prone to blowdowns. The trail splits shortly before Oldman Lake. The right fork heads directly for Pitamakan Pass while the left leads to the campsites on the lake.

The National Park Service (NPS) has four designated campsites, at which

*Oldman Lake in Glacier National Park. Mike Sample photo.*

*Pitamakan and Dawson Passes*

wood fires are not permitted, in the timber by the lake.

An outhouse stands nearby. Campers are required to use the designated sites to minimize man's impact on this beautiful spot.

Flinsch Peak dominates the western skyline. You may see a family of beavers at the far end of the lake in the twilight hours. Twenty-inch cutthroat cruise the shoreline. And on the northern slopes above the lake, a white cloud of beargrass stands as thick as anywhere in the park in late July.

The area around Oldman Lake seems to be natural habitat for grizzlies. Chances are slim of seeing one of the great bruins, let alone having any trouble, but play it safe: It's really their turf. Read over "Hiking Bear Country" (page 8) before taking this hike.

From Oldman Lake to No Name Lake is a distance of about 7.5 miles; almost all of it is dry by early August, so carry water. Some hikers elect to bypass the camp at No Name Lake and hike all the way out on the second day. This makes for a long day, partly because this segment of the hike begins with an elevation gain of 1,400 feet.

To reach Pitamakan Pass from Oldman Lake, take the short cutoff trail almost straight north from the outhouse instead of going back to the trail junction. This cutoff trail is not maintained. The climb to Pitamakan is short and steep—1,000 feet up in about a mile. You will find the pass is actually a saddle in a ridge. Before turning left (west) to follow the trail up the ridge, pause for a look down at Pitamakan Lake 800 feet below you.

Very quickly after leaving the saddle, the hiker encounters two well-marked junctions in the trail; in each case take the trail to the left. Less than a mile from Pitamakan Pass, you cross the Continental Divide. Due west stands mighty Mount Stimson rising 6,000 feet above the Nyack Creek valley.

From here, the trail goes in a southerly direction, paralleling the Continental Divide along the shoulders of Mount Morgan and Flinsch Peak to Dawson Pass, where you cross the Divide again. While nearly level through this section, the trail traverses steep slopes of "roller bearing" scree, which is dangerous when wet. Because dangerous snow banks lie across these slopes until late June or early July, the NPS opens this trail later than most. Check with the Two Medicine Ranger Station before planning an early trip.

Dawson Pass is a favorite hangout for mountain goats, which are quite tame in this region. Dawson is also a favorite jumping-off spot for people who wish to make the steep walk up the south face of Flinsch Peak.

From Dawson Pass, the trail drops very rapidly through Bighorn Basin to No Name Lake. The lake deserves a more descriptive "no-name," for it lies at the base of sheer Pumpelly Pillar. It's an evocative pool, especially in the first moments of sunlight on a quiet morning.

Again, there is a cluster of three campsites (no wood fires) and a nearby outhouse. The campsites are near the creek just before it empties into the lake. Like Oldman Lake, this area is quite "buggy" in July—bring some bug dope.

A fishing rod isn't of much use here. For some reason, the tiny trout which dimple the surface of the lake haven't made it big in recent years.

Leaving No Name Lake, the hiker moves down the valley about two miles to a trail junction. The left fork goes along the north shore of Two Medicine Lake three miles to the trailhead. The right fork goes only a short distance to another junction, where the hiker can either turn west a short distance to Twin Falls or east to the head of the lake, where a boat picks up paying customers from the dock to return to the foot of the lake. If interested in a boat ride (which cuts about two miles off the last leg of this trip), inquire about the schedule at the boat concession stand near the trailhead before beginning the hike.—Mike Sample

## 57   Iceberg Lake

General description: A ten-mile round trip day hike to a beautiful lake in a spectacular setting.

General location: On the east side of Glacier National Park eight miles west of Babb.

Special attractions: High probability of seeing mountain goats and other wildlife.

Special caution: Of all hikes in this book, this one is probably the most dangerous in terms of possible encounters with grizzlies.

*Iceberg Lake*

*For more information:* Write Superintendent, Glacier National Park, West Glacier, MT 59936 or call (406) 888-5441.

Technically, Iceberg Lake doesn't have icebergs, but it comes as close as any place in Montana. Chunks of ice float around in the lake—usually until September. However, the "icebergs" are larger and more scenic in July and August.

Find the trailhead by driving along the eastern boundary of Glacier National Park eight miles north from St. Mary to Babb and then twelve miles west into the park to Many Glacier. The trail starts from a parking lot behind Swiftcurrent Motel. Or you can join the trail at the north side of the bridge over the outlet of Swiftcurrent Lake.

Except for a short section at the very beginning, this trail climbs only 200 feet per mile, a rate most people find comfortable. Wide and relatively smooth, the trail leads through fields of wildflowers. Large flickers with pronounced reddish coloring and swooping flight patterns nest in the ghost trees along the trail.

At the 2.5-mile mark, the hiker passes by lovely Ptarmigan Falls as it plunges over rocky layers to a deep emerald pool. Shortly thereafter, a clearly marked trail junction indicates a right turn for those wishing to see Ptarmigan Lake and Tunnel—and willing to make the stiff, 2.5-mile climb to get there. The Iceberg Lake trail goes straight for another 2.5 miles to the lake, making this a ten-mile round trip.

During the summer months, the National Park Service installs a bridge over Iceberg Creek just before the lake. However, this bridge is removed each fall to prevent it from washing out in the spring. So hikers who take this trip after mid-September can plan on getting their feet wet here.

On the last segment of this hike, mountain goats and bighorn sheep are commonly seen on the grassy slopes above and to the right. Like the rest of Swiftcurrent Valley, this is prime grizzly habitat. Be alert and make noise. You may sacrifice solitude, but it would be safer to take this trip with a group, possibly the ranger-conducted walk scheduled almost every morning in July and August.—*Mike Sample*

## 58   *Gateway Pass, Gateway Gorge*

*General description:* A three-day hike for experienced hikers.
*General location:* Twenty miles west of Dupuyer in the Bob Marshall Wilderness.
*Maps:* Swift Reservoir, Gateway Pass, Gooseberry Park, and Morningstar Mountain USGS Quads; and the Lewis & Clark National Forest Map (Rocky Mountain Division).
*Special attraction:* Spectacular scenery—and lots of it.
*For more information:* Write District Ranger, Rocky Mountain Ranger District, Lewis & Clark National Forest, Box 340, Choteau, MT 59422 or call (406) 466-2951.

An experienced hiker can make this thirty-two mile trip in three days, but the scenery is so spectacular that you may stay longer.

The trailhead is easily located by turning west off U.S. 89 at Dupuyer onto a

*Gateway*

Miles

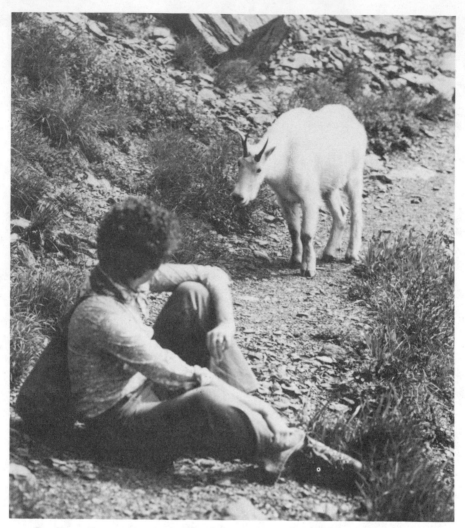

*Back country visitor meets back country resident. Mike Sample photo.*

gravel Forest Service road. Follow this road for eighteen miles until you reach Swift Dam. Then, take the road to the right that passes in front of the dam and goes along the north side of the reservoir. The trail starts at the end of this road. After a heavy rain, the road along the reservoir may be impassable, and you'll have to add an extra two miles to your trip by walking to the trailhead.

After climbing onto a small knob, the trail follows the South Fork of Birch Creek, gradually climbing through thick forests of Douglas fir with a few meadows rich in wildflowers. You reach Gateway Pass at the fourteen mile mark. The trail stays high, and in another mile, you reach Big River Meadows, a great campsite surrounded by open hillsides and mountain panoramas.

From here the trail drops gradually along Gateway Creek and through the awe-inspiring Gateway Gorge. It's about four miles from Big River Meadows to the Strawberry Creek Trail. After leaving the gorge, take the Strawberry Creek Trail north to the East Fork Trail which puts you about twenty miles into the hike and at a good second campsite.

From the Strawberry Creek/East Fork trail junction, the trail climbs easily through forests and meadows for about six miles along the creek to Badger Pass, where the scenery is hard to equal. From that high point, the trail climbs another 600 feet before dropping into the North Fork of Birch Creek. The trail then follows this stream which has very interesting rock formations and little water-falls. One side drainage has a sheer rock wall similar to those found in the Canyonlands of southern Utah. After eight miles of easy hiking, you come out on the north shore of Swift Reservoir where you started.

The trail is well-used and easy to follow. It has several rocky sections and the stream crossings can be tricky especially after a good rain or early in the summer of a heavy snow year. The trail along Strawberry Creek has a few boggy sections.

The overall elevation gain is 1,600 feet. Water is available throughout the trip, and mosquitoes usually aren't a problem after June. It's best to wait until July anyway, so the passes will be free of snow.

Although grizzly bears inhabit this area, hunting pressure keeps them very wary of man. So the chance of an incident is as remote as this trail.

This hike has dozens of possible campsites, but Big River Meadows and a site at the Strawberry Creek/East Fork trail junction are two top choices. Both have good water supplies. Big River Meadows has the edge on scenery, but hikers must haul firewood from the edge of the meadow. Strawberry Creek has plenty of firewood.

Nearly all of this hike is in the spectacular Rocky Mountain Front addition to the Bob Marshall Wilderness, designated in 1978. Unfortunately, the north side of the North Fork of Birch Creek Valley was left out of the wilderness, and has come under increasing interest of oil companies. Let your congressman know what you think of the North Fork Valley remaining unprotected, open to industrial development.

Although Gateway Gorge is probably the highlight of the trip, you won't be disappointed at the rest of the hike, which is probably one of the most beautiful in Montana.—*Elaine and Art Sedlack*

# 59  *Our Lake*

*General description:* A seven-mile round trip suitable for a day or overnight hike.

*General location:* Twenty-nine miles west of Choteau in the Rocky Mountain Front.

*Maps:* Our Lake USGS Quad, and the Lewis & Clark National Forest Map (Rocky Mountain Divison).

*Special attractions:* A very pristine mountain lake with good fishing and mountain goats inhabiting the slopes above the lake.

*For more information:* Write District Ranger, Rocky Mountain Ranger District, Lewis & Clark National Forest, Box 340, Choteau, MT 59422 or call (406) 466-2951.

This is a popular overnight or day hike with a well-maintained trail, outstanding scenery, good fishing, and excellent opportunities to view wildlife.

To find the trailhead, drive north from Choteau on U.S. 89 for five miles before

*Our Lake*

turning west on County Road #144, which follows the Teton River. Follow this paved road, which doesn't cross the river, for about fifteen miles until you see the sign for Ear Mountain Ranger Station. Here, turn south on County Road #109 (South Fork Road). Cross the Teton River and follow the South Fork of the Teton River for nine miles until the road ends. Take trail #184 which begins where the road ends.

Although it's only 3.5 miles to Our Lake (sometimes called Hidden Lake), expect a fair climb, as the trail climbs 1500 feet to the lake.

The last half-mile to the lake switchbacks up a steep slope which can be hazardous if tried before the snowbanks disappear. Thus, it's best to wait until July or August to try this hike.

Motorized vehicles are banned on this trail, and other signs of man are uncommon. Mosquitoes aren't much of a problem except some years in June. Bears are common in the area. There is a good source of water at about the three-mile mark, but the rest of the trail is dry, especially in late August and September.

Hikers can almost always spot mountain goats on the alpine slopes behind Our Lake. If they're lucky, they can also see bighorn sheep near Rocky Mountain, the highest peak in the Bob Marshall Wilderness (9,392 feet). In addition, expect to see marmots and pikas. Asters, daisies, and lupine seem to prevail among the abundant supply of wildflowers along this trail. Skunkflower is common on the alpine slopes above the lake.

The lake has four campsites, which are the only signs of man on this trip. In addition, some hikers camp below the waterfall about one-half mile before the lake. Others stay at one of several good campsites in the basin beyond the lake.

Although there is a good selection of campsites, all of them are high altitude and thus wood is in short supply. A backpacking stove for cooking is necessary.

Since access is easy, the lake is heavily used at times. Still, the fishing remains good. Ten-inch rainbows make up most of the catch. The lake also has cutthroat trout, but they're harder to catch.

For moderate hikers, there is a good side trip to the saddle west of the lake above the basin. From this saddle, hikers can view the Chinese Wall, the backbone of the Bob Marshall Wilderness. The distance to the saddle is approximately three-fourths of a mile.

This spectacular mountain country has been left out of the Bob Marshall Wilderness, and has been opened to oil and gas leasing by the Forest Service. Conservationists are pushing for a Bob Marshall Completion Bill which would protect these areas on the fringes of the present wilderness.—*Dave Orndoff*

## 60 *Chinese Wall*

*General description:* A long, rugged hike which crosses the Continental Divide twice in the heart of the Bob Marshall Wilderness.

*General location:* Thirty miles west of Augusta.

*Maps:* Benchmark, Pretty Prairie, Prairie Reef, Slategoat Mountain, Three Sisters, Bungalow Mountain, Amphitheatre Mountain, and Haystack Mountain USGS Quads; and the Forest Service's Bob Marshall Wilderness Map.

*Special attractions:* High alpine scenery along the Chinese Wall in one of the most remote places in Montana.

*The Chinese Wall, the backbone of the Bob Marshall Wilderness. U.S. Forest Service photo.*

*For more information:* Write District Ranger, Rocky Mountain Ranger District, Lewis & Clark National Forest, Box 340, Choteau, MT 59422 or call (406) 466-2951.

This sixty-mile loop takes at least five days for the veteran hiker but deserves longer than that to fully enjoy the heart of the Bob Marshall country. With two passes to cross, each nearly 8,000 feet, it pays to take it easy and enjoy the scenery of this very remote area.

143

Take Forest Service road #235 thirty miles west from Augusta (the Benchmark Road) to reach the trailhead adjacent to the South Fork Campground. Almost immediately after leaving the parking area, the trail (#202) crosses a packbridge and enters the Sun River Game Preserve in which no hunting is allowed. The huge bridge is one of several built after the disastrous 1964 floods but before passage of the Wilderness Act limited the number of such massive construction projects in wilderness areas.

The next 3.5 miles of trail receives heavy use by horses and may be quite ripped up. However, once past this one bad stretch, trail conditions improve considerably for the remainder of the hike. This stretch of trail also parallels the South Fork of the Sun River through the recommended Renshaw addition to the Bob Marshall Wilderness.

You officially enter the Bob Marshall near the Sun River Forks. A half mile past the official entrance sign, the trail crosses the West Fork of the Sun on another of those huge packbridges. The trail (now signed as #203) follows the West Fork through a series of beautiful lowland meadows to Indian Point Guard Station. A good first night's camp can be found in any of the meadows along the river before the trail reaches the guard station. There is excellent fishing for cutthroat trout in the West Fork. Campsites and level ground become more scarce once the trail passes the guard station.

A mile past the guard station, the trail intersects the White River Pass Trail (#211 and #138) which crosses the West Fork at a ford. At this point, some three days and forty miles later, you will complete your loop around the Chinese Wall, but for now, continue up the West Fork.

After three cold but minor stream crossings, the trail climbs out of the sparsely timbered valley of Burnt Creek and reaches the high flower fields at the base of the Chinese Wall. The trail (now #175) wanders through alpine meadows in the shadow of the sheer, thousand-foot limestone cliffs of the Wall. Camping is prohibited on much of this stretch, to protect the fragile meadows from overuse. Travellers must therefore reach Larch Hill Pass or stop before the Moose Creek trail junction if they plan to spend the night on the Wall.

Wildlife is plentiful along the Wall Trail, with elk, deer, coyote, and grizzly frequently seen; so follow the rules for camping in bear country.

The adventurous hiker can reach the top of the Wall by walking south from Larch Hill Pass, or by scrambling up Trick Pass at the head of Moose Creek. Trick Pass is not on any map and would seem to exist only in the imagination of some deranged mountaineer. But it is the only obvious goat trail going to the top, where a piece of the Wall has slumped down into the Moose Creek cirque.

Even if you do not choose to climb the Wall itself, the views eastward down the glacial carved troughs of Moose Creek and Rock Creek are spectacular enough, with the Deep Creek Mountains rising above the broad valley of the North Fork of the Sun River.

More views open up to the north and west as the trail crosses the Continental Divide at Larch Hill Pass (now signed as trail #112) and enters the huge bowl of the upper White River. Silvertip Mountain and Lone Butte tower over this subalpine valley in the very heart of the Bob Marshall. The area is so remote that Silvertip Mountain is at the center of a township-sized section of land which doesn't even have any trails in it!

*Chinese Wall*

Campsites are plentiful in the upper White River valley, but fishing is poor until the trail passes below Needle Falls, another scenic wonder hidden deep in the Bob. At the falls, the White River drops hundreds of feet after shooting out from under a natural bridge carved out of stone.

At the White River Forks, the trail climbs steeply eastward up and over the Continental Divide at White River Pass and drops down to the Indian Point Guard Station. From the guard station, retrace your steps down the West Fork of the Sun and up the South Fork to Benchmark and the completion of the hike.

The Chinese Wall will receive most of its visitors during late July and the month of August. If you want to avoid crowds and experience some solitude, your best bet is to go sometime before the Fourth of July or after the first of September. Before the Fourth, snow drifts along the Chinese Wall Trail and high-water stream crossings at the West Fork and the White River may make travel difficult (and in some especially heavy snow years, downright impossible), so check out conditions with the Forest Service before making the trip. Fishing is also worse during the high water of early summer.

The autumn can be a particularly beautiful time to take this hike, especially in early September. The summer crowds will have thinned out considerably by then, and hunting season in the White River Valley will not have opened yet. The Chinese Wall itself is included in the Sun River Game Preserve, and therefore is closed to hunting. Hikers who would prefer to avoid hunters altogether can do so by dropping down Moose Creek and following the west bank of the North Fork and the South Fork of the Sun back to Benchmark.

Ever since the late 1970s, energy companies have been attempting to open up the Bob Marshall Wilderness area to speculative exploration for natural gas. Fortunately, however, they have been stopped by the overwhelming opposition of people throughout Montana who have staunchly supported protecting the Bob. In fact, the Bob Marshall vs. the energy companies battle was the issue that catalyzed national concern over the possible development of our wilderness areas by the oil interests. Take this hike and you'll agree with the thousands of others who have worked to "Save the Bob!"—*Ed Madej and Rosemary Rowe*

# 61    *Renshaw Mountain Renshaw Lake*

*General description:* A pleasant two day hike through a proposed addition to the Bob Marshall Wilderness.

*General location:* Twenty miles west of Augusta.

*Maps:* Patricks Basin, Pretty Prairie, Double Falls, Wood Lake, and Benchmark USGS Quads; and the Lewis & Clark National Forest Map, Rocky Mountain Division.

*Special attractions:* A subalpine lake with good fishing, plus expansive views of the Rocky Mountain Front.

*For more information:* Write the District Ranger, Rocky Mountain Ranger District, Box 340, Choteau, MT 59422 or call (406) 466-2951.

This easy twelve-mile hike passes through a variety of terrain in the Rocky Mountain Front and offers some good lake fishing as well. You'll need two vehicles to do this hike properly, leaving one at the Benchmark Creek trailhead along the Benchmark road and another near the Willow Creek Work Station at

Renshaw Mountain Renshaw Lake

the start of the trek.

To reach Willow Creek, take Forest Service road #235 twenty miles west from Augusta. Just outside the Forest Service boundary, road #235 turns left (now called the Benchmark road), while Forest Service road #233 goes straight ahead for about one mile to the Willow Creek turnoff. With luck, and no mud, you can turn left at the Scoutana Girls Ranch into Willow Creek and drive two miles to a

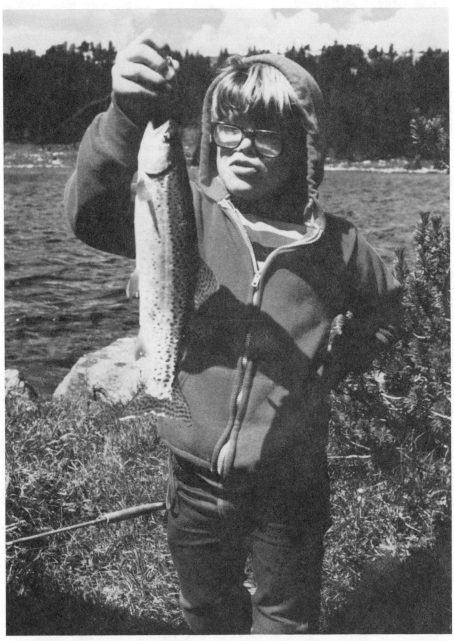

*Wild trout add to the back country vacation. Bill Schneider photo.*

gate on private land where the trail starts. The other vehicle should be driven down the Benchmark road for another fifteen miles to where the Benchmark Creek trail comes in on the right.

Back at Willow Creek, go through the gate (remembering to close it!) and follow trail #204 past the private inholding.

The country gets interesting at the very beginning, as the trail climbs up Willow Creek Canyon past a series of beautiful waterfalls. To the north is the bulk of Fairview Mountain, one of the higher peaks along the Rocky Mountain Front. Hikers shouldn't drink Willow Creek water; there is usually a cattle herd grazing in its headwaters up in the high country.

Past Willow Creek Canyon, the trail passes through the flower covered Fairview Plateau, a favorite haunt for bighorn sheep and elk. The plateau and the nearby Patricks Basin are prime grizzly habitat, so keep your eyes open and your camp clean.

Crossing the plateau, the trail drops into the headwaters of Fairview Creek and offers attractive views of Renshaw Mountain to the northwest.

Just past a crossing of a sidestream (Renshaw Creek), there is a junction with trail #243. Turn right on the trail, which goes uphill for several miles to Renshaw Lake. It's easy to walk past the lake on the trail, so use your topo map to guide you up to the lake on one of the many sidetrails which lead about 100 yards and fifty feet up to the lake basin.

Renshaw Lake is one of the very few subalpine lakes in the Rocky Mountain Front. It's used as a base camp for hunters in the fall and gets visited by a few trail bikers. The Lewis and Clark National Forest hasn't closed this fragile area to motorized vehicles.

After eating your fill of pan-sized rainbow trout and leaving the lake, turn left up the trail to a low divide between Renshaw Creek and Lange Creek. Here an unmarked trail (# 256 on the Forest Service map) takes off uphill to the left. For about one hundred feet it seems to go straight up, but once you gain the northern shoulder of Renshaw Mountain, the worst is over. The peak of Renshaw Mountain is an easy scramble to the south, and the trail itself offers great views of the Deep Creek Mountains along the Rocky Mountain Front to the north.

One more scenic attraction awaits the hiker as the trail drops into an unusual limestone gorge as it descends Benchmark Creek.

If you're impressed with the country along this hike, you'll be glad to know that all of it has been recommended as an addition to the Bob Marshall Wilderness by the Forest Service. Give the folks of the Bob Marshall Alliance a hand, and write your congressman asking that the Renshaw area be added to the wilderness system.—*Ed Madej and Rosemary Rowe*

# 62    Mount Wright

*General description:* A walk up to an old fire lookout with tremendous views.
*General location:* Thirty miles west of Choteau.
*Maps:* Mt. Wright USGS Quad and the Lewis and Clark National Forest Map, Rocky Mountain Division).
*Special attractions:* One of the best mountaintop views of the northern Bob Marshall Wilderness.

*Mount Wright*

*For more information:* Write the District Ranger, Rocky Mountain Ranger District, Lewis and Clark National Forest, Box 340, Choteau, MT 59422 or call (406) 466-2951.

The old lookout is now gone, but the trail to the 8,855-foot summit of Mt. Wright remains. For those in average physical shape and with no mountaineering experience, this is the perfect hike to catch some views which stretch from Glacier National Park to the Scapegoat Wilderness.

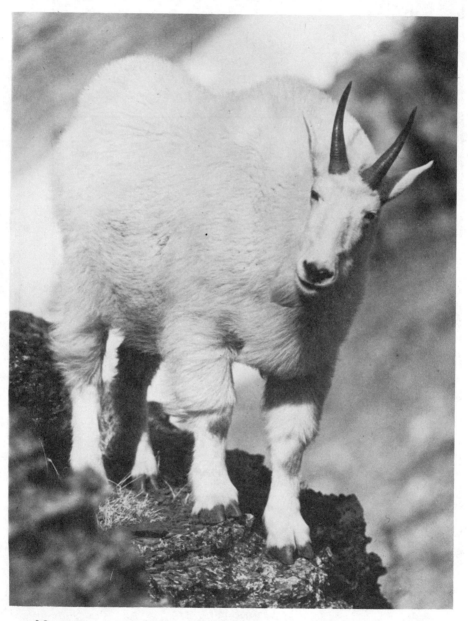

*Mountain goats, a favorite of wilderness visitors. Harry Engels photo.*

Drive four miles north of Choteau and take the Teton River Road (FS road #144) westward into the Rocky Mountain Front. After entering Forest Service land, the road passes Cave Mountain Campground, a very pretty car campground, on the left. Continue along the North Fork of the Teton River, past the Teton Pass Ski area, and down to the West Fork Ranger Station. Just before the bridge crossing the Teton River, a small sign will point to the Mt. Wright trailhead on the left.

The trail starts in an old clearcut and begins to climb to the north on a closed-off logging road. The route is well marked, since a Youth Conservation Corps group signed the trail several years ago. After one-half mile, the trail leaves the clearcut and enters the forest.

Switchbacking up the southeastern slope of the mountain, hikers may catch glimpses of mountain goats on Mt. Wright's south ridge, as the trail breaks out of the sparse tree cover. Two miles from the trailhead, you'll reach a small pass to the east of the main summit.

Above timberline now, the trail is very faint in these meadows. The actual trail cuts across a steep bushy slope to the west. It isn't hard to find. More adventuresome hikers might want to follow the old telegraph poles to the plateau above.

Whichever route you choose to reach the plateau, it would be wise to avoid going up there in a storm, since the barren, windswept reaches are totally exposed. The trail continues over the plateau to a low saddle on the north-south ridge dead ahead. Once on the ridge, it is a short hike to the summit.

The views on the summit are some of the best to be found anywhere in the northern Rockies. Directly north is the knife-edged top of Mt. Patrick Gass, named after a lieutenant in the Lewis and Clark expedition. To the east is the thin, steep ridge of Choteau Mountain and the endless expanse of the northern Great Plains. With a good regional map (the Lewis and Clark National Forest Map is useful), the hiker can pick out Mt. Saint Nicholas in Glacier Park; the long limestone cliffs of the north Chinese Wall; and the large bulks of Old Baldy and Rocky Mountain Peak to the south. Literally hundreds of other peaks stretch across the horizon on a cloudless day.

The descent from the summit should take you less than two hours, while the ascent can stretch as long as four or five hours. The 3,500-foot elevation gain may deter families with young children, but the trail doesn't require any mountain climbing experience, just strong lungs and legs.

The route is totally waterless, so fill up before you start. Try this one early in the season (June or early July) so that a few snowfields are still around to slake your thirst near the summit. The exposed, southward-facing slopes can be a real scorcher of a trip in August.—*Ed Madej and Rosemary Rowe.*

# 63    *Devils Glen*

*General description:* A short and easy hike along a wild river.
*General location:* Fifteen miles southwest of Augusta.
*Maps:* Steamboat Mountain and Caribou Peak USGS Quads, and the Lewis and Clark National Forest map (Rocky Mountain Division).
*Special attractions:* Waterfalls and good fishing along a beautiful river.

*Devils Glen*

*For more information:* Write the District Ranger, Rocky Mountain Ranger District, Lewis and Clark National Forest, Box 340, Choteau, MT 59422 or call (406) 466-2951.

Floating the lower Dearborn River has become very popular, but fewer people bother to hike the river's upper reaches through Devils Glen. This is the perfect family hike, with low mileage, virtually no elevation gain, and a fish-filled river.

Take the Elk Creek Road southwest from Augusta to Bean Lake, or take county road #434 north from State Highway 200, which branches off 27 miles southwest of Simms. At Bean Lake, take the Dearborn River Road #577 westward into the mountains.

Past the Diamond X Ranch, the road can get muddy and rutted, but two-wheel-drive pick-ups can reach the end of the road and the trailhead. Other vehicles may have to park a quarter-mile away.

The trail immediately crosses the Dearborn River and stays on the north side for four miles. The crossing can be a little tough at high water, so wait until July to take the family along.

The Dearborn River flows through a broad valley here, with spectacular waterfalls interspersed with deep pools. Summertime fishing for cutthroat is excellent along this stretch of river. After about three miles, the trail begins to climb into a rockpile coming off the southern slopes of Steamboat Mountain. This is called Devils Glen.

Hikers can camp anywhere along the river at this point, but on busier weekends, you might want to ford the stream and camp on the southern side in the trees, or continue past Devils Glen for a mile or two more. The fishing is equally good above the glen, but the valley is more heavily wooded and slightly less scenic.

For the hiker bored with just fishing and appreciating the rushing river, you can hike north up the rocky slopes to the summit of Steamboat Mountain, which offers stunning views of the Rocky Mountain Front and the Great Plains.

This entire area is a recommended addition to the Scapegoat Wilderness. If enough people visit the area and talk to their congressmen about it, it might become part of the Scapegoat some day.—*Ed Madej and Rosemary Rowe.*

## 64  *Deep Creek, North Fork of the Sun River*

*General description:* A three- or four-day hike through some little-visited country in the Rocky Mountain Front area.

*General location:* Twenty miles west of Augusta.

*Maps:* Patricks Basin, Arsenic Peak, Our Lake, Gates Park, and Glenn Creek USGS Quads; and the Lewis and Clark National Forest Visitors Map for the Rocky Mountain Division.

*Special attractions:* A variety of jagged limestone peaks and large lowland meadows.

*For more information:* Write District Ranger, Rocky Mountain Ranger District, Box 340, Choteau, MT 59422 or call (406) 466-2951.

This outstanding thirty-five mile loop hike passes through some of the most spectacular country to be found along the Rocky Mountain Front and in the eastern portions of the Bob Marshall Wilderness. It can be done in three days, but for the sake of your feet, take at least four.

The trail starts at the Mortimer Gulch Campground on the Gibson Reservoir. Take county road #208 west from Augusta to Gibson Dam. Then turn right and drive along the north side of the reservoir until you reach Mortimer Gulch campground. The trailhead is in the trees across the road from the campground. Be sure to fill up your water bottles here before hitting the trail, since the first five miles are mostly a dry, uphill slog.

Heading north on trail #252, you'll enter the Deep Creek Further Planning Area on the Lewis and Clark National Forest. There, you will be rewarded by incredible views of the Rocky Mountain Front to the south, as you reach the head of Mortimer gulch. Ignore the trail which breaks off to the left at the four-mile mark (the trail isn't marked on the map); instead turn right and drop into Blacktail Gulch. Head north on trail #223, a National Recreation Trail, which leads into the south fork of Deep Creek.

After crossing Deep Creek at the site of an outfitter's camp, follow the stream bank westward until a well-defined trail (#128) becomes apparent. This is a remnant of an old seismic road bulldozed up the drainage in the late 1950s. Follow this track to Biggs Creek Pass and the official entrance into the Bob Marshall Wilderness.

A scramble up the goat trails on the hillside to the west of the pass provides outstanding views of the North Fork of the Sun River Valley and tantalizing views of the Chinese Wall in the distance.

The trail now drops down into Biggs Creek and skirts the southern slope of Rocky Mountain Peak, at 9,392 feet the highest peak in the Bob Marshall Wilderness. Six miles and one stream crossing later, the trail pops out of the timber into a large meadow called Biggs Creek Flat. Turn south on trail #110 (which eventually becomes trail #201), which sixteen footsore miles later will bring you back to Mortimer Gulch and your waiting car.

This loop has many attributes which commend it as one of the state's premiere hikes. The valley of the North Fork of the Sun River, for example, is one of the largest lowland valleys outside of Alaska that is preserved in a completely wild condition. The trail wanders through huge lowland meadows which offer a chance to see elk, deer, and an occasional grizzly, along with awesome views of the surrounding mountains.

generally stays back from the river, requiring a little extra effort to get down to the water.

As you might expect, with all this to offer, the North Fork portion of this hike will be heavily used during the peak summer season, although the Deep Creek stretch receives very light use. To avoid the crowds, go before the Fourth of July, but be prepared for a short bit of snow on Biggs Creek Pass, and a few mosquitoes. Or go before hunting season (September 1-15). Summer crowds will be gone, and the fall hordes won't have descended yet.

There are numerous fine places to camp along this loop. The South Fork of Deep Creek has two sites used by outfitters during the fall hunting season and a scattering of level sites near the stream. On the Biggs Creek-Sun River stretch, campsites are essentially unlimited, with open, aspen-ringed meadows being especially attractive.—*Ed Madej and Rosemary Rowe*

*Deep Creek, North Fork of the Sun River*

# 65   Halfmoon Park

*General description:* A three-day hike for experienced hikers.

*General location:* Sixteen miles southwest of Augusta in the Scapegoat Wilderness.

*Maps:* Scapegoat Mountain and Jakie Creek USGS Quads, the Scapegoat Wilderness Map, and the Lewis & Clark National Forest Map (Rocky Mountain Division).

*Special attractions:* Good views of Scapegoat Mountain, perhaps the highlight of the Scapegoat Wilderness.

*For more information:* Write District Ranger, Rocky Mountain Ranger District, Lewis & Clark National Forest, Box 340, Choteau, MT 59422 or call (406) 466-2951.

This rugged, three-day hike takes you to the heart of the Scapegoat Wilderness. By budgeting an extra day, you'll have time to climb the unusual lump of limestone called Scapegoat Mountain. Halfmoon Creek runs right by this glaciated mountain, which at 9,204 feet is the second highest peak in the Scapegoat Wilderness. It's a thirteen-mile one-way hike into Halfmoon Park, not including the extra mileage needed to climb Scapegoat Mountain.

Find the trailhead by taking Forest Service Road #196 southwest from Augusta until the road deadends on Elk Creek near Cataract Falls. Take trail #215 over Elk Pass and down Smith Creek to Jakie Creek. Turn left on Jakie Creek trail #214, which goes to Welcome Pass.

After crossing Welcome Pass, turn up Dearborn River Trail #206 for about four miles, until you reach trail #216 which leads to Halfmoon Park.

You can either retace your steps back to the Dearborn River via Telephone Creek or make a small loop and see new country. Instead of returning on the same trail east from Halfmoon Park, go south on trail #216 until you reach the Dearborn River where the trail turns east and goes back to the Telephone Creek junction.

The hike has well-maintained trails with plenty of water except for a three-mile stretch from Smith Creek over Welcome Pass down to the Dearborn River. Since this hike extends into the Scapegoat Wilderness, no motorized vehicles are allowed. Take this hike anytime between late July and late September.

This hike isn't for fanatic fishermen. There are fish in the upper stretches of the Dearborn River, southeast of Welcome Creek Ranger Station, but they're small and scarce.

However, elk and deer are quite common, especially along Halfmoon Creek and on the slopes of Scapegoat Mountain. Bears—black and grizzly—are also common. But these are wild bears, so if hikers keep a clean camp, the chances of a bear/man confrontation are remote.

Wildflowers, particularly lupine, are present, but not unusually abundant for western Montana. However, the Dearborn River drainage grows some super huckleberry and elderberry crops.

There are many good campsites along this trip, perhaps the choicest being Welcome Creek (halfway point), Halfmoon Creek, and Green Fork Creek. All have ample firewood, easily accessible water, and spectacular scenery.

*Halfmoon Park*

Many hikers who go to Halfmoon Park allow an extra day to climb mighty Scapegoat Mountain. There is a trail from Halfmoon Creek over the ridge to Green Fork Creek. Then, go southwest up Green Fork Creek to the end of the glaciated valley. From here, find a goat trail that takes you out of this cirque onto the ridge. Walk east along this ridge to the summit. The view from the top is totally impressive.—*Dave Orndoff and Ed Madej*

## 66    *Alpine Park*

*General description:* A steep but short six mile hike to a high subalpine meadow in a little-used part of the Scapegoat Wilderness.

*General location:* Ten miles northwest of Lincoln.

*Maps:* Arrastra Mountain and Coopers Lake USGS Quads, and the Scapegoat Wilderness Map (1976).

*Special attractions:* The large, subalpine valley of Meadow Creek.

*For more information:* Write the District Ranger, Lincoln Ranger District, Helena National Forest, Box 234, Lincoln, MT 59639 or call (406) 362-4265.

This trip will take you into the far southern portion of the Scapegoat

*Alpine Park*

Wilderness, up to a pretty subalpine valley off the main travel routes in this popular wild area. Although the trailhead is in the Lolo Forest, the major portion of the trip lies in the Lincoln Ranger District of the Helena National Forest.

Turn north from Montana 200 sixteen miles west of Lincoln (two miles west of the Montana 271 intersection) onto the Rock Creek road, which leads to the Whitetail Ranch and Coopers Lake. After seven miles of driving across the level expanse of Kleinschmidt Flat, turn right toward Forest Service road #4106 and the Dry Creek Trailhead, which appears in another two miles.

The trail (labeled the Meadow Creek Trail on the topo maps) switchbacks steeply from the valley floor, climbing some 2,300 feet to the 6,800-foot pass into the Meadow Creek drainage. In three miles, the route passes several small ponds, the only water sources in the appropriately-named Dry Creek watershed.

As the trail reaches the higher slopes, views open up to the southwest, overlooking the broad valley of Kleinschmidt Flat. Kleinschmidt is a glacially bulldozed plain, formed by large glaciers which ground their way out of the Scapegoat Mountains into the Blackfoot Valley during the last ice age. The Scapegoat Mountains today are too low to support permanent snowfields, but still bear the signs of past glacial advances.

Dropping down from the broad pass which lies on the southern boundary of the Scapegoat Wilderness, the trail enters Alpine Park along Meadow Creek. Here, some six miles from the road, are several good camping sites in the scattered meadows along the stream. The mixture of forest and meadow continues for two miles down to where Meadow Creek leaves Alpine Park and joins the East Fork of Meadow Creek.

Alpine Park can serve as a fine base camp for further explorations of the surrounding meadows, for fishing in Meadow Creek and Meadow Lake (further downstream) or for the steep four-mile round trip up the old trail to the summit of Arrastra Mountain. Arrastra Mountain provides some interesting views of the remote peaks to the north deeper in the Scapegoat Wilderness.

Alpine Park is grizzly country, although problems with hikers and bears are few. Make sure to keep a clean camp and follow the usual safety precautions.
—*Karen Renne*

# 67    Gates of the Mountains

*General description:* An overnighter through one of Montana's smaller wilderness areas.

*General location:* Twenty miles northeast of Helena.

*Maps:* Upper Holter Lake, Candle Mountain, and Hogback USGS Quads; and the Helena National Forest Map.

*Special attractions:* Several historic points from the Lewis and Clark Expedition.

*For more information:* Write District Ranger, Helena Ranger District, Helena National Forest, Federal Building, Drawer 10015, Room 498, Helena, MT 59626 or call (406) 449-5490.

The 28,560-acre Gates of the Mountains Wilderness has the variety representative of most wildlands—open parks, deep canyons, craggy peaks, etc.,—with one exception: no lakes. More than compensating for this void, however, is a rich history.

*Hikers looking into the Meriwether Canyon from the Gates of the Mountains Wilderness. U.S. Forest Service photo.*

The trail starts at Refrigerator Canyon. To get there, drive northeast from Helena on County Highway 280 for about fifteen miles until you cross the Missouri on the newly constructed York Bridge. After crossing the bridge, drive for about four miles to the tiny community of York.

Here, turn north on road #224 and drive the well-maintained gravel road until it junctures with the Beaver Creek Road #138. Turn east (right) on the Beaver Creek Road and drive about five miles until you see a well-marked trailhead for Refrigerator Canyon. The last five miles on the Beaver Creek Road can be dangerous because of sharp, blind corners and logging truck traffic. So if you're driving, don't be caught gawking around at the scenery. Let the passengers take in the steep-walled Beaver Creek Canyon with its whitish, limestone cliffs and beautiful stream.

This hike requires more logistics than usual. It's an eighteen-mile, point-to-point hike that ends at Meriwether Campground on the Missouri River. You must leave a vehicle or have somebody pick you up at Gates of the Mountains Boat Club.

Gates of the Mountains, Inc. (458-5241) offers tours of the scenic "Gates of the Mountains" section of the Missouri several times daily; these tours stop at

*Refrigerator Canyon, on the edge of the Gates of the Mountains Wilderness, is usually 12-20 degrees cooler than the surrounding country. U.S. Forest Service photo.*

Meriwether Campground on the way up and back. When you reach Meriwether Campground, you have to wait for the next boat. However, check the schedule before you leave, so you don't miss the last one. Also, bring a few dollars to pay for the ride.

To get to the Gates of the Mountains boat dock, take I-15 north from Helena for about sixteen miles and turn right at the Gates of the Mountains exit. Follow the paved road two miles to the boat dock.

This trail can, of course, be taken in reverse, but most hikers find the boat ride a refreshing conclusion.

From the trailhead, trail #260 gradually climbs about one-half mile to Refrigerator Canyon. Even on the hottest summer day, it's cool in this extremely steep, narrow canyon.

After Refrigerator Canyon, the trail gradually switchbacks about three miles to the Moors Mountain junction. Trail #260 continues on to the right to Moors Mountain. You turn left on trail #259 to Bear Prairie.

About five miles later, you reach the wildflower-carpeted Bear Prairie, one of the largest and most gorgeous mountain meadows in the Helena area. You can camp here or hike another mile to Kennedy Springs, which sits in a similar but slightly less impressive meadow. Kennedy Springs has a reliable source of water

0             1             2 Miles

right in the meadow, while at Bear Prairie you'll need to hike down the slopes of the Willow Creek trail, several hundred yards to the north, for some H$_2$0.

From the Moors Mountain junction through Kennedy Springs (about seven miles), the trail is fairly level and well-maintained. The only confusing spot occurs just after Kennedy Springs in a large meadow where the trail swings to the right to the top of a ridge and then starts its descent to Meriwether Campground, where the Lewis and Clark Expedition camped almost two centuries earlier. The last five miles switchback steeply downhill—another good reason why hikers rarely take this trip in reverse.

After June, this trail is devoid of water with the exception of Kennedy Springs and a short section of Meriwether Creek for the last mile or so of the hike. On the plus side, the dry climate holds down the mosquitoes. This area has the advantage over many other wildlands because the snow usually frees the area early in the year, even as early as late April in dry years.—*Bill Schneider*

*Gates of the Mountains*

# 68   *Hanging Valley*

*General description:* A steep, eight to twelve mile day hike in a little known area.

*General location:* Twenty miles northeast of Helena.

*Maps:* Hogback Mountain and Snedaker Basin USGS Quads, and the Helena National Forest Map (1977).

*Special attractions:* A deep, narrow canyon with impressive limestone towers.

*For more information:* Write District Ranger, Helena Ranger District, Federal Building, Drawer 10015, Room 498, Helena, MT 59626 or call (406) 449-5490.

After exploring this section of the Big Belt Mountains, you'll wonder how part of Utah, complete with narrow canyons and unusual rock formations, ended up in Montana.

The trailhead lies at the Vigilante Campground in the Helena National Forest, six miles past York on FS road #4021, the old Figure Eight Route. To get to York take county road 280 northeast of Helena for fifteen miles, across the new Missouri River Bridge. The Figure Eight Route used to go beyond Vigilante Campground until the massive floods of May, 1981 buried the road under tons of gravel in Trout Creek Canyon. Hanging Valley is actually a dry tributary of Trout Creek, entering the canyon from a point high on the southern wall. You'll be able to pick out where you've been from Trout Creek Canyon once you've taken the hike.

0          2          4 Miles

*Hanging Valley*

The trail (#248) starts at the back of the campground and is marked with a smart national recreation trail sign. The path climbs a dry hillside for three miles to a low pass between Trout Creek and Magpie Creek. During late May, the trail is lined with hundreds of pink fairy slipper orchids and blue clematis flowers just below the pass.

At the pass, turn left onto trail #247, which will lead you to the top of the mountain which forms the southern rim of Trout Creek Canyon. Here the views are tremendous on a clear day, with the Flint Creek Range appearing from over the Continental Divide to the west and the Spanish Peaks near Bozeman visible some one hundred airline miles to the south.

The rest of the trail is not shown on Forest Service maps, but is well constructed and practically impossible to lose. Past the summit, the trail switchbacks down a heavily wooded slope for half a mile into Hanging Valley, past huge Douglas firs which have escaped the logger's axe. The trail follows the dry watercourse into the canyon.

Limestone pinnacles fifty feet tall tower over the trail, which soon becomes a route just a few feet wide at the bottom of a narrow canyon. After the trail passes under a small natural bridge, a rickety wooden ladder aids the hiker in descending a five-foot-high rock step in the trail and adds excitement to the trip. During heavy snow years, such as the winter of 1982, the trail at this point may be snow-choked and impassable into mid-June.

The trail deadends on the lip of a dry waterfall several hundred feet up a sheer rock face on the southern wall of Trout Creek Canyon—hence the name Hanging Valley. A metal fence installed by the Forest Service allows the hiker to lean over and gawk at the canyon walls, which bear a close resemblance to those of Bryce Canyon in Utah.

Retrace your steps to Vigilante Campground, where you can briefly hike up Trout Creek Canyon and try to pick out Hanging Valley, high on the southern rim.

Aside from a few snow fields in the spring, the trail is waterless, so fill up your canteens at the campground. Although the twelve-mile round trip can be done easily in one day by most well conditioned hikers, there are a few dry campsites along the trail for those wishing to make it an overnighter. The trip may prove too steep for younger hikers, but it should not be missed by anyone wanting to see a part of the Southwest right here in Montana.—*Ed Madej and Rosemary Rowe*

## 69   Red Mountain

*General description:* An easy cross-country mountain climb.

*General location:* Eighteen miles southwest of Helena.

*Maps:* Jefferson City USGS Quad and the Helena National Forest Map.

*Special attractions:* A short climb with a super view on the outskirts of one of Montana's largest cities.

*For more information:* Write District Ranger, Helena Ranger District, Helena National Forest, Federal Building, Drawer 10015, Room 498, Helena, MT 59626 or call (406) 449-5490.

Montana has many mountains to climb, but not many are so close to a city nor so easily climbed. Red Mountain is one of those wonderful exceptions.

To start this hike drive west from Helena on U.S. 12 for nine miles to the

*Red Mountain*

Rimini turnoff. Turn left (south) and drive seven miles to the ghost town of Rimini. (Don't fret—Helena commuters have moved in and driven out the ghosts.) Drive south through Rimini and go another 3.6 miles. Park where the road takes a sharp right and climbs a steep hill, .3 miles past the City of Helena water ditch and cabin. The trail takes off to the left just before this sharp bend in the road.

This trailhead isn't signed and can be easily missed. Watch for an abandoned miner's cabin in the brush on your left and fifty yards before the trailhead. Also watch for a blaze on a ponderosa pine on the left edge of the road at the trailhead. If you come to a major fork in the road, you've driven about a half-mile past the trailhead.

The trail—which is actually an abandoned mining road—starts out following a small, unnamed stream and goes past some mining ruins. Follow the stream about a half-mile until it turns off to the right. Here, strike off straight uphill on a cross-country course. Head for a small pass which you'll see ahead and slightly to your left.

Although it's uphill all the way, there is only one really steep pitch in the three-mile trek to the summit of Red Mountain. After climbing this rock slide, you emerge on a saddle at the south side of Red Mountain. From this saddle, enjoy an easy walk to the summit.

The first part of the trail has good supplies of wild strawberries and huckleberries, plus plenty of wildflowers. The trip from the saddle to the summit goes through a forest of veterans of a war against the long, cruel winters at this 8,150-foot altitude. Some of the trees are more ghostly than the ghost town below.

The view from the summit of Red Mountain is one of Montana's grandest. On a clear day, you can see ten Montana counties. Mountain ranges in view include the Big Belt, Bridger, Gallatin, Madison, Ruby, Tobacco Root, Highland, Pintler, and Flint Creek. Also, you can see the Peerless Jenny, Sally Bell, Linda, Julia, Crescent, and other abandoned mines whose names have been lost in time.

Drinking water is available from the small stream at the start, but the rest of the trip is dry. Snowbanks usually cling to the summit until early July.

Although only a six-mile round trip which any hiker can make in a day, you can camp on the summit. Be sure to check the weather forecast for a clear night, preferably at the full moon, so you can get all the benefits of sleeping so close to the stars.—*Herb B. Gloege*

## 70    *Mount Helena Ridge*

*General description:* A fairly rigorous day hike.

*General location:* On the south edge of Helena.

*Maps:* Helena USGS Quad and Helena National Forest. (Neither map shows the trail.)

*Special attractions:* Superb east-of-the-divide scenery from a trail starting on the city limits of Helena.

*For more information:* Write District Ranger, Helena Ranger District, Helena National Forest, Federal Building, Drawer 10015, Room 498, Helena, MT 59626 or call (406) 449-5490.

Although this seven-mile, point-to-point trail was recently declared a National Recreational Trail by the Forest Service, it receives very little use. This is even more amazing when one considers how scenic and accessible it is.

The northern end of the trail is probably the easiest trailhead in the state to find. Simply drive up Adams Street (in southwest Helena) until it deadends at the Mount Helena parking lot on the city limits. To set up the shuttle, drive south on South Park Avenue until it forks, just out of town. Take the right fork and drive five miles, near to Park City, where a dirt road will bend to the right off the main road. Leave your other vehicle here until you finish the hike.

Mount Helena is a 620-acre city park with about twenty miles of hiking trails. There are at least three ways to hike the first three miles, but the easiest route goes west from the parking lot. Follow this well-maintained trail for a half-mile until it forks. Take the right-hand fork and stay on it for 1.5 miles until you reach a trail junction with a picnic table on top of a small saddle (just past a series of switchbacks).

If you chose to take the left (steeper) fork, the trail will pass right under Mt. Helena's northern cliffs, and intersect with the Backside Trail, which will lead to

*Mount Helena Ridge*

the picnic table.

At the picnic table, take the right-hand trail that goes west along a ridge. Stay on this trail all the way—about five miles from this point—to Park City. Since the trail past this point isn't heavily used, it can be hard to follow at times. It's marked with rock cairns and silver, retangular trail markers on trees.

About one-fourth mile past the picnic table, the trail runs through an open, grassy saddle and temporarily disappears in the ungrazed grass. At this point, the trail bends to the left, to go around the eastern edge of a small knob.

In another one-fourth mile, the trail takes a sharp right. Be careful not to follow the trail going straight (south).

After these two confusing spots, the trail is easy to follow for two miles or so. Then, the ridge becomes a series of small hills where the trail hasn't been marked well. You can usually find it through this one-mile section by staying close to the top of the ridge. The most confusing section begins after crossing a fence on Forest Service "stairs." (You'll have to take the hike to see what that means.) Stay alert and stay on the crest of the ridge and you won't get lost.

At about the five-mile mark, the trail intersects with a jeep road coming up from the left (east) from Grizzly Gulch. Follow this jeep track for another quarter mile, where the trail will resume again on the left.

From here to Park City, the trail is well marked. This is probably the most scenic part of the hike, as you can often look back and see the Mount Helena Ridge and Mount Helena itself, which is several hundred feet elevation below you. The City of Helena also appears frequently in the distance.

The last half-mile of the trail switchbacks down a south-facing, grassy slope just above Park City and a small cluster of rural ranchettes. When you reach a jeep road, walk down it (east) to a well-maintained road where your vehicle should be waiting for you. As you'll see, you could have made your shuttle a bit easier by driving up this road, but parking is limited.

Unfortunately, the trailhead at this end hasn't been marked, so it's almost impossible to find the first time. That's why it's better to leave your vehicle at the head of Grizzly Gulch and walk the extra one-half mile.

Since this is a ridgetop trail in a rather dry part of the state, there is no water.

Contrary to other suggestions in this book, you might want to give the Forest Service a call and thank them for developing such a fine hiking trail so close to an urban area.—*Bill Schneider*

## 71 Manley Park

*General description:* An overnight hike into the heart of the Elkhorn Mountains.
*General location:* Twenty miles southeast of Helena.
*Maps:* Clancy USGS Quad and the Helena National Forest Map.
*Special attractions:* Gorgeous high elevation meadows and large waterfall.
*For more information:* Write District Ranger, Townsend Ranger District, Helena
   National Forest, Box 29, Townsend, MT 59644 or call (406) 266-3425.

Instead of snow-capped peaks, the Elkhorns have lush, high elevation meadows surrounded by gently rolling forests. Poe and Manley parks offer excellent examples.

When Forest Service planners rate wilderness quality, they often give areas of high, craggy peaks the highest score. The Elkhorns have a limited supply of such geology, but the scenery still rivals that of many Montana mountain ranges.

To find the trailhead, drive eleven miles south from Townsend on U.S. 287. Then take a right, and drive nine miles west on a paved road to Radersburg. Go through town and follow the only major gravel road (known locally as the Hall Creek Road, which might not be shown on maps) heading northwest from Radersburg. Follow this road eighteen miles to the trailhead, while watching for a Forest Service sign saying Poe Park. The trailhead is three miles past the new road plowed into Crow Creek Falls.

From the trailhead, it's a two-mile stroll into Poe Park. Although you gain about 800 feet in these two miles, most of the climb comes in the first half-mile.

*Bull elk in a September battle. Harry Engels photo.*

The view from Poe Park is something to behold, especially with the carpets of wildflowers. However, don't be looking around so much that you miss a trail marker. The trail temporarily disappears in the lush grass, but you can stay on it if you keep your eyes peeled for FS trail markers and blazes on trees. If you lose the trail, head for the west edge of the park where the trail enters the timber and again becomes easy to follow.

When you reach Little Tizer Creek, you hit a trail junction. You can get to Crow Creek with either fork, but if you go right, you miss Manley Park which is as gorgeous as (if not more than) Poe Park, and the view is even better. So bear left.

Watch carefully for another junction less than a mile after Little Tizer Creek. You must take a sharp right and head up a steep, but short, trail to Manley Park.

Most hikers prefer Manley Park for a campsite. The disadvantage is absence of water. Either you must camp at Little Tizer Creek or haul enough water up to Manley Park. Hauling water might be work, but the view from Manley Park rewards your extra effort.

The trail in Manley Park is easy to follow until about halfway through; then, it gradually disappears, as you approach the timber on the north side. With some care, you can find where it leaves the big meadow.

After a short, steep drop down to Crow Creek, you hit the Crow Creek trail on the north side of the stream. You come out by the abandoned Wildcat Mine and a private cabin—the only signs of civilization along the otherwise remote hike.

From here, the trail follows Crow Creek for about eight miles back to the Hall Creek Road. If you don't have a vehicle there, you'll have to hike or jog up the road to the Poe Park trailhead.

The trail goes through a parcel of private land (an old mining claim) around the beautiful Crow Creek Falls. You might have to scramble around this private land in the narrow canyon, unless the Forest Service has negotiated public access rights through the property.

The whole situation demands a better explanation: Crow Creek Falls was once public land. It was legally given away to gold miners under the archaic 1872 Mining Law. This obsolete, destructive law allows miners to take over public land which may or may not have mineral potential and close it to public use. The miner who inherited the old claim at the Falls decided in 1981

| 0 | 1 | 2 | 3 | 4 | 5 Miles |

*Manley Park*

to plow a road up to the site and obliterate the trail, all without the permission of the Forest Service. After the miner illegally bulldozed the road, received a minimal fine for his misdeed, and caused quite a public controversy, the Forest Service meekly granted him legal access to dredge-mine the falls, completing the desecration of the crown jewel of the Elkhorns.

As this is written, the miner is proposing a hydroelectric dam and reservoir on Crow Creek, and the Forest Service is negotiating for public access to what was once public land. Call the Townsend Ranger District for an update before you take this hike.

Although there isn't any water in Manley Park, if you search the southwest corner of Poe Park you can find a spring at the headwaters of Dewey Creek. Little Tizer and Crow creeks have water as well.

If you stay overnight in Poe or Manley park, you stand a good chance of seeing elk in the early morning or late evening. Crow Creek has a good supply of pan-sized brookies and rainbows for anglers who like to fish smaller streams.

The Elkhorn Mountains have a wilderness quality unlike other ranges—a quiet, gentle, easy beauty. Technical mountain climbers might frown on the Elkhorns, but for the rest of us, it's difficult to surpass. And it's so accessible—close to Bozeman, Butte, and Helena.

The Forest Service, however, doesn't see it that way. The agency has opposed wilderness designation for the Elkhorns, which limits the chance of these mountains ever receiving lasting protection. The Forest Service is, however, considering designating the Elkhorns as a wildlife management area, which would provide some protection.

What the public wants—wilderness or development—may mean the difference for the Elkhorns, so pass your comments along to the Forest Service and your elected representatives.—*Bill Schneider*

## 72   Elkhorn and Crow Peaks

*General description:* A strenuous day hike.

*General location:* Fifteen miles southeast of Helena.

*Maps:* Clancy USGS Quad and either the Deerlodge National Forest Map or the Helena National Forest Map.

*Special attractions:* Views of the entire Elkhorn Mountains from the two highest peaks in the range.

*For more information:* Write the District Ranger, Jefferson Ranger District, Deerlodge National Forest, Whitehall, MT 59759 or call (406) 287-3223.

Hikers who have become experienced to the point where they can consider cross country hiking or rock climbing might use this hike to break the ice. Although more than half the hike is trailless and it goes to the summits of the highest peaks in the Helena area, it's reasonably safe, with little chance of getting lost.

The trail begins at Elkhorn, a historic mining camp on the southern end of the Elkhorn Mountains. To get there from Helena, drive twenty-eight miles south on I-15 to Boulder. Take the Boulder exit from the Interstate and go five miles south of town on State Highway 69. Here turn left onto a gravel road. There is a large

*Elkhorn/Crow Peaks*

sign for Elkhorn marking this corner.

The gravel road immediately crosses the Boulder River and then dead ends. Turn right and follow the same gravel road for about thirteen miles to Elkhorn, bearing left on two junctions along the way. Go through Elkhorn and park at the northeast corner of town just before the road turns south to the cemetery. The trail—actually a jeep road—heads north out of town.

Most hikers start walking here, but if you have a four-wheeler you can drive another mile on a jeep road until you see the road jut off to the right and up a steep grade. Park here even though there's a sign saying "Four-wheel Drive Vehicles Only." In reality, the road to the Iron Mine is too rough for any vehicle. On the Forest Service map, it's marked as Trail #72, so it must be more suited to Vibram soles than steel-belted radials.

From Elkhorn, it's about three tough miles to the Iron Mine, an abandoned mining camp on the west slope of Elkhorn Peak. After exploring this old mine, backtrack down the trail less than a quarter-mile. Here, leave the trail and head straight up for about a half-mile until you reach the top of the ridge. Follow the ridge north for about another mile to the top of Elkhorn Peak. After leaving the Iron Mine Trail, it's cross-country hiking.

Here, you're 2,800 feet above Elkhorn, and the view is something to behold, especially to the north where you can see the entire Tizer Basin, the heart of the Elkhorn Mountains. To the southeast lies 9,414-foot Crow Peak, slightly higher

*Pika, a delightful little denizen of most high rocky slopes. Harry Engels photo.*

than Elkhorn Peak—9,381 feet.

Pick your way to Crow Peak along the saddle between the two mountains. Be sure to bear slightly to the north so you can look down steep cliffs into Hidden Lake, and, a little farther, Glenwood Lake. Both lakes are nestled in steep, glacier-scoured cirques with sheer cliffs on three sides, opening only to the north.

From the Iron Mine to Crow Peak, watch for mountain goats, a favorite of hikers in this area. The Elkhorn/Crow complex supports fair numbers of these white-clad mountaineers. Also prepare your heart for the surprise flush of a blue grouse from the weather-beaten whitebark pines between the two peaks.

Unless you spend too much time taking in the vistas, you can easily make it to Crow Peak and back (about ten miles total distance) in one full day. It is, however, a rugged, cross-country hike that may be too tough for small children or poorly conditioned hikers.

Bring drinking water, as there's only one small stream (about halfway to the Iron Mine), and even that one may dry up by late summer. Snow clings to the area into June and even into July on heavy snow years, so plan a late summer or early fall conquest. Mosquitoes can be a problem early in the season at the Iron Mine.

In 1981, the 83,000-acre Elkhorn Wilderness Study Area was recommended for special consideration as a wildlife management unit, in recognition of its outstanding wildlife resources. The Elkhorns were not designated wilderness, but managing the area for wildlife should minimize destructive development of the area. Let the Forest Service know your thoughts on this matter.—*Bill Schneider*

# 73   Casey Peak

*General description:* A day hike up the most prominent mountain in the northern Elkhorns.

*General location:* Ten miles southeast of Helena.

*Maps:* Clancy USGS Quad and the Helena National Forest Visitors Map.

*Special attractions:* Good views of the Helena Valley and the Elkhorn Mountains.

*For more information:* Write the District Ranger, Helena Ranger District, Federal Building, Drawer 10015, Room 498, Helena, MT 59626 or call (406) 449-5490.

Casey Peak dominates the skyline to the southeast of Montana's capital city. Although somewhat less impressive than Crow and Elkhorn Peaks in the southern part of the range, a trip to the summit of Casey is well worth the time, especially if you live and work within sight of the peak.

To reach the trailhead, take Interstate 15 south from Helena. At Montana City, exit east onto a paved road. Within one-half mile, turn right at a school onto a gravel road. Follow this road until FS Road 294 departs to the left. Follow FS Road 294 until you pass Jackson Creek. Continue past Jackson Creek to the next turnoff to the left, a small road with a locked gate. Park here. The trail begins in the woods just past the turnoff and bypasses the private inholding to which the road leads.

The trail (#343) ascends gradually through the forested slopes along the East Fork of McClellan Creek to Casey Meadows, a large open area. Do not head out into the meadows. Hug the treeline on your right and soon you will see where

*Casey Peak*

Trail #301 heads toward Teepee Creek over the shoulder of Casey Peak to the south. A trail sign marks the junction.

Hike the Teepee Creek Trail until a signed trail to the summit of Casey Peak departs to your left. This trail will take you all the way to the summit with no scrambling involved. All you need is determination.

The Casey's summit is a large rubble heap crowned by the remains of a well-weathered and severely blasted fire lookout. To the north spread commanding views of the Helena Valley and the Big Belt Mountains.

When you've torn yourself away from the summit, there are two choices concerning your trip down. If you are short on time and darkness is near, retace your steps down McClellan Creek to the trailhead. If plenty of daylight remains, follow the summit trail back down to trail #301 and continue on it to the left. Trail #301 will intersect with trail #302, which follows Teepee Creek northward to your car. These two trails are hard to follow in places where they wind through meadows and disappear into the forests, so you'll need some extra time for trail finding.

The Casey Meadows area is popular in the winter with cross-country skiers. The lower parts of the trail usually are icy, but the meadows generally have good powder. Casey Peak sometimes is ascended on skis in winter, but this requires a two-day trip with a base camp in the meadows.—*Rosemary Rowe*

## 74    *Edith-Baldy Basin*

*General description:* A moderate, overnight round trip for beginners or rugged loop for experienced hikers.
*General location:* Thirty miles southeast of Helena in the Big Belt Mountains.
*Maps:* Mount Edith and Duck Creek Pass USGS Quads and the Helena National Forest Map.
*Special attractions:* A lake-filled basin in a small mountain range.
*For more information:* Write the District Ranger, Townsend Ranger Station, Helena National Forest, Box 29, Townsend, MT 59644 or call (406) 266-3425.

Driving along the highway and seeing Mount Edith and Mount Baldy in the distance, you would never guess that a spectacular, lake-filled basin, accessible to all hikers, lies nestled in their northeastern shadow.

To begin the hike, drive east of Townsend on U.S. 12 for about three miles and turn left (north) on the major paved road skirting the east side of Canyon Ferry Reservoir. Drive north for about five miles and turn right (east) on a well-marked Duck Creek Pass Road. Follow this road for about twelve miles to the top of Duck Creek Pass where the trail begins on the right (south) side of the road.

The first three miles are actually a rough jeep road which bumps its way to a Mountain Bell microwave tower on Baldy Ridge, about one mile before the summit of 9,472-foot Mount Baldy. Be sure to bring water along because there isn't any for the first one-half of the hike.

At the microwave tower, there is a trail that drops off the ridge to the east into Hidden Lake. If you aren't an experienced hiker in good condition, take this trail into the basin. However, if you're in good shape and knowledgeable on cross-country hiking, you can make a spectacular loop out of this hike.

Hikers who opt for a shorter, easier trip can camp at Hidden Lake or continue on to any of the other lakes, set up a base camp, and stay for several days,

*Edith-Baldy Basin*

visiting new lakes every day. Then, they can retrace their steps to Duck Creek Pass.

More ambitious hikers can head cross country toward the summit of Mount Baldy. All along this ridge, the vistas are incredible, with the Smith River drainage to the east and Canyon Ferry Reservoir to the west. Expect to see mountain goats around the summit of Baldy and Edith.

After leaving the top of Baldy, you drop rapidly for one-fourth mile into the saddle between the two peaks. Then, you gradually work your way over several false summits to the top of 9,384-foot Mount Edith, with Upper Baldy Lake on your left most of the way. It's four miles between the two summits, but it will be four miles of the most scenic hiking you've experienced. Although it's cross-country, the terrain is fairly easy to traverse. In addition to mountain goats, this area seems to attract unusually large numbers of golden eagles.

From the top of Edith, you can see a penetrating limestone formation known as the "needles" to the north and Edith Lake to the northwest. Follow a series of rock cairns toward this gorgeous, high altitude lake.

About one mile before Edith Lake, you intersect the main trail through the Edith-Baldy Basin. Turn right on this trail (which you crossed on the way to the summit of Edith), and work your way back through the basin to Hidden Lake and then up to a series of tough switchbacks to the jeep road leading back to your vehicle.

Although Edith and Baldy are rock and talus, the basin is heavily timbered. Most lakes have suitable campsites. However, some lakes don't have trails to them. You'll want to spend at least one night in the basin before heading home.

The loop is twenty to twenty-five miles—depending on how many lakes you visit— about one-third of it cross-country. The shorter hike into Hidden Lake and out is only eight miles round trip.

Although the ridge is devoid of water, the basin has plenty. This area accumulates a surprising amount of snow, so wait until at least late June—August if you want to escape the mosquitoes.

Many of the lakes have good fishing for cutthroat or rainbows. Only one, Hidden Lake, seriously shows the hand of man, as motorcyclists have severely scarred the terrain around the lake.

Although this may come as a surprise after a pleasant backpack in this scenic, alpine basin, the 20,000-acre roadless area has been recommended for "non-wilderness" through the Forest Service planning process. If you disagree, write or call the Helena National Forest in Helena.—*Bill Schneider*

# 75    *Little Blackfoot Meadows*

*General description:* A ten-mile round trip along the upper reaches of the Little Blackfoot River.

*General location:* Twenty miles southwest of Helena.

*Maps:* Basin USGS Quad and the Helena National Forest Visitors Map.

*Special attractions:* A large, marshy meadow in a subalpine basin.

*For more information:* Write District Ranger, Helena/Canyon Ferry Ranger District, Helena National Forest, Federal Building, Drawer 10015, Helena, MT 59626 or call (406) 449-5490.

Little Blackfoot Meadows, within easy driving distance of Helena, is a one-way hike over gentle terrain. This large subalpine basin along the Continental Divide receives heavy use during hunting season but is rarely frequented at other times of the year.

To reach the trailhead, turn south off U.S. Highway 12 one mile east of Elliston onto FS road #227. After fifteen miles of gravel road, you will pass Kading campground on your left. The road ends just past the campground.

Leave your car here and continue on foot along a rough jeep track (trail #329). After a mile and a half, the jeep track forks. Take the fork leading downhill to the banks of the Little Blackfoot, where you must ford the stream if the foot log which bridged the river before May, 1981 floods hasn't been replaced. Rainbow and brookies frequent the pools along this stretch of stream, so bring your fishing rod along.

Continuing up the east bank of the stream, the trail passes through some low-lying marshy areas before climbing a dry side hill. Good views of the meadows and the mountain-rimmed basin can be obtained by briefly leaving the trail and

*Little Blackfoot Meadows*

climbing uphill into the obvious open area, just before the second crossing of the Little Blackfoot.

From the second crossing, it is an easy stroll of about a mile to the Little Blackfoot Meadows. Campsites are plentiful on the higher ground surrounding the beaver ponds, for those wishing to make this an overnighter. Day trippers should turn around at this point, which will make the hike a solid ten-mile round trip.

The meadows make a good base camp for exploring the surrounding roadless country. Trails lead up to the rounded, rocky summits of Cliff Mountain, Electric Peak, Thunderbolt Mountain, and Bison Mountain on the Continental Divide.

Grizzly bears have been sited occasionally in the area, which attests to its wildness. Unfortunately, the Forest Service has timber sales planned for the fringes of this roadless country, so its wild days may be numbered.

For those wishing a gentle introduction to hiking or overnight camping, there could be no better place to start than with a trip to Little Blackfoot Meadows.—*Rosemary Rowe*

## 76    Bear Trap Canyon

*General description:* A long but easy hike along a trout-filled river.
*General location:* Thirty miles west of Bozeman along the Madison River.
*Maps:* Norris USGS Quad and the Bureau of Land Management's Public Lands in Montana Map #33—Madison.
*Special attractions:* A rare hike with a primitive flair along a major river with nationally famous trout fishing.
*For more information:* Write District Manager, Butte District, Bureau of Land Management, P.O. Box 3388, 106 N. Parkmont, Butte, MT 59702 or call (406) 494-5059.

If you're a trout fisherman, you've undoubtedly heard of the Madison River, one of the most highly acclaimed streams in the United States. However, you probably haven't heard of a special hiking trail developed by the Bureau of Land Management (BLM) along the Madison in rugged Bear Trap Canyon. For hikers who fancy large trout, this is a seven-mile slice of heaven.

To find the trailhead, drive west from Bozeman on U.S. 289 for about thirty miles. Immediately before you cross the Madison River, watch for a dirt road turning left from the highway and a sign for the Bear Trap Recreation Area.

After driving four miles on this dirt road, you come to a small parking lot and the boundary of the primitive area. The well-marked trail starts at the parking area.

The trail winds along the river for seven miles, gaining a mere 500 feet in elevation. In past years, hikers could leave a vehicle at Montana Power's Ennis Dam Power House at the end of the hike. For safety reasons, however, Montana Power has closed access to this area, making this, in fact, a fourteen-mile round trip.

Since the trail follows the river, there's plenty of water. However, most hikers bring their own water as they fear the river water might not be suitable for drinking. Also, bring plenty of insect repellent, as the mosquitoes can be bad, especially in early summer. Many hikers (especially families) choose to stay overnight to

*Bear Trap Canyon*

take advantage of the early morning and late evening fishing.

There are several campsites, the first at the point where Bear Trap Creek joins the river. Bring your backpack stove, as firewood can be scarce along the narrow canyon.

Also, bring a garbage bag—not only for your own trash, but to carry out junk left by thoughtless hikers. The trail and campsites receive fairly heavy use. With that much traffic, there's often a few who haven't gotten the word about packing out what they carry in.

The area is closed to motorized recreation, so the signs of civilization (except some litter at the campsites) are scarce. Since it remains free of snow most of the year, you can take the hike anytime between April and November. The heaviest use occurs when the fishing is good, especially during the salmon fly hatch in mid-June to early July.

The major drawing card is, of course, fishing. Rainbows and browns two to four pounds and larger are common.

However, the hike would still be attractive without a fishing rod. The trail wanders through a spectacular canyon with sheer rock cliffs and abundant wildlife. This includes rattlesnakes, so be alert, and don't forget your snake bite kit.

In 1981, Bear Trap became one of the first BLM areas in the state to be recommended for wilderness designation. Conservation groups have included the canyon in their proposal for a Lee Metcalf Wilderness in the Madison Range. Bear Trap Canyon is connected to the Spanish Peaks by a strip of roadless Forest Service land called Cowboy Heaven. The altitudinal gradient from 4,500 feet along the Madison River to over 10,500 feet in the Spanish Peaks presents an unparalleled opportunity to preserve the wide variety of life zones found in Montana.

This represents one of the best hiking trails on BLM land in Montana. Next time you run into somebody from that federal land-managing agency, suggest that Montana could use a few more such trails.—*Mike Comola*

# 77   Spanish Peaks

*General description:* A long, multi-day loop.
*General location:* Forty miles southwest of Bozeman on the western edge of the Spanish Peaks Primitive Area on the northern tip of the Madison Range.
*Maps:* Spanish Peaks USGS Quad and the Spanish Peaks Wilderness Management Unit Map from the Gallatin National Forest.
*Special attractions:* Spectacular, high mountain scenery.
*For more information:* Write District Ranger, Bozeman Ranger District, Gallatin National Forest, 601 Nikles, Bozeman MT 59715 or call (406) 587-5271.

The Spanish Peaks rank among the most popular hiking areas in Montana. Although this hike traverses the fringe of the primitive area, it doesn't venture into the most heavily used portions. It does, however, provide the same incredible scenery that made the Spanish Peaks Primitive Area nationally famous.

To find the trailhead, drive south from Bozeman down U.S. 191. About ten miles south of Gallatin Gateway and just before entering the Gallatin Canyon, take a right (west) up Spanish Creek at a marked turn-off. After five miles, turn left (south) up the South Fork of Spanish Creek. Drive about eight miles along the South Fork until you reach a campground by the Spanish Creek Guard Station where the trail begins.

This is a twenty-six-mile loop going up the South Fork and coming back to the same trailhead through the headwaters of Camp and Cuff Creeks. Take at least three days to fully enjoy the scenery.

The hike starts with a gentle, eight-mile hike up the South Fork on trail #407. Stay on the same trail as it leaves the South Fork and climbs to the west through a large group of small, subalpine lakes until you veer right on trail #446 down Camp Creek. You could shorten the hike by taking trail #410 down Falls Creek, but you retrace your steps down the South Fork and miss some outstanding vistas.

The trail has more water than most, but take precautions to prevent the threat

*The moose, largest of the deer family and commonly observed from back country trails. Harry Engels photo.*

*Spanish Peaks*

of giardia. The trail is well maintained and easy to follow all the way with the minor exception of a few meadows towards the end of the hike.

You can camp at several excellent sites along the South Fork or, depending on how early you hit the trail, you might make it to the high lakes where the scenery popularizes the campsites. Camp at any of the lakes in this subalpine plateau. Plan on using your stove to cook however, as firewood is scarce.

Most of the lakes have pan-sized cutthroat or rainbows. And the South Fork has good fishing for small brookies.

The trip is loaded with side trip possibilities—Spanish Lakes, the upper reaches of Falls Creek, several excellent climbs to scenic summits—to name a few. You might decide to spend an extra day to get acquainted with this land of rock and thunder.

This area is part of a currently popular wilderness proposal. If designated wilderness by Congress, this area would be the northernmost corner of a tremendous, 300,000-acre wilderness ranging south to the Taylor-Hilgard region and including much of the wild country in the Madison Range. If you have a chance, lend your support to this proposal.—*Art Foran*

## 78   The Helmet

*General description:* A long day hike or moderate overnighter including a healthy climb.

*General location:* Eighteen miles southeast of Ennis in the Madison Range.

*Maps:* Cameron and Sphinx Mountain USGS Quad and the Gallatin National Forest Travel Plan Map (south half).

*Special attractions:* The Sphinx and the Helmet, truly unique geological formations.

*For more information:* Write the District Ranger, Madison Ranger District, Beaverhead National Forest, Box 366, Ennis, MT 59729 or call (406) 628-4254.

The Madison undoubtedly has some of Montana's finest hiking. Oddly, only the northern section, the Spanish Peaks, has ever become popular with hikers.

The area south of the Spanish Peaks all the way to the Hilgard Basin on the southern tip of the range offers as much as or more than the Spanish Peaks. The loop trail between the Sphinx and the Helmet nicely illustrates this fact.

The trail starts at Bear Creek Ranger Station which can be found by turning east off U.S. 287 at Cameron and following a gravel road for three miles before it turns right (south). Continue south on the good gravel road for 1.5 miles until it turns left (east) and goes another mile to Storey Ranch (as indicated on the Cameron Quad). Here, turn south again for less than a mile before angling off to the southeast along Bear Creek to the Bear Creek Ranger Station. Park your car here.

Trail #326 follows the Trail Fork of Bear Creek to the northeast for about two miles before it joins trail #325. (The first mile or so is actually a rough jeep road, but it's best to hike it.) Trail #326 (not shown on the topo maps) heads east to Manley Camp; you take trail #325 to the saddle between the Helmet and the Sphinx—which is another three miles, where you experience most of the 2,300-foot elevation gain.

From this saddle, you have two logical side trips—climbs to the summits of the Helmet and the Sphinx—which, incidentally, do resemble a helmet and a sphinx. The Helmet takes less than two hours and the Sphinx slightly more. They're both easy, nontechnical scrambles and well worth the effort.

The Sphinx has the edge on vistas, with much of the Madison Range visible from the 10,876-foot summit—including the Yellow Mules country to the northeast (which still has grizzly bears); and Kock Peak, Shedhorn Ridge, No Man Ridge, and the Taylor Peaks to the south. At the summit, stay clear of the edge, lest you fall over an incredibly steep cliff into the Indian Creek valley.

After the climbs are behind you and you're back in the saddle, continue down the north side on trail #325 into the Middle Fork of Bear Creek. Near the bottom, you will intersect a trail following the creek back to a point just west of the Bear Creek Ranger Station—a trailhead you drove past on the way up.

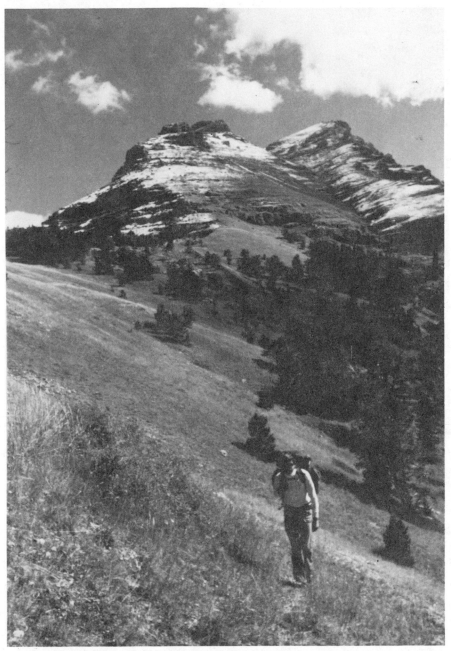

*Climbing towards the saddle separating the Helmet and in the background, the Sphinx. Bill Schneider photo.*

It's about five miles out to the road, making this a tough, ten-mile hike, not including the mountain climbs. The Middle Fork and one stream on the climb are the only reliable water sources, so plan on carrying water with you.

When you hit the road, you must walk less than a mile up the Bear Creek Road

*The Helmet*

to your vehicle. Or you can leave the trail just before it ends and head south cross-country to the Bear Creek Ranger Station and your vehicle.

If you're camping, pick one of several good sites along the Middle Fork. There's plenty of firewood, and you can spend some time after supper trying to spot a member of the area's large moose population.

Although there is a current proposal to designate much of the Madison Range as a unified Lee Metcalf Wilderness, extending from the Spanish Peaks to the Hilgard Basin, it has run into several obstacles. One of the most serious is the checkerboard land ownership in the area, with private and public sections intermingled. For example, the Helmet and part of the Sphinx belong to Burlington Northern. Take a minute to pass your feelings for the area on to your elected representative.—*Bill Schneider*

## 79  *Lizard Lakes*

*General description:* An easy hike for strollers who appreciate gentle, alpine scenery.

*General location:* Forty-five miles south of Bozeman; twelve miles south of Big Sky Resort.

*Maps:* Sphinx Mountain USGS Quad and the Gallatin National Forest Travel Plan Map (south half).

*Special attractions:* Alpine forests, meadows, and lakes.

*Mule deer, perhaps the most common big game animal along wilderness trails.*

*Lizard Lakes*

*For more information:* Write District Ranger, Bozeman Ranger District, Gallatin National Forest, 601 Nikles, Bozeman, MT 59011 or call (406) 587-5271.

Because of volcanic activity long ago, there's a special scenic quality about the Madison and Gallatin Ranges. Strangely shaped buttes and fortresses rest atop plateaus of timber and meadows. Small lakes are tucked away in unexpected places. Every turn in the trail brings a fresh surprise.

To find the trailhead, take U.S. 191 south from Bozeman. About sixteen miles past Big Sky, look for the Taylor Fork Road heading west. About eight miles up this road, take the fork to the right (Cache Creek Road) and follow it about three miles to the trailhead (Trail #173).

Go north on this trail for one mile to the Taylor Fork/Indian Creek divide, an uphill walk (about 1,000 feet elevation gain) through aspen thickets and open meadows interspersed with sagebrush and wildflowers. The pass is at 8,500 feet. The large mountain off to the northwest is Sphinx Mountain. From this location it actually looks like a sphinx.

From this pass, the trail follows the east ridge, wandering through mosaics of timber and open grass. Stay on this ridge as it turns north. About three miles from the pass, the trail favors the east side of the ridge as it angles down to Lizard Lakes.

One lake is near the trail. Another is one-half mile downstream from the outlet. Sometimes the higher lake is dry, producing interesting contours of color from the aquatic vegetation. The lower lake has fair fishing for pan-sized cutthroat.

Altogether, it's about a nine-mile round trip. Wait until July for the snows to leave. Bring drinking water; it's dry all the way to Lizard Lakes.—*Pat Caffrey*

## 80  Hilgard Basin

*General description:* A moderate backpack into a lake-filled, high-altitude basin.
*General location:* Forty miles south of Ennis or twenty-two miles northwest of West Yellowstone on the southern end of the Madison Range.
*Maps:* Hebgen Dam USGS Quad and the Gallatin (south half) and Beaverhead (east half) National Forests Travel Plan Maps.
*For more information:* Write District Ranger, Hebgen Lake Ranger District, Gallatin National Forest, Box 520, West Yellowstone, MT 59758 or call (406) 646-7369.

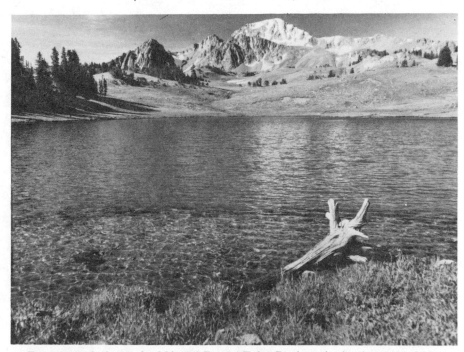

*Expedition Lake in the Hilgard Basin, Echo Peak in the background. Mike Sample photo.*

*Hilgard Basin*

Of all the Madison Range's natural wonders—the Spanish Peaks, the Sphinx/Helmet complex, Taylor Peaks, and all the rest—the Hilgard Basin might top the list for hiking enjoyment.

To find the trailhead, turn north on the Beaver Creek Road off U.S. 287 two miles west of Hebgen Reservoir or twenty-eight miles southwest of Ennis along Quake Lake. Follow the Beaver Creek road for about six miles until it ends at Polomageton Park where the trail begins. Two trails start from this trailhead; take the one marked "Hilgard Basin."

The trail gradually climbs along Sentinel Creek at first, then the incline steepens as the trail and creek get closer to Expedition Pass, for a total elevation gain of 2,720 feet. It's seven miles to the basin, all on a well worn trail, which, although not hazardous, could definitely use some maintenance.

One mile before the Sentinel Creek Trail reaches Expedition Pass, the Hilgard Basin Trail will turn off to the south. At a high saddle, the splendor of the Hilgard Basin unfolds before you, with Expedition Lake and several others in the foreground and Echo Peak creating a perfect backdrop.

Spend a few minutes taking in the views, then drop into the basin and pick one of many campsites along Expedition, Sunset, Ha Hand, Blue Paradise, Crag, or one of the other lakes.

This is high country with only a limited supply of wood. So plan on using your backpack stove, leaving the area's scarce wood supply to add to the aesthetics.

Most of the lakes used to support trout populations, but the harsh winters have frozen out many of the fish. In 1982 only Expedition, Crag, and Blue Paradise lakes seemed to be any good for fishing.

It would be your big loss to head back the next day without spending at least one day exploring and fishing in the basin. For climbers, the basin acts as a base for several climbs, with 11,214-foot Echo Peak being the most popular and 11,316-foot Hilgard Peak—the highest point in the Madison Range—being the most technical.

In recent years, Hilgard Basin has become increasingly popular. Such a wonderland can stay undiscovered only so long, especially with the publicity which wilderness proposal for the area has gotten.

However, Hilgard Basin is among the most fragile of hiking areas, so take every precaution not to leave marks of your visit.—*Bill Schneider*

# 81   *Coffin Lake*

*General description:* A five-mile hike up to a high mountain lake in a little-used area.

*General location:* Twelve miles west of West Yellowstone, Montana.

*Maps:* Hebgen Dam and Targhee Pass USGS Quads, and the Gallatin National Forest Travel Plan Map.

*Special attractions:* High alpine country along the Continental Divide.

*For more information:* Write the District Ranger, Hebgen Lake Ranger District, Gallatin National Forest, Box 520, West Yellowstone, MT 59758 or call (406) 646-7369.

Contrary to popular misconception, the Madison Range does not end with the Taylor-Hilgards, but continues south across Quake Lake into the little-visited

*Coffin Lake*

Lionhead Mountains. Familiar only to a few locals, the Lionhead features several high mountain lakes surrounded by ten thousand foot peaks.

Drive west from West Yellowstone on U.S. 20/191, which leads to Cherry Creek, Rumbaugh, and Spring Creek Campgrounds on Hebgen Lake. After going past these three campgrounds, about 9.5 miles from U.S. 20/191, you'll reach the Watkins Creek trailhead.

Trail #209 will take off to the right up Coffin Creek. Two more miles will bring you to Coffin Lake.

Coffin Lake serves as a good base camp to explore the surrounding area, or a nice place just to sit and fish for the lake's elusive cutthroat trout. Hikers can wander over to Upper Coffin Lake and scramble to the flat-topped summit of

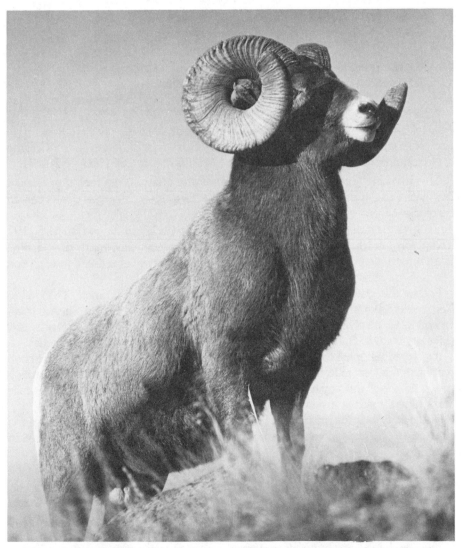

*The majestic bighorn sheep, a rare sight along hiking trails. Harry Engels photo.*

Coffin Mountain to the north. Here views of the rest of the Madison Range and the vast expanse of Yellowstone Park are stunning. A herd of bighorn sheep also make the area their home, and seem to show little fear of hikers.

By climbing out to the lake basin toward the south, you can gain the Continental Divide and gaze down at the many lakes in the headwaters of Targhee Creek in Idaho. One visitor to these lakes reported that he could find absolutely no signs of previous use by hikers, not even the omnipresent fire rings of old hunters' camps.

The Coffin Lakes lie in the recommended Lionhead Wilderness Area, which, although approved by the Forest Service, has received little attention from conservationists. Hopefully, hikers will be impressed enough with this area to encourage congressional action on the Forest Service's recommendations.—*Ed Madej*

## 82    Ramshorn Lake

*General description:* A long day hike or easy overnighter.
*General location:* Forty-five miles south of Bozeman.
*Maps:* Crown Butte USGS Quad and the Gallatin National Forest Travel Plan Map (south half).
*Special attractions:* Gentle back country and good fishing.
*For more information:* Write District Ranger, Bozeman Ranger District, Gallatin National Forest, 601 Nikles, Bozeman, MT 59715 or call (406) 587-5271.

This area isn't scenic in the same sense as the Mission Mountains or Glacier National Park. It offers more of a gentle, quiet beauty—not rugged peaks carved by glaciers.

To find the trailhead, drive south through the Gallatin Canyon on U.S. 191 about forty miles from where it crosses I-90—or ten miles south of Big Sky. Watch for a sign to 320 Guest Ranch on the left (east) side of the highway. You can see the guest ranch from the road.

Follow this gravel road until it ends one-half mile past the ranch. The trail to Ramshorn Lake starts where the road ends. Although the Forest Service is attempting to resolve the situation, the bridge across the Gallatin River is still privately owned. So thank somebody at the 320 Ranch for allowing access.

It's a gradual uphill for six miles to Ramshorn Lake—a fairly easy hike except, perhaps, the last mile where the trail gains elevation rapidly. It goes through heavy timber all the way with a few open parks—particularly around the four-mile mark where there is a series of big meadows.

The trail is well maintained and receives considerable use by horses from the guest ranch. Motorized vehicles are restricted on the lower portions of the trail in summer.

The trail follows Buffalo Horn Creek most the way. So drinking water is usually available.

Although the area doesn't seem to support many deer, elk are everywhere. Also, watch for bighorn sheep, moose, and black bears. Since Ramshorn Lake lies just north of Yellowstone National Park, a few grizzly bears inhabit the area.

The lake has all sizes of cutthroat trout, including some over three pounds. But as usual, they're hard to catch.

Ramshorn Lake

The best campsite is at the lower end of the lake near the outlet. There's plenty of firewood and good drinking water.

For rock climbers, 10,269-foot Ramshorn Peak (just east of the lake) offers an easy scramble.

For rockhounds, there are some extremely interesting geologic formations about one-half mile from the lake on the way to Ramshorn Pass, just north of Ramshorn Peak. Petrified wood can be found on Ramshorn Peak.

The trail brings hikers into the Porcupine-Buffalo Horn-Hyalite Wilderness Study Area. The fate of this area is being cast, so you might want to pass your ideas for future management on to the Forest Service.—*Bill Cunningham*

## 83    Hyalite Lake

*General description:* A long day hike or moderate overnighter to an alpine lake.
*General location:* Twenty miles south of Bozeman.
*Maps:* Fridley Peak USGS Quad and the Gallatin National Forest Travel Plan Map (south half).
*For more information:* Write District Ranger, Bozeman Ranger District, Gallatin National Forest, 601 Nikles, Bozeman, MT 59715 or call (406) 587-5271.

To find the trailhead, drive south from Bozeman on State Highway 243 (marked #345 on the Montana State Highway Map) for about seven miles before turning left on a gravel road to Hyalite Basin. This junction is marked with Forest Service signs. Drive about twelve miles to the Hyalite Reservoir, then turn left and drive around the north side of the reservoir. When the road forks, turn left and go past Window Rock Ranger Station to the end of the road.

While walking 5.5 miles south and 1,800 feet up this well maintained trail, you pass eleven waterfalls cascading in stairstep fashion out of a red-rocked mountain bowl. Although none of them are large waterfalls, each has its own unique character, as their names suggest: Grotto, Arch, Twin, Silken Skein, Champagne, Chasm, Shower, Devil's Slide, Apex, S'il Vous Plait, and Alpine. The progression of waterfalls lures the hiker onward to see the next cascade. The hike seems to pass quickly, although you may spend four or five hours before climbing out of the timber into the wide bowl which holds Hyalite Lake.

This lake is justly popular with the people in the Bozeman area, but as is so often the case, the usage occurs mostly at the lower end by dayhikers who come for a short walk to see a couple of the waterfalls. By the time you reach the lake, you may have the surrounding country to yourself.

Do not count on trout for dinner; the lake is too shallow to stay liquid in some winters. Instead, enjoy the spectacular vistas, which incude Fridley Peak to the southeast and Hyalite Peak just to the southwest. A large meadow stretches around the lake and expands out to the base of Fridley Peak. Possible campsites are numerous; the only problem is deciding which view you favor the most.

Birds seem to like the basin. On the edges of the timber, Clark's nutcrackers and grey jays flash their black and white patterns; Stellar jays catch the eye with their irridescent blue crests. And out in the meadows hover hummingbirds, attracted by the profusion of wildflowers. Especially abundant are the paintbrush, lupine, fleaband, and four o'clocks.

In the evening you may hear or see a deer come down for a drink at the

*Hyalite Basin in the Gallatin Range. Mike Sample photo.*

lakeshore. Spotting an occasional elk, mountain goat, or bear is a possibility. Most assuredly, a few marmots will whistle their attention to you as you explore the bowl.

Winter releases its grip on the Hyalite Basin quite late by lowland standards. The snowbanks may not melt off the trail until late June. And winter may return quickly, making late September and October trips a gamble.

While at the lake, the hiker should consider a couple of short but interesting side trips which depart from the outlet of the lake. One is an easy two-mile walk to the top of Hyalite Peak (10,299 feet) for views down into Horseshoe Basin and out into the Yellowstone River country. The other is a two-mile hike across a neighboring cirque and up a ridge to the Hyalite/Squaw Creek Divide. Both pro-

*Grotto Falls on the way to Hyalite Lake in the Gallatin Range. U.S. Forest Service photo.*

vide high vantage points from which to enjoy the beautiful Gallatin Range.—*Mike Sample*

*(Because of their close proximity, the hikes to Hyalite and to Emerald and Heather lakes are on the same map—Editor.)*

## 84    Emerald and Heather Lakes

*General description:* A long day hike or moderate overnighter to two beautiful mountain lakes.

*General location:* Twenty miles south of Bozeman.

*Maps:* Fridley Peak USGS Quad and the Gallatin National Forest Travel Plan Map (south half).

*For more information:*  Write District Ranger, Bozeman Ranger District, Galla-

*Emerald Basin in the Gallatin Range. Mike Sample photo.*

tin National Forest, 601 Nikles, Bozeman, MT 59715 or call (406) 587-5271.

To find the trailhead, drive south from Bozeman on State Highway 243 (marked #345 on the Montana State Highway map) for about seven miles before turning left on a gravel road to Hyalite Basin. This junction is marked with Forest Service signs. Drive twelve miles to the Hyalite Reservoir, then turn left and drive around the north side of the reservoir. At a fork in the road, turn left onto the East Fork Road and continue past the turnout for the short hike to Palisade Falls until the road ends at the trailhead. (Note: the Fridley Peak Quad map does not show this last two-mile segment of the road.)

Although somewhat rocky in places, the trail is generally well maintained. Over the 5.5-mile gradual uphill pull to Emerald Lake, the hiker emerges from the thick forest to gain increasingly expansive views of the rugged cliffs to the east. These cliffs eventually pinch in and meet the mountainous ridgeline from the west to form the walls of the cirque which holds Emerald and Heather Lakes and a few unnamed potholes.

Once at Emerald Lake, the hiker has a wide choice of campsites in the meadows interspersed around the lake with sparse stands of subalpine timber. A rough trail departs from the west side of Emerald and travels less than a half-mile up 250 more feet in elevation to Heather Lake. From the trailhead to Heather Lake the trail climbs a total of about 2,000 feet, yet there aren't any prohibitively steep pitches.

*Hyalite Lake, Emerald & Heather Lakes*

Heather Lake does not have as many potential campsites as does Emerald. The wall of the cirque falls sharply down to the shore of Heather on the west side, while rock shelves and snowbanks protrude on the other shores. Both lakes offer fair fishing for pan-sized trout.

The eleven-mile round trip should require only about five hours of hiking—not including time spent relishing the beauty of these high altitude lakes. The hike may be too much for small children.

The trail follows the East Fork of Hyalite Creek most of the way, so unlike many hikes, drinking water is readily available. Wait until July to try this hike, however, as the area remains clogged with snow through June.

About 1.5 miles from the trailhead, the East Fork tumbles over Horsetail Falls—a sight well worth seeing. The falls are plainly visible from the trail; the sound of falling water will be a tonic for anyone who has stayed out on the plains too long.

Perhaps the highlight of the trip is the incredible display of wildflowers. Color is everywhere, even rivaling Glacier National Park's natural flower beds. You'll find glacier lilies, columbine, lupine, paintbrush, alpine forget-me-nots, shooting stars, and many more.

These lakes are just north of Yellowstone National Park, but the chance of stumbling into a grizzly bear is remote. Nonetheless, take the standard precautions. The chances of seeing deer, black bears, elk, or mountain goats are good.

Although the trail receives above average use, most hikers apparently have taken care not to leave signs of their passing. But please pay special attention to wilderness camping manners, as this is fragile, beautiful, alpine country.—*Mike Sample*

## 85  *Sacajawea Peak*

*General description:* A two-mile hike to the top of the highest peak in the Bridger Range. For beginners who are almost ready to go on to bigger and better things.

*General location:* Fifteen miles north of Bozeman.

*Maps:* Sedan 15 minute USGS Quad and Gallatin National Forest Map.

*For more information:* Write District Ranger, Bozeman Ranger District, 601 Nikles Ave, Box C, Bozeman, MT 59715.

Hundreds of Bozeman area residents have been up Sacajawea Peak. Find out why. Pack the car with a picnic lunch. Bring water, as none is available on the hike. Take the kids and the dog. Drive a little over twenty miles up the Bridger Creek Road, going past the Bridger Bowl Ski Area. About two miles past Battle Ridge Campground, turn off to the west (left) and take the road to the Fairy Lake Campground, about seven more miles. This road is okay for your car, but leave your trailer at home, Park at Fairy Lake.

Note the massive furrowed limestone on the east face of Sacajawea Peak just above the lake. Find the trailhead and head up the two mile, 2,000-foot climb to the summit. The trail will take you up to the saddle between Sacajawea Peak and Hardscrabble Peak, where you take the trail to the south (left) and follow its twists and turns up to the top. On a clear day you can see half the hiking areas this book describes.

Sacajawea Peak

On a nice weekend in the summer you will most certainly encounter other hikers on the trail and at the summit. This won't be the time and place for wilderness isolation and introspection, but rather a place to meet friends and neighbors who just thought they'd take a couple hours to work up a sweat and see how swell Montana is.—*Pat Caffrey*

# 86 Big Snowies Crest

*General description:* A long, but fairly easy, hike on a flat ridge in a little-known mountain range.

*General location:* Twenty miles south of Lewistown.

*Maps:* Crystal Lake, Jump Off Peak, and Half Moon Canyon USGS Quads; and the Lewis & Clark National Forest Map (Jefferson Division).

*Special attractions:* Flat alpine prairie, ice cave, unrestricted views of Eastern Montana from the Missouri River to the Beartooth Plateau.

*For more information:* Write District Ranger, Judith Ranger District, Lewis & Clark National Forest, Box 484, Stanford, MT 59479 or call (406) 566-2292.

The Big Snowies consist of one massive, broad-based ridge flanked by cirques and streams. The main western segment of this ridge runs for twelve miles and ranges from 8,500-8,700 feet in elevation.

The trail to the ridge can be reached by turning south from U.S. 87 onto the Crystal Lake Road about eight miles west of Lewistown (or five miles east of Moore). From there, it's about twenty-two miles to Crystal Lake. The trailhead for trail #405 is at the south end of the lake near the campground. The trail climbs over 2,000 feet in 3.2 miles to the crest of the Big Snowies. At this point, the hard hiking becomes a stroll across level prairie-style tundra interspersed with mangled thickets of trees.

Here, at the top, trail #405 junctures with the Crest Trail #493. Take this trail and follow it either way along the ridge. It isn't always easy to follow and is often marked only by rock cairns. If you lose the trail, stay on high ground until it materializes again.

There is no water anywhere along the Crest Trail. Day hikers must carry up what they need. Overnighters can usually melt snow for their water, if they wish. Massive snowdrifts form near the top of the Crest and last through September.

For a good day hike to a rare ice cave (which is only 1.5 miles past the Crest Trail junction) go 1.2 miles to the west, then look carefully for a trail (#524) branching off to the south. In .3 mile this trail leaves the Crest and goes out on the south slope through scattered trees and rocks to the cave. This cave is one room-full of ice from a combination of water seeping out of the rock and snow blowing in through the entrance. A flashlight is helpful but not necessary.

For a good overnighter, try Greathouse Peak, ten miles past the Crest Trail junction, going east. This "peak" is at 8,730 feet the high point of the range. Getting there is one surprise after another. The trail crosses large expanses of alpine grasses which give incredible visual harmony to the endless prairies off to either side, 4,000 feet below. Then, there is a stretch called "Knife Blade Ridge," where the mile-wide Crest narrows to a few feet and drops off abruptly on either side. Finally, the trail dips into a primitive little pass where there is a four-way trail junction. Stay on the obvious ridge trail to reach the top of Greathouse Peak. From here, you can retrace your route to Crystal Lake or choose one of four trails which descend directly from the peak area to trailheads you'll need a good map and a little luck to find by vehicle.

This is a wilderness study area being considered for wilderness designation under the late Senator Metcalf's Montana Wilderness Study Act. It is a strange area, gentle yet primitive and remote—an easy place to traverse, but also where a spirit of timeless wildness prevails.—*Pat Caffrey*

0          1          2          3  Miles

# 87  Crazy Mountains

*General description:* A moderately strenuous twenty-three-mile, four day hike crossing two high ridges.

*General location:* Twenty-five miles north of Big Timber.

*Maps:* Crazy Peak, Campfire Lake, and Amelong Creek USGS Quads; and the Gallatin National Forest Travel Plan Map (north half).

*Big Snowies*

*Special attractions:* Rugged, alpine scenery, refreshing streams and lakes, and mountain goats.

*For more information:* Write District Ranger, Big Timber Ranger District, Gallatin National Forest, Box A, Big Timber, MT 59011 or call (406) 932-3647.

The Crazies stand majestically above the plains near Livingston and Big Timber. Well-developed glacial scouring has produced the enchanting valleys which contain numerous high elevation lakes. Beautifully sculptured peaks and serrated ridges radiating from the core of the range rise over 11,000 feet, offering views of the surrounding mountains and prairies.

This hike is designed for at least three nights, giving participants a glimpse of how pleasant life can be in the heart of goat country, the Crazy Mountains.

The trailhead on the east side of this hike is at Half Moon Campground, which is located about twenty-five miles northwest of Big Timber. Drive twelve miles north of Big Timber on U.S. 191 until you see the road turning left up the Big Timber Canyon. This gravel road winds for another ten-twelve miles across private property, eventually through two gates before you arrive at the Forest Service's Half Moon Campground below Big Timber Canyon.

The route for the first mile and a half beyond Half Moon Campground is a hastily bulldozed jeep road, which was built in 1981 with hopes of dredge-mining for gold at Twin Lakes at the canyon head. This has been temporarily stopped by the Forest Service, but check with the Gallatin Forest for an update.

After less than a mile, take a short side trip to the south to see Big Timber Falls, a roaring waterfall set deep in the canyon rock.

The jeep track ends at the western side of section five on your map. Here the actual trail remains (#119), but you may still see some signs of helicopter mining activity above Twin Lakes.

Two well-constructed bridges are traversed at the two-three mile mark, providing ample support in crossing Big Timber Creek even during high runoff periods. Another mile along the trail, Granite Peak stands out as the dominant feature of the landscape. This peak is also the location of a long side trip possibility. At the base of the mountain, a trail turns off left to Blue Lake.

The Blue Lake trail almost immediately crosses Big Timber Creek on a log jam. Then, it switchbacks up for a mile along a rock slide, through forest, and past a couple of abandoned cabins before reaching a vantage over Blue Lake, a mountain gem with a fair supply of small rainbow trout for anglers. The trail ends at this point with a view of Crazy Peak, highest in the range. However, cross-country hiking will provide access to alpine lakes—Blue, Granite, and Thunder Lakes—all over 8,000 feet. Pear and Druckmiller Lakes, also nearby, sit in a deep cirque approaching 9,000 feet. A base camp set up at Granite Lake could occupy the back country enthusiast for many days with climbing, fishing, and deep thought around the shores of these incredible lakes.

Meanwhile, back on the way to Twin Lakes, the trail skirts Granite Peak for about one mile. Moderate climbing and a route crossing an avalanche path are encountered after five miles of traveling from Half Moon Campground. The trail breaks out into open meadows beside the Lower Twin Lake. Camp on one of the drier sites. Take in the hard-to-beat views of the surrounding mountains. Or follow the trail around the first lake and look for a cozy campsite along the stream

*Outstanding scenery along the Big Timber Canyon trail in the Crazy Mountains. Bruce Chesler photo.*

that separates Twin Lakes. There is an adequate supply of firewood at both sites.

From Upper Twin Lake, the trail begins a steep ascent. Plan on at least an hour for this 2,000-foot trudge. Switchbacking across the high, open country, hikers are treated to wildflowers and cascading brooks. The stiff climb is more than rewarded on top with an awesome view of the Big Timber Creek drainage and surrounding ridges. From this pass a short scramble along the ridge to the north will put you on top of Conical Peak.

Dropping down one mile into the South Fork of Sweetgrass Creek drainage, the trail reaches Glacier Lake. This alpine lake is fed by sheer waterfalls and a long summer snowmelt. Due to the irregular, rocky topography, campsites along this beautiful lake are hard to find. Stay around the area for lunch; drink some of its sparkling, chilled water; and watch the icebergs float across the bluegreen lake.

The trail leaves Glacier Lake and drops steadily for over a mile through the trees until a crossing of the South Fork is necessary. No bridge is located at this point, and the crossing can be dangerous during spring runoff.

Another one-fourth mile downstream you cross a series of meadows which may temporarily obscure the trail, as will rock slides in the area. There are some choice campsites located in this part of the valley. Plan on spending your second night at either the meadows or at the stream's junction with the Middle Fork of Sweetgrass Creek two miles downstream. The Middle Fork has fair fishing for small cutthroat.

Where the South Fork joins the Middle Fork, the trail begins heading upstream through forested slopes on the way to Moose and Campfire Lakes. The next two miles wind upstream to Moose Lake. Above Moose Lake, the trail switchbacks 800 feet up in one mile to Campfire Lake. Don't get this large body of water confused with the small trailside pools that lie in depressions nearby. Campfire Lake is a big, irregularly-shaped beauty which reflects the surrounding peaks and

0          1          2          3          4 Miles

ridges nicely and has good fishing for twelve to fourteen-inch rainbows. Campsites around this lake have been abused in the past, so be extra careful, particularly with your fire, if you must have one. And consider packing out trash left by thoughtless visitors.

From Campfire Lake, the trail climbs another 1,000 feet to the divide separating the Middle Fork of Sweetgrass Creek and Trespass Creek drainages. At this 9,500-foot vantage point, the well-defined Crazy Mountain high country is at eye level. Goat tracks cross rock and snowfields, which lie precipitously above green valleys and shining lakes. The Bridgers, Absarokas, Castles, and Spanish Peaks are all visible on a clear day—an inspiring view to say the least. From this

*Crazy Mountains*

point, the lakes of the Sweetgrass drainage shine invitingly in the morning sun; and to the east, the endless expanse of prairie overwhelms visitors unaccustomed to such vistas.

Dropping steeply into the basin at the head of Trespass Creek, the trail winds across talus slopes and through lush meadows for about two miles before entering the trees. The remaining five miles of this hike follow the east side of Trespass Creek, crossing two small tributaries of this stream.

The Tresspass Creek trail comes into Cottonwood Creek Canyon and joins another roughly bulldozed road that goes up the canyon to a second-home subdivision right in the heart of the Crazies. This is another legacy of the "checkerboard" ownership of these magnificent mountains. You should have arranged to leave another vehicle somewhere along this road to complete your shuttle. Check with the Forest Service as to road conditions on this jeep track, which eventually, down the canyon, turns into the Cottonwood Creek Road and joins U.S. 89 at Clyde Park.

You may find it hard to believe after this back country adventure that there is no formal wilderness proposal for the Crazy Mountains. The reason? Most of the mountain range is "checkerboarded" with private land, which is being developed as second home sites and mining claims. If you want the Crazy Mountains to remain wild, let your congressional delegation know.—*Bruce Chesler.*

# 88   Cottonwood Lake

*General description:* A moderate overnighter or long day hike.
*General location:* Forty miles northeast of Livingston in the Crazy Mountains.
*Maps:* Campfire Lake and Crazy Peak USGS Quads and Gallatin National Forest, Livingston Ranger District.
*For more information:* Write the District Ranger, Livingston Ranger District, Gallatin National Forest, Route 62, Box 3197, Livingston, MT 59047 or call (406) 222-1892.

The first mile of this trail retraces the last mile of the Crazy Mountain Traverse hike. Although the two hikes could be combined, it would turn into a long, strenuous backpack.

To find the trailhead for the Cottonwood Lake trip, take U.S. 89 fourteen miles north of Livingston to Clyde Park. About a half-mile past Clyde Park turn right on a heavily used gravel road (known locally as the Cottonwood Creek Road) and follow it northeast for fifteen miles to the Ibex Guard Station Junction. Instead of turning left to the guard station, continue going straight up the Cottonwood Creek Road. The trail begins about two miles past the guard station junction where the road is blocked to motorized vehicles, except motorcycles and snowmobiles, with a barrier of large rocks.

In the last few miles, you go through three gates. However, don't fret; this is a public road. Be sure to close the gates.

The first mile (going past the Trespass Creek trail junction) is a gated jeep road. By using your topo map, you should be able to find the trail where it picks up again past a large opening, which is—believe it or not —the site of a proposed subdivision for vacation homes. The "checkerboarding" between private and public land in the Crazy Mountains and in other Montana national forests makes

*Cottonwood Lake*

this development possible.

Where the trail crosses the stream and leaves this private land, check out the narrow canyon, with several waterfalls, which isn't visible from the trail. It's about 200 yards upstream from the stream crossing.

The trail is heavily used and well-maintained—with one exception. Towards the end of the hike, the trail passes through some glacial moraine, sometimes disappearing in the rocks. However, at this point in the hike you really don't need a trail as you can look ahead and see where the lake is.

The Crazies get lots of snow, so wait until late summer for this trip. The trail has at least four good sources of drinking water, but there's a 1.5-mile dry stretch between the outlet of Long Lake to a group of small ponds just before Cotton-wood Lake.

The lower end of the lake has several excellent campsites. However, don't forget your stove, as firewood is scarce and should only be used in an emergency. The lake has a good population of pan-sized cutthroat.

If you have extra time at this lake, try a couple of exciting side trips. Perhaps the best is to head east from the lake for a two-hour climb up to Grasshopper Glacier. The unusually large glacier lies on the major north/south crest in the Crazy Mountains and offers a spectacular view into the Big Timber Creek drainage which is dotted with lakes. You can also see 11,214-foot Crazy Peak, the highest in the Crazy Mountains.

This is a difficult, but not technical climb. With caution it can be made by most hikers.

For a shorter side trip, take an easy fifteen-minute scramble south from the lake up a rocky slope to the divide between Rock Creek Lake and Cottonwood Lake. From here, you can see many of the major peaks in the Crazies.

When you get back from the hike, take a few minutes to encourage the Forest Service to hurry up efforts to resolve the land use conflicts created by checker-board ownership.—*Bill Cunningham*

# 89 *Middle Fork, Lost Fork of the Judith*

*General description:* A fairly demanding three-day loop.

*General location:* One hundred miles southeast of Great Falls in the Little Belt Mountains.

*Maps:* Sand Point and Ettien Springs USGS Quads and the Lewis & Clark National Forest Map (Jefferson Division).

*Special attractions:* Large roadless area with major streams and 1,000-foot limestone cliffs.

*For more information:* Write District Ranger, Judith Ranger District, Lewis & Clark National Forest, Box 484, Stanford, MT 59479 or call (406) 566-2292.

Of all the large roadless areas in Montana, the Middle Fork of the Judith may be the least popular with hikers—not because it doesn't have good hiking, because it does; but because few wilderness travelers know about it. The 81,000-acre *de facto* wilderness has great stream fishing for native cutthroat, a large big game population, and vistas to rival any wildland.

To find the trailhead, take U.S. 12 east from White Sulphur Springs for about eighteen miles until you reach the small town of Checkerboard. Go about one mile east of Checkerboard and turn left (north) on a gravel road (Forest Road #274) to the Whitetail Guard Station, about ten miles north of the highway. Go past the guard station and stay on this road. There are several road junctions, but you'll stay on the track by sticking with the major, heavily traveled road. Go about five miles past the guard station to the trailhead for Trail #433 to Burris Cabin.

Unlike most hikes, this trail loses elevation rapidly from the trailhead, as it drops from the ridgetop three miles to the Lost Fork of the Judith and to Burris Cabin, an abandoned homestead. As will become obvious, there has been extensive abuse by motorcycles along this section.

If you started late in the day, you might want to camp along the Lost Fork above Burris Cabin. There's plenty of good sites, complete with firewood and a beautiful stream filled with native cutthroat.

Right at Burris Cabin, the trail junctures with the trail following the length of the Lost Fork. Take the trail northwest up Burris Creek for about five miles until you reach Sand Point, a 8,211-foot knob on the divide separating the Lost Fork and Middle Fork drainages.

After relishing the view for a few minutes, go northwest for about a half-mile to a trail junction. Take a right here and head down (north) about three miles into the Middle Fork of the Judith River.

You come out on the bottomland at the Middle Fork Ranch, now abandoned. Don't camp on this private land. Take a right and head downstream, selecting one of many good campsites along the Middle Fork.

Like the Lost Fork, the Middle Fork offers excellent cutthroat fishing and scenery, especially towering limestone cliffs. From the Middle Fork Ranch, you're actually walking on a lightly traveled jeep road for about six miles downstream until you reach the point where the Lost Fork joins the Middle Fork. Take a right at this trail junction and follow the Lost Fork about seven miles upstream to the Burris Cabin, where you must retrace your steps three miles uphill to your vehicle.

All told, this is about a thirty-mile loop trail that introduces hikers to much of the Middle Fork of the Judith Wilderness Study Area. The Forest Service is presently contemplating the fate of the area, so contact the Lewis & Clark National Forest in Great Falls with your suggestions for future management.—*Bill Cunningham*

## 90   *Highwood Baldy*

*General description:* A strenuous day hike.
*General location:* Thirty miles east of Great Falls in the Highwood Mountains.
*Maps:* Highwood Baldy and Arrow Peak USGS Quads and the Lewis and Clark National Forest Map (Jefferson Division).
*Special attractions:* An outstanding view of the high plains from the summit of Baldy Mountain.
*For more information:* Write District Ranger, Judith Ranger District, Lewis & Clark National Forest, Box 484, Stanford, MT 59479 or call (406) 566-2292.

The Highwoods are one of Montana's isolated mountain ranges that rise like

0          1          2          3   Miles

*Middle Fork, Lost Fork of the Judith*

islands from a grass ocean. Hiking in them can be as pleasant as straddling the Continental Divide.

Find the trailhead by taking U.S. 87 east from Great Falls for about three miles, then turn north on paved county road #228. Follow this road north for a few miles before it turns east. After about fifteen miles of pavement, the road turns to gravel and follows Highwood Creek to Highwood Guard Station. Go right at the road fork near the guard station and follow a rough jeep track for about one mile until the trailhead appears on the right.

From the jeep track the trail goes up the Deer Creek drainage. As you approach Mount Baldy, it gets steep, primitive, dry, and difficult to follow. Be sure to bring water.

It's about three miles and a 2,600-foot elevation gain to the summit of Baldy. Only experienced hikers should try this hike. It's a six-mile round trip that takes even good hikers a full day.

During July and August, mosquitoes and deer flies can be a problem along the first mile of this hike where the jeep road parallels Highwood Creek. There is no bear danger.

August through October is best for this hike. If you can hit it just as the aspen and cottonwoods turn gold, you can experience east-of-the-divide scenery at its very best.

Motorized vehicles are permitted on this trail. The area—especially the last half of the hike—is as wild as any wilderness area. Wildlife is fairly abundant, and most wildflowers common east of the divide as well as high-mountain species can be found.

The high point of the trip—in more ways than one—is Mount Baldy. From the 7,600-foot summit, hikers get an awe-inspiring view of the prairie environment, the high plains of Montana.

From Baldy, ambitious hikers can add four miles to their hike with a cross-country side trip to Pinewood Peak, to the west of and easily visible from the summit of Baldy. If you try for both summits in one day, make sure you have enough time; don't get caught in the dark.

Few hikers make this an overnight backpack. Some hikers stay overnight two miles up the road at Briggs Creek in Thain Creek Campground, which is fairly heavily used by recreational vehicle campers.—*Larry Thompson*

## 91    Bear Paw Baldy

*General description:* A short, but rugged, day hike to the highest point in the Bear Paw Mountains.

*General location:* Twenty-five miles south of Havre on the Rocky Boy Indian Reservation.

*Maps:* Warrick USGS Quad.

*Special attractions:* A super view of nearly all the isolated mountain ranges of central Montana.

The hike to Mount Baldy in the Bear Paw Mountains resembles the trip to Mount Baldy in the Highwood Mountains east of Great Falls. However, this hike is shorter and the view slightly more impressive.

The trailhead is easy to find. Simply follow Highway 234 south from Havre for

*Highwood Baldy*

*Bear Paw Baldy*

about twenty-five miles until you reach Teepee Campground near Rocky Boy Recreation Area, a local ski resort. The trail begins at the far end of the campground.

It's a mere 1.5 miles to the summit of Baldy. Don't attempt it, though, unless you're an experienced hiker. The trail is poorly maintained, rocky, without water, and has a 2,200-foot elevation gain—a little too hefty for a beginner.

The entire hike is on the Rocky Boy Indian Reservation. The area is very rugged and remote—too rugged, in fact, for motorized vehicles. After leaving the Teepee Campground, all signs of man disappear.

Although few—if any—hikers make this an overnight backpack, many stay at Teepee Campground and try some of the excellent fishing in the beaver ponds in lower Beaver Creek. A tribal fishing permit is required.

221

The view from the top of Mount Baldy is unsurpassed. Be sure to pick a clear day (August through October) for this hike, so you can get the full impact of this vista. Almost all the isolated mountain ranges in eastern Montana are visible.

If you have extra time, you might try hiking cross-country for about three miles (six miles round trip) into the headwaters of Eagle Creek. You will pass through some unusually moist, dense forests for eastern Montana.—*Larry Thompson*

## 92 West Butte

*General description:* An easy 1.5-mile trek in the Sweetgrass Hills. A moderate climb, but you can take your time.

*General location:* Thirty-five miles northeast of Shelby.

*Maps:* USGS 15 minute Quad.

*Special attractions:* Views of the Sweetgrass Hills and the prairies of Montana and Alberta. On a clear day, the peaks of Glacier Park are visible. Recommended for early summer when everything is green.

*For more information:* Write Bureau of Land Management, Malta, MT.

Before you write off this wheat-and-oil-producing area as a source of wild exhileration, hop in the car and drive to Sunburst, which is about twenty-six miles north of Shelby on Interstate 15. At the freeway exit, turn east on the county road and follow it straight for ten miles. Then it will curve north. There are several side roads, but just stay on the main travelled route that leads to the south side of 6,983-foot West Butte, which you can now see up close and personal.

Park just south of the butte and notice the large cleft-type gully down the middle of it. Stroll up the grassy shoulder just west (left) of the gully. Near the top of this shoulder it's a little steep, and you may have to scramble up some loose rock, but you should soon find a game trail which angles to the north (left) and takes you on up to the summit. There, over 3,000 feet above the prairie, the Indians used to scout the horizon for the tell-tale cloud of a buffalo herd. You'll be glad if you have time to spend, a coat to keep out the wind, and some drinking water. If you ever called the prairie your home, this one's a must.—*Pat Caffrey*

## 93 Pine Creek Lake

*General description:* A steep five-miler up the east side of Paradise Valley to a beautiful mountain lake.

*General location:* Fifteen miles south of Livingston.

*Maps:* Emigrant and Mount Cowen USGS Quads and the Gallatin National Forest Travel Plan Map (south side).

*For more information:* Write District Ranger, Livingston Ranger District, Gallatin National Forest, Route 62, Box 3197, Livingston, MT 59047 or call (406) 222-1892.

To begin this hike, drive south of Livingston five miles. Then, turn east (left) onto the old highway at the sign "East River Road" and go about eight more miles. Past the cabin community of Pine Creek 0.7 miles, turn east (left) on a gravel road marked with Forest Service signs and go to the end of this road, where there is a Forest Service campground and the trailhead for this hike.

In the summer of 1981, volunteers from the American Hiking Society improved and maintained the trail, the first mile of which is deceptively flat. At the end of

*West Butte*

this flat stretch, you stand at the foot of beautiful Pine Creek Falls. This is far enough for some of you who have heard about the next four miles. In those four miles, the trail climbs more than 3,000 feet. But for others, the allure of a mountain lake held in a glacial cirque is too much to resist. Draw some water at the falls because the trail is usually dry.

Because the trail climbs 1,000 feet per mile, most people take between three and four hours to reach the lake. On the bright side, coming out takes only two. Therefore, this could be a day hike. But there is a good campsite near the outlet and good fishing for pan-sized cutthroat to keep the backpacker occupied. Plan on using your stove, as firewood is scarce.

The lake lies beneath 10,941-foot Black Mountain in an obvious glacial cirque. On the north side of the lake, the bedrock shows pronounced striations where the glacier shoved its rocky load across the granite. At the outlet, a broad slab impounds the lake.

The best time to visit Pine Creek Lake is from July 15 to September 30. Any earlier will mean wading through snowdrifts on the last part of the trail; in October, those drifts may reappear quickly. If you prize solitude, wait until after Labor Day; before school starts the trail is heavily used by youth camps.

Overly friendly ground squirrels, marmots, pikas, and a few mountain goats are common around the lake.

If you have extra time, hike around to the east end of the lake and climb the divide to look into Lake McKnight and the Davis Creek drainage. There is no trail

Pine Creek Lake

into McKnight Lake, and the country is so rough and remote that few hikers ever walk its shores.

One of the pleasures of camping at Pine Creek Lake is the chance of seeing alpenglow on the peaks. As the sun moves lower in the west and begins to set behind the Gallatin Range, the atmosphere deflects a portion of the color in the spectrum, leaving a pronounced reddish hue to the last few moments of sunlight. When the conditions are right and this red light bounces off the polished rock surfaces just north of the outlet, the effect is startling. With only a little poetic license, one could say it looks like the peaks are on fire.—*Mike Sample*

# 94    Elbow Lake, Mount Cowen

*General description:* A rugged overnighter.

*General location:* Twenty miles south of Livingston in the Absaroka Mountains, now part of the Absaroka-Beartooth Wilderness.

*Maps:* Emigrant and Mount Cowen USGS Quads and the Gallatin National Forest Travel Plan Map (south half).

*Special attractions:* Mount Cowen, an incredible mass of rock and the highest point in the Absaroka Range.

*For more information:* Write District Ranger, Livingston Ranger District, Gallatin National Forest, Route 62, Box 3197, Livingston, MT 59047 (406) 222-1892.

The rugged North Absaroka range forms the east wall of the Paradise Valley south of Livingston along the Yellowstone River. Of all these perilous peaks, 11,206-foot Mount Cowen is the highest.

To find the trailhead, drive south of Livingston on U.S. 89 for about twenty miles to the large Forest Service sign directing you to turn left (east) across the Yellowstone River and onto the Mill Creek Road. Follow the Mill Creek Road for ten miles to the East Fork of Mill Creek Road. Take a left on this road and go 1.5 miles to the trailhead, which is located one-fourth mile before the Snowy Range Ranch.

The trail skirts around the south side of Snowy Range Ranch for a little more than a mile before crossing the East Fork on a new bridge to a trail junction. Be careful to take the Upper Sage Creek Trail, which immediately starts steeply to the northwest.

After the trail crosses Sage Creek, it starts an unrelenting climb, switchbacking up and across a dry hillside. You probably will want to carry water on this stretch. Otherwise, there is plenty of water along the trail even in late August. Check with the Forest Service about snow conditions before trying an early summer trip.

Elbow Lake is about nine miles from the trailhead. Hikers need to gain almost 3,500 feet of elevation, making this a tough hike for all but the well-conditioned. Start early and plan to make the entire hike in one day as good campsites are non-existent along the way.

Camp at the lower end of Elbow Lake or just below the outlet. Fishing may produce some cutthroat. Explore the nearby nameless lake to the northeast by following the stream which enters Elbow Lake's east side. Incidentally, the unnamed lake has no fish, but some nice campsites. And for spectacular views of Mount Cowen, hike up the little valley on the east side of Cowen to the top of the

**Elbow Lake**

ridge. You may spot some mountain goats as well.

Mount Cowen does lure a fair number of climbers, but do not attempt it unless you know what you are doing. Unlike most of the other peaks in the Absaroka range, this massive pinnacle is not a walk-up.—*Art Foran*

## 95   Lake Pinchot

*General description:* A week-long backpacking vacation.

*General location:* Fifty miles south of Big Timber, in the Absaroka-Beartooth Wilderness.

*Maps:* Mount Douglas and Cutoff Mountain USGS Quads and the Gallatin National Forest Travel Plan Map (south half).

*For more information:* Write District Ranger, Big Timber Ranger Station, Gallatin National Forest, Box A, Big Timber, MT 59011 or call (406) 932-3647.

Reaching Lake Pinchot and investigating the nearby treasures of the Lake Plateau region of the Absaroka-Beartooth Wilderness is more than a hike. Actually, it's more like a vacation.

Don't even think about hiking into this area and out the next day. Instead, plan on at least two days in addition to two days to get in and out. Bring plenty of food—because once you're there, you'll probably decide to stay at least a week.

The trailhead is at Box Canyon Guard Station, forty-nine miles south of Big Timber on the Boulder River Road, of which the last twenty four miles are bumpy and dusty. Park at the guard station and take the Trail #27 marked "Rainbow Lakes 12 miles."

The trail gradually climbs through timber and open parks along the East Fork of the Boulder River for about 3.5 miles before crossing on a sturdy bridge. If you started late, you may wish to stay the first night at an excellent campsite just before the bridge.

After crossing the East Fork, the trail follows the river for a quarter-mile before climbing away through heavy timber. Along the river, you'll notice several trout-filled pools, so be prepared to fight off temptations to stop and rig up your fly-casting gear.

After two more miles, Trail #27 goes straight toward Slough Creek Divide. You turn left on trail #28.

About 200 yards after the junction, you pass little Lake Kathleen on your left. Then, two miles later, you reach another junction, where Trail #30 breaks off to the right and heads for Columbine Pass. You stay left on Trail #28.

Just before you reach the next junction at the eleven-mile mark, you pass along the left side of a large, wet meadow. Watch for moose.

At the eleven-mile junction, you have several options. Depending on how tired you are and where you intend to camp, you can (1) go straight for another two miles over the Stillwater Divide to Lake Pinchot, (2) turn left and switchback up a steep hill one mile to Rainbow Lakes, or (3) veer right for a very steep, half-mile climb to 9,472-foot Fish Lake, one of the highest in Lake Plateau.

Lake Pinchot is probably the best choice for a base camp for such an extended trip. However, the immediate area has hundreds of excellent campsites along the

*Wounded Man Lake in the Lake Plateau section of the Absaroka-Beartooth Wilderness. Bill Schneider photo.*

*Lake Pinchot*

lakes. Thus, you might choose to make a temporary camp and look for a site that is especially appealing.

Once you've established your base camp, start taking advantage of the numerous adventures all around you. For anglers, there are two dozen lakes within the reach of an easy day hike. For climbers, there are 11,298-foot Mount Douglas, 11,153-foot Chalice Peak, and other summits to reach.

Most of the lakes have rainbow trout or hybrids. However, Fish Lake has cutthroat. Although a few lakes are barren, most have good fishing with some rainbows over two pounds.

On the way home, take the trip between Lake Pinchot and Rainbow Lakes. In addition to passing by Wounded Man Lake, you go through a collection of gemlike lakes on an alpine plateau. It's only a two-mile hike. The trail is heavily used and signed, but it doesn't show on the maps. It leaves the main trail on the northwest corner of Wounded Man Lake and comes out between Middle and Upper Rainbow Lakes.

To avoid returning to your vehicle on the same trail, you can take the Upsidedown Creek trail that can be found at the foot of Lower Rainbow Lake. This may be slightly shorter, but it involves steep, downhill hiking. It hits the Boulder River Road about two miles north of Box Canyon Guard Station.

The only unpleasant part of this hike is the first day—hiking twelve to fourteen uphill miles with a loaded pack. If you endure this, however, you will almost certainly say it was worth it.

The area is about as heavily used as any hiking area in Montana. However, the large number of campsites dilutes the crowd to a tolerable level.

The climate in this high country often leaves something to be desired, with rain fairly common. So bring good rain gear.

The climate also restricts the hiking season to about one month—the last week in July and the first three weeks in August. Before this time, expect to be hiking through last year's snowbanks. And after it, be prepared for early season snowstorms.

A week in this hiker's wonderland will undoubtedly be an always-remembered vacation. So expect a few remorseful moments when you realize that you must return to your hectic lifestyle back home. For the first few days at home, civilization will never have been so unpleasant.—*Bill Schneider*

# 96   Aero Lakes

*General description:* A long day hike or moderate overnighter to two high altitude lakes with outstanding fishing.

*General location:* Three miles northeast of Cooke City near the northeast entrance to Yellowstone National Park.

*Maps:* Cooke City USGS Quad and the Custer National Forest Map (Beartooth Division), even though this hike is in the Gallatin National Forest.

*For more information:* Write District Ranger, Gardiner Ranger District, Gallatin National Forest, Box 5, Gardiner, MT 59030 or call (406) 848-7321.

The Beartooth Plateau—now part of the Absaroka-Beartooth Wilderness—is the second largest contiguous area in the U.S. over 10,000 feet in elevation. It has hundreds of lakes ranging in size from potholes to major lakes like the Aero Lakes.

*Aero Lakes*

To reach the trailhead from Cooke City, drive east two miles to a turnoff marked with a large Forest Service sign as the Goose Lake jeep road. Drive northeast about two miles up this dirt road to a cluster of old buildings. An inconspicuous trailhead on the right shoulder of the road has an old Forest Service sign directing you to Lady of the Lake—which is also the trail to Aero Lakes.

Once at Lady of the Lake (1.5 miles from trailhead), turn left and walk up the meadow on the north side of the lake where two trails depart.

The left trail heads north and then turns west to Long Lake. You take the right trail, which leads almost due north one mile to the junction of Star and Zimmer creeks. Continue north along Zimmer Creek another mile until you see a crude trail switchback up the steep right side of the canyon. If you are following Zimmer Creek and see a stream coming in from the left, you have gone too far up the drainage.

The scramble up the switchbacks is steep, but short. Suddenly, you emerge from the timber and stand above Lower Aero Lake. Be sure to notice the dramatic contrast between the treeless ridge and plateau with the timbered country just below.

It's about five miles into Aero Lakes. The trail isn't shown on the USGS maps, but it's fairly obvious on the ground because of the fairly heavy use it receives.

The shoreline around Lower Aero is rocky and punctuated with snowbanks. There are a number of places to camp, but perhaps the best is on the grassy north side where a point juts out into the lake. Don't expect a campfire on this treeless site.

To proceed on to Upper Aero Lake, follow the stream which connects the two lakes. Another good camping spot is just below the outlet of the upper lake. This provides a good view of the lake and the prominent Mount Villard with its spiny ridges. It also makes a good base camp for fishing both lakes and for exploring east to Rough Lake and then north up the Sky Top Lake chain.

Fishing is one of the prime reasons for coming to the Aero Lakes. The fishing here, like most mountain lakes, is tempermental, but both lakes offer outstanding fishing in number and size. Upper Aero Lake has cutthroat, while Lower Aero has both cutthroat and brook trout. They are stocked every four years and thus have two age classes of fish—the young, upcoming trout and the lunkers.

At this altitude, the summer season is very short; the ice may not free the lakes until mid-July. Because the tundra is quite wet on the plateau, there tends to be a prodigious number of mosquitoes when the wind isn't blowing. Bug dope is mandatory until the first hard frost.

Enjoy the Absaroka-Beartooth Wilderness for what it is—wild and spectacular. At Aero Lakes, you're at least five miles from the nearest machine. At night, no city lights or heavy auto fumes block your view of the stars. There are nearly a million acres of pristine land around you, more than enough for a lifetime of wandering.—*Mike Sample*

## 97    Rock Island Lake

*General description:* An easy day hike or overnighter.

*General location:* Ten miles east of Cooke City, just north of the Montana border in the Absaroka-Beartooth Wilderness.

*Maps:* Cooke City USGS Quad and the Custer National Forest Map (Beartooth Division), even though this hike is in the Gallatin National Forest.

*For more information:* Write District Ranger, Gardiner Ranger District, Gallatin National Forest, Box 5, Gardiner, MT 59030 or call (406) 848-7321.

Rock Island Lake differs from many high elevation lakes. Instead of forming a small, concise oval in the end of a cirque, it sprawls in every direction. A hiker will tire simply trying to walk all the way around it.

For hikers planning overnight stays, the lake has several good campsites—especially two choice spots on the south shore east of a section of rocky shoreline. The lake contains large brook trout that—like most big fish—take patience and skill to catch.

The selection of side trips in this area is incredible. You can go in for a day or stay a week, going to a new lake or seeing new sights every day.

Because Rock Island Lake is so accessible—seven miles round trip on a near-level trail—it would be a perfect choice for a family planning to try out the Absaroka-Beartooth Wilderness. Drinking water is readily available on the trail and at the lake, but the mosquitoes are bad in early summer. Although you could find enough wood for a campfire at the lake, consider using a stove for cooking. The area receives heavy use, and if every hiker had a fire, it would soon show signs of overuse.—*Bill Schneider*

*Rock Island Lake*

# 98    Tempest Mountain and Granite Peak

*General description:* A long, steep backpack to Tempest Mountain, a traditional launching point for ascents of Montana's highest peak, strictly for experienced, well-conditioned hikers.

*General location:* In the heart of the Beartooth Mountains eighty miles southwest of Billings.

*Maps:* Alpine and Cooke City USGS Quads and the Custer National Forest Map (Beartooth Division).

*Special attractions:* An excellent chance to view or climb Montana's highest mountain, 12,799-foot Granite Peak.

*For more information:* Write District Ranger, Beartooth Ranger District, Custer National Forest, Route 2, Box 110, Red Lodge, Mt 59068 or call (406) 446-2103.

Hikers have a choice of two trailheads for this hike. Both are found by driving south from Columbus on State Highway 78 and after fourteen miles taking a left (still on 78) at Absarokee. A few miles out of Absarokee, the road forks.

For the most commonly used route, drive one mile west of Fishtail, and take the left fork of the road up the West Rosebud drainage. The trailhead is next to the Mystic Lake power plant.

Either trailhead gets you to the same place, the saddle between Prairieview Mountain and Froze-to-Death Mountain. The Mystic Lake route is two miles shorter with 400 feet less elevation to gain, but includes a very steep series of switchbacks. The East Rosebud route has a less steep gradient, more scenery, and potential campsites for hikers who don't wish to get to the shoulder of Tempest Mountain in one day. Either way, this hike is definitely for rugged types; just reaching the saddle where the two trails meet is a climb of 3,500 feet from Mystic or 3,900 from East Rosebud Lake.

Once at the saddle, the hiker turns southwest and follows a series of cairns around the north side of Froze-to-Death Mountain. The destination is a group of rock shelters at approximately the 11,600-foot level of Tempest Mountain. Tempest Mountain is really a plateau, and the rock shelters are on the west edge 1.6 miles north of Granite Peak. The shelters are rock walls (perhaps three feet high) built over the years to protect campers from the strong winds which frequently blast the area. Behind these walls are some of the few square feet of flat ground to place sleeping bags without making uncomfortable adjustments to this rocky "moonscape."

By the time the hiker reaches the rock shelters, he has traversed approximately ten miles from the trailhead and climbed more than 5,000 feet. He crossed timberline just before reaching the saddle. No plants or grasses can survive the climate and elevation at the rock shelters except hardy lichens. Rock, ice, and sky are the predominate elements.

There are some advantages to hiking and camping in such an austere place. The wind is so prevalent that few mosquitoes ever attempt takeoffs from ground zero. The bear danger is nil. And, of course, the high altitude grants superb views in all directions.

Along the west edge of the plateau leading up to Tempest, the view of Granite Peak is awesome. Granite buttresses rise almost vertically from the Huckleberry

*Granite Peak, the highest summit in Montana. Mike Sample photo.*

Creek canyon to form a broad wall nearly a half mile wide. The north face is heavily etched with fissures running almost straight up between the buttresses. Granite Glacier clings to the center of the wall. At the top, a series of pinnacles builds from the west side up to the peak.

To those who are skilled in technical climbing, Granite is an easy ascent in good weather, but for those with little experience, it is dangerous. Probably the best advice is to go with someone who knows what he is doing and who has the proper equipment. Especially important is a good climbing rope for crossing several precipitous spots. The easiest approach is across the ridge which connects Granite to Tempest and then up the east side.

Check with the Forest Service for more information before attempting this

*Granite Peak*

climb. In recent years, not one summer has passed without mishaps and close calls, mostly due to bad judgement. One sobering concern is the extreme difficulty in rescuing an injured person from Granite.

People have tried this hike and climb at almost all times of the year, but August and early September are the most logical choices. Even then, sudden storms with sub-zero wind chills are a real possibility. Snow can happen anytime. And the thunderstorms around Granite Peak are legendary. Be prepared with warm and windproof clothing and preferably a shelter which will hold together and stay put in strong wind.

Whether or not you climb Granite, take the time to walk up to the top of Tempest. To the north and 2,000 feet below are Turgulse and Froze-to-Death Lakes. On a clear day, one can see perhaps 100 miles out onto the Great Plains. And if one moves a little east towards Mount Peal, one can look southwest over Granite Peak's shoulder to Mount Villard and Glacier Peak, both over 12,000 feet.

As one might guess, there is little wildlife at this altitude. Nearer the saddle where there is grass and other hardy alpine plants, mountain goats are commonly spotted. An occasional golden eagle soars through this country looking for marmots and pika. Down closer to the trailheads a few mule deer and black bears make their summer homes.

If you use the East Rosebud trailhead, you may wish to take an alternate way back. From the east edge of the plateau to the west-northwest of Turgulse Lake you can drop down into the bowl which holds Turgulse and hike past Froze-to-Death Lake and Phantom Lake (good fishing for cutthroat) and then sidehill back to rejoin the trail above Slough Lake. There is no trail for most of this route, and some investigating between Froze-to-Death and Phantom may be necessary, but it is an interesting way out for the adventuresome. And high adventure is what this hike is all about in the first place. —*Mike Sample*

## 99   *Sundance Pass*

*General description:* A fairly rugged, three-day hike for more experienced hikers.

*General location:* On the northeast side of the fabulous Beartooth Range, about ten miles southwest of Red Lodge.

*Maps:* Alpine and Mount Maurice USGS Quads and the Custer National Forest Map (Beartooth Division).

*Special attractions:* Spectacular mountain scenery, especially the view from Sundance Pass, and excellent fishing.

*Special attractions:* Spectaclar mountain scenery, especially the view from Sundance Pass, and excellent fishing.

*For more information:* Write District Ranger, Beartooth Ranger District, Custer National Forest, Route 2, Box 110, Red Lodge, MT 49068 or call (406) 446-2103.

In addition to being one of the choicest backpacking trips in the Beartooth Mountains, the Sundance Pass hike is only a short drive from the Billings area.

Find the trailhead by taking U.S. 212 southwest from Red Lodge for about ten miles and take a right at the Lake Fork of Rock Creek. A short, paved road leads to a turn-around and the trailhead.

This is a fairly difficult (3,900-foot elevation gain), twenty-one-mile, point-to-point hike that ends at Camp Senia in the West Fork of Rock Creek just south of Red Lodge. Most hikers who take this trip arrange for somebody to pick them up at Camp Senia or leave a vehicle there.

Although many hikers take three days for this trip, it can easily be extended by taking scenic side trips. The main route passes by three lakes—Keyser Brown, September Morn, and Sundance; but several others can be the targets of side trips.

One of these is Black Canyon Lake, which lies just below Grasshopper Glacier and is a short side trip. The trail to Black Canyon Lake is a rough but short hike, about 1.5 miles. Part of it is rock talus with no trail, and there is a steep climb as you get close to the lake. The hike to Black Canyon is probably too tough for families or poorly conditioned hikers. There is almost no place to camp at this high, rugged lake— only a few marginal places on the lower end. Fishing for large cutthroat can be great, but you have to hit it just right. It's usually very windy at Black Canyon during mid-day.

First and Second Rock Lakes can be reached by a fisherman's trail from Keyser Brown Lake. Dude Lake is one mile on a rough, steep trail from Quinnebaugh Meadows. And there's a steep but good trail from Quinnebaugh

*Keyser Brown Lake from the Sundance Pass trail. U.S. Forest Service photo.*

*Sundance Pass*

Meadows to Lake Mary. Occasionally, the saddle to the north from Lake Mary is used as a cross country route to Crow, Sylvan, and East Rosebud lakes.

Lost Lake is a short, quarter-mile, steep climb from the main trail. This is a very heavily used lake and shows it. The trail to Lost Lake leaves the main trail about a half-mile before the trail crosses the Lake Fork of Rock Creek, the same place where the Black Canyon Lake Trail takes off.

The lakes on the main route and on the side trips offer good fishing, mostly for pan-sized trout. Fishing seems best in Black Canyon and Dude lakes, with the former having large—but hard to catch—cutthroat trout. Stream fishermen often try their luck in Lake Fork and West Fork of Rock Creek, but it's poor fishing for small trout.

It's best to wait for this hike, as Sundance Pass usually isn't snow-free until July 15. This delay also avoids the peak season for mosquitoes and no-see-ums, which can be quite bad in this area, especially on the West Fork side.

Besides superb fishing, the hike has spectacular scenery. From Sundance Pass, for example, hikers can see 12,000-foot mountains and the Beartooth Plateau, the largest contiguous area above 10,000 feet in North America. Hikers are also treated to glaciers and obvious results of glaciation, exposed Precambrian rock, and waterfalls.

Hikers have a good chance of spotting wildlife, particularly pika, ground squirrels, and marmots. Also watch for mountain goats, deer, golden eagles, and gyrfalcons. Goats are frequently seen from First and Second Rock lakes. An occasional black bear will be spotted, but bear danger is very low.

As with wildlife, wildflowers are present, but not terribly abundant. Fireweed, stonecrop, bluebells, and four o'clocks are some of the most common species.

Water is plentiful except near Sundance Pass. And the trail is well marked and maintained throughout.

The main route has several good campsites: Keyser Brown Lake (heavily used, but good fishing for pan-sized trout), September Morn Lake (lightly used and good fishing for pan-sized trout), Sundance Lake (seldom used with no fish, but very scenic view of 12,548-foot Whitetail Peak), Quinnebaugh Meadows (poor fishing, but great view of 3,000-foot cliff off Silver Run Plateau), and any number of good campsites along the Lake Fork or West Fork of Rock Creek.

Since this area is part of the Beartooth Wilderness, motorized vehicles aren't allowed. This entire drainage is probably used as heavily as any wild area in Montana. Consequently, the FS has hired a ranger to enforce several protective measures such as a prohibition of camping on lakeshores. These special regulations are listed at a sign on the trailhead. Obey them for two reasons—they are strictly enforced, and they are necessary to protect this fragile drainage.—*Mike Sample*

# 100 *Strawberry Hills*

*General description:* A short day hike in an area of buttes and badlands.
*General location:* Eight miles east of Miles City.
*Maps:* Government Hill USGS Quad and the BLM's Custer #29, National Resource Lands map.

*Strawberry Hills*

*Special attractions:* Pretty prairie scenery among the wooded plateaus of south-eastern Montana.

*For more information:* Write the District Manager, Miles City District, Bureau of Land Management, P.O. Box 940, Miles City, MT 59301 or call (406) 232-4331.

Hiking opportunities on the scattered tracts of public land in eastern Montana are limited; that's why this hike among the badlands south of the Yellowstone River is such a pleasant surprise to people looking for an easy outing on the Montana prairies.

Drive eastward from Miles City on U.S. 12 for about eight miles, until the highway begins to ascend the pine-covered plateau just east of the town. As the road climbs Government Hill, turn off to the left at the sign for the Strawberry Hills Recreation Area.

Past the parking area, the trail (in the form of a rough jeep track) steeply climbs the western flank of Strawberry Hill. A quarter-mile from the trailhead, the route crosses a metal cattleguard and enters an area frequently used for target practice by the local rod and gun clubs. Once past this point, you have escaped most of the people that bother to drive out to the Strawberry Hills.

The route wanders seemingly aimlessly through the eroded basin on the north side of Strawberry Hill. Here, you have a choice of three interesting destinations for your wandering. The low ridges to the north provide good views of the valley of the lower Yellowstone River, with pine-covered plateaus appearing to float on the summer heat waves on the far horizon. Just pick out a grass-covered slope which isn't too steep and head for the top, keeping one eye out for the small prairie rattlers which frequent these hills. Bring your snakebite kit.

The rock formations which make up these buttes are sure to prompt you to examine them more closely. The red layer of rock, from which the Strawberry Hills get their name, is sometimes called "clinker" and was theoretically formed when underlying coal seams caught fire, baking the upper layers of sedimentary rock. Upon closer examination, the rock is not uniformly red, but has streaks of grey, blue, and black scattered on a freshly broken surface. Rock hounds will enjoy puttering about the clinker layers, but avoid the crumbly cliffs, which offer poor rock climbing and razor sharp handholds.

By picking a route to the south, you can climb up onto the pine and meadow covered summit of Strawberry Hill itself. The meadows are particularly pretty in April and May, when springtime moisture encourages the prairie's brief flower show of pasque flowers and arrowleaf balsam root.

Continuing along the rough jeep track will eventually take you, in about a mile, to a spectacular red-topped conical butte. You can climb this butte on its eastern ridge. It provides intriguing views of the broken country in the Terry Badlands across the Yellowstone River to the north.

After doing as much, or as little, wandering about the prairie as you like, retrace your steps to the parking area and your vehicle.

Spring or fall are best for this prairie walk, since summertime is frequently brutally hot in eastern Montana. Make sure to bring adequate water along, because none is available in the Strawberry Hills area.—*Ed Madej*

# Afterword

## The Wilderness Challenge

Many hikers, I suspect, view the "wilderness challenge" as the adventure of braving wild country with only what they carry on their backs. They briefly flee the comfortable life to risk survival along some austere divide, and return home the victor.

It almost seems like our *right* to at last have the opportunity to visit a place on earth that has been primarily affected by the forces of nature, where the imprint of man's hand is substantially unnoticeable.

Yes, we can "challenge" it. We can climb the highest peak, float the wildest river, seek out the most hidden of the mountain's secrets. In Montana, we can even challenge the mighty grizzly bear, the wilderness king, and temporarily become the most feared creature on the mountain.

This challenge lures us to the blank spots on the map. It seems ingrained in our birthright—and most likely will for generations to come.

But today's hikers face an even more fierce, more difficult, more time-consuming, and more frustrating challenge. Now, we must rise to the challenge of saving the last wilderness.

Never has the oft-quoted adage of Will Rogers—"They ain't makin' any more of it."—been so revelant. Another famous thinker, Aldo Leopold, also emphasized the point by writing, "Wilderness is a resource that can shrink, but not grow."

How true. But it must grow to help dilute the rapidly increasing number of hikers.

I suppose the day will come when most wilderness areas have restrictions on the number of human visitors. However, increasing the size of the wilderness resource would certainly make this day a more distant probability.

It's also true that the label "wilderness," when officially designated by Congress, can attract hikers, leading to more crowded conditions. However, limitations on recreational use is undoubtedly preferable to the alternative—gradual destruction.

In years past, I spent many wonderful days in my favorite roadless areas—which were almost unknown—never meeting another hiker and relishing the uncommon solitude. Too bad it never lasts. These areas are now severely threatened with various development schemes which would be much worse than seeing other hikers. Much worse.

In pioneer times, land could be logged, mined, or homesteaded, then abandoned, slowly reclaiming its wild character. Indeed, this has happened in many places throughout Montana. And of course, this is sitll scientifically possible, but as we all know, ever more unlikely.

Knowing this, it hurts to hear politicians talk of "balance," as they prepare to give their guarded support to the violation of yet another unprotected roadless area. In the lower 48 states, the ratio is now 99 percent nonwilderness and 1 percent wilderness, as legally defined by the Wilderness Act of 1964.

Yet, in almost every speech by wilderness opponents or politicians trying to please everybody, we hear cries for balance.

"I'm in favor of wilderness," they predictably say, "but not in this area. We need balance; we can't have all wilderness."

I wonder how many of these podium-thumpers really understand the existing inequity. If every remaining acre of roadless country south of Canada became part of the Wilderness Preservation System (created by the Wilderness Act of 1964), we *wouldn't even come close* to balance. The pitiful one percent might, at best, climb to three percent.

Here lies our challenge—to make America understand the wisdom of wilderness, to keep the bulldozer out of the last remnants of wild America, to preserve for future hikers a few examples of what it used to be like.

This challenge can't be taken lightly. Compared to winning congressional protection for a threatened roadless area, climbing the highest peak or surviving the elements is remarkably easy.

In a time when economics dictates most decision-making, pleas to designate wilderness aren't always eagerly received. But wilderness can be an economic bonanza to a community, especially for Montana's third largest industry—recreation and tourism.

Claims that wilderness destroys the local economy illustrate only one of the many myths plaguing wilderness preservation efforts. Other myths include: Only the rich, elite, young, and strong use wilderness. Domestic livestock grazing isn't possible or practical in wilderness. Wilderness locks out sportsmen and other recreationists. Wilderness is bad for wildlife. Wilderness isn't multiple-use. Wilderness locks up vital minerals. We have too much wilderness already.

These are pure myths, and quite the opposite is true in each case. So if you're confronted with these false statements, get the facts and set the record straight. Don't let it pass without a reply; there's too much at stake. The integrity of the last American wilderness is on the line. And even more important, the decisions on what to do with the remaining roadless areas will be made in the next few years.

The Montana Wilderness Assn.—and other conservation groups listed at the end of this section—have the facts to support pro-wilderness claims and dispel myths. They even have detailed information on many of the unprotected areas mentioned in this guide. Making the decision-makers relate to these facts is your challenge.

I dislike projecting wilderness as a giant battleground. But in reality, that's a fair description. The battle over wilderness has been—and will be in the future—as bitterly fought as any domestic political issue.

Hikers—and other people who use and adore wilderness—must be the soldiers in this war. Otherwise, the day when the last roadless area is protected as wilderness will soon dawn.—*Bill Schneider*

---

# *Conservation Organizations*

Montana Wilderness Association
Box 365
Helena, MT 59624

American Wilderness Alliance
4260 E. Evans
Denver, CO 80222

Sierra Club
330 Bush St.
San Fransisco, CA 94108

The Wilderness Society
1901 Pennsylvania Ave. N.W.
Washington, D.C. 20006

Montana Wildlife Federation
Box 901
Missoula, MT 59801

# Appendix I

## Always check the checklist

Hikers can—and will—take almost anything they choose into the mountains. But without a complete checklist it's remarkably easy to forget an essential item. The following list is "over complete"—there are items on it that hikers rarely use. Still, it's always good sense to take a final look at a checklist before loading the pack into the car. The extra minute is usually worth it.

## Clothing

_____ Shirt
_____ Pants
_____ Underwear (extras)
_____ Windshirt
_____ Vest
_____ Belt and/or suspenders
_____ Jacket or down parka
_____ Turtleneck
_____ Poncho or rainsuit
_____ Gloves
_____ Hat
_____ Bandana
_____ Walking shorts
_____ Sweater
_____ Swimming suit
_____ Balaclava or headband

## Cooking

_____ Matches (extras)
_____ Matches (waterproof)
_____ Waterproof match case
_____ Stove
_____ Fuel bottles (filled)
_____ Funnel
_____ Foam pad for stove
_____ Cleaning wire for stove
_____ Cleaning pad for stove
_____ Cleaning pad for pans
_____ Fire starter
_____ Cook kit
_____ Pot gripper
_____ Spatula
_____ Cup
_____ Bowl/plate
_____ Utensils

_____ Dish rag
_____ Dish towel
_____ Plastic bottle

## Food and drink

_____ Cereal
_____ Bread
_____ Crackers
_____ Cheese
_____ Margarine
_____ Powdered soups
_____ Salt/pepper
_____ Main course meals
_____ Snacks
_____ Hot chocolate
_____ Tea/coffee
_____ Powdered milk
_____ Drink mixes

## Photography

_____ Camera
_____ Film (extra)
_____ Extra lenses
_____ Filters
_____ Close-up attachments
_____ Tripod
_____ Lens brush/paper
_____ Light meter
_____ Flash equipment

## Fishing

_____ Rods
_____ Reels
_____ Flies
_____ Dry fly floater (silicone)
_____ Lures

_____ Leader
_____ Extra line
_____ Swivels
_____ Hooks
_____ Spit shot/sinkers
_____ Floats
_____ Bait

## Miscellaneous

_____ Pocket or Swiss Army knife
_____ Whetstone
_____ Compass
_____ Topo map
_____ Other maps
_____ Sunglasses
_____ Flashlight
_____ Batteries (extra)
_____ Bulbs
_____ Candle lantern
_____ First aid kit
_____ Snakebite kit
_____ Survival kit
_____ Repair kit
_____ Suntan lotion
_____ Insect repellent
_____ Zinc Oxide (for sunburn)
_____ Toilet paper
_____ Space blanket
_____ Binoculars

_____ Nylon cord
_____ Plastic bags
_____ Rubber bands/ties
_____ Whistle
_____ Salt tablets
_____ Emergency fishing gear
_____ Wallet/I.D. cards
_____ Money
_____ Ripstop tape
_____ Notebook & pencils
_____ Field guides
_____ Toothpaste and tooth brush
_____ Dental floss
_____ Mirror
_____ Garbage bag
_____ Book
_____ Towel
_____ Safety pins
_____ Scissors
_____ Trowel
_____ Water purification tablets
_____ Car key
_____ Signal flare
_____ Watch
_____ Extra parts for stove, pack, and tent
_____ Solar still kit
_____ Rubber tubing

# Appendix II

## Finding Maps

For the hikes listed in this book, hikers need basically two kinds of maps—USGS Quadrangles and various Forest Service maps. The USGS maps can be ordered directly from the Geological Survey's Denver Distribution Center, or (hopefully!) at the list of stores accompanying this appendix. When ordering maps from Denver, be sure to request an *Index of Topographic Maps of Montana.* Many of the stores listed may not have that critical map you need in stock at the moment you need it. In any case, it's good to have your Quads in hand before you head off for the trailhead.

To order topographic maps from Denver, send a letter to the following address for an index and price list:

• United States Geological Survey, Branch of Distribution, Federal Center, Building 41, Denver, Colorado 80225.

Forest Service Maps can be obtained from the addresses listed along with each hike, or if you would like a complete set of maps of the ten national forests and twelve Forest Service wilderness areas in Montana, write to the following address:

• United States Department of Agriculture, Forest Service, Northern Region, Federal Building, P.O. Box 7669, Missoula, Montana 59807, Attention: Information Receptionist.

As of summer, 1982, maps of individual national forests and wilderness areas are $1 each, while national forest travel plan maps are free for the asking.

For the hikes on Bureau of Land Management areas listed in this guide, write to the address listed with each hike or request maps in BLM's National Resource Lands in Montana map series from the following address:

• United States Department of Interior, Bureau of Land Management, Montana State Office, 222 North 32nd Street, P.O. Box 30157, Billings, MT 59107

Montana stores carrying USGS Quads (topographic maps):

Big Timber, MT 59011
    Bob's Sport Shop
    230 McLeod

Billings, MT 59101
    Selby's ESCO
    405 S. 24th
    Montana Oil and Gas Commission
    15 Poly Drive

Bozeman, MT 59715
    The Beaver Pond
    1716 West Main
    The Powderhorn
    35 East Main
    Selby's ESCO
    233 East Main

Butte, MT 59701
    Montana Bureau of Mines and Geology
    Main Hall—Montana Tech
    West Park

Great Falls, MT
    Bighorn Wilderness Equipment
    600 Central Ave.
    Blend's Copy Shop
    509 First Avenue North

Helena, MT
    The Base Camp
    334 North Jackson
    State Publishing Company
    Airport Road
    Capital Sports and Western
    1092 Helena Ave
    Hustad Center

Kalispell, MT 59901
    Books West
    Main & First Streets West
    The Sportsman
    Junction Highways 2 & 93

Lewistown, MT 59457
    Don's Inc.
    207 West Main Street

Livingston, MT 59047
    Dan Bailey's Fly Shop
    209 West Park Street

Missoula, MT 59801
    Missoula Blueprint
    1613 South Avenue West
    The Trailhead
    501 South Higgins Ave.
    Hi Country Pack & Ski Shop
    Southgate Mall
    Selby's ESCO
    1914 North Avenue West

West Yellowstone, MT 59758
    Pat Barnes Tackle Shop
    105 Yellowstone Ave.
    Bud Lilly's Trout Shop
    39 Madison Ave.
    Eagles Trading Post
    7 Canyon Street